AF526644

Folklore and Transformative Reflections

Assumptions and Resumptions of Indian Writers in English

Lata Mishra

AUTHORSPRESS

Worldwide Circulation through Authorspress Global Network
First Published 2013
by
Authorspress

Editorial
Q-2A Hauz Khas Enclave
New Delhi-110 016

Marketing
E-35/103, Jawahar Park
Laxmi Nagar, Delhi-110 092

e-mails: authorspress@rediffmail.com; authorspress@hotmail.com
Website: www.authorspressbooks.com

Folklore and Transformative Reflections:
Assumptions and Resumptions of Indian Writers in English

ISBN 978-81-7273-702-3

DISCLAIMER

The contents of all the articles included in this volume do not necessarily reflect the views of the editor. The authors of the articles are responsible for the opinions, criticisms and factual information presented. The contributors are also responsible for ensuring the proper adherence to the scientific rules of writing and copyright regulations. While the editor have tried their best to carefully review, format and make necessary corrections in the manuscripts, if there are still any lapses, the onus lies only with the authors of the articles.

Printed in India at Tarun Offset, Delhi.

Dedicated to

My Mother

a woman of infinite strength and incredible wisdom,
whom I love and miss so much...

Preface

Folklore and myths have been an eternal part of every culture since ages. Humans have always enjoyed story-telling, may it be in the form of myths, histories, folktales or legends. Levi-Strauss compares myth to a window through which cultures can be studied. India is a land of diverse cultural patterns. These variegated cultural patterns have existed within the framework of different religious, linguistic and regional traditions. This accounts for a wide range of stories and mythological legends, which emerge from all walks of life in this country. They are in fact the cultural ethos of our country. The oral tradition in India has won an authority and accomplished unbelievable achievements. This holds true with all ancient texts which have been taken over by word of mouth from the teacher to his disciples.

Myths may be considered as an early science, the result of man's first attempt to explain what he saw around himself. Human intellect has formulated and expressed the ideas of perennial value and eternal truths in ancient texts but the plurality of truths contained in scriptures formed by a blend of history, folklore and empirical knowledge is limited by finiteness of human mind as well as culture of the time.

In present times when there is growing consciousness for human rights among all sections of society, especially in the area of women and marginalized ones, and the faith in authoritative structures is failing, literary writers are increasingly becoming interested in finding out the meanings in these myths and folklore, and refashioning them. The literal meanings of folklore are unacceptable to this new culture and thus arises the need to recreate the ancient stories, transposing them with new symbolic meaning. Writers re-appropriate, re-tell and revise these tales with new creativity and revolutionary changes, so that openings can be made for new meanings to appear. For Levi-Strauss, myth is a mode of communication. A culture's mythology casts light on the culture's *shared unconscious.* A culture can be best understood by attempting to know and appreciate its mythos. All the writers have their own assumptions, presumptions and biases as they engage their texts. Mythological characters express indigenous thinking about sexual roles and relationships. Indeed, to a great extent, they are a means by which indigenous tradition has thought about sexual roles and sexual identity. Through the use of folktales and myths in their work fictionists provide an integral analysis of the modern world. Their ability to make pertinent points about the real world is marvellous.

The present anthology on Indian Literature in English is devoted exclusively to the rich tradition of mythology and oral literature of India's indigenous peoples. It is strongly felt that such work with the oral traditions of indigenous peoples in India would further open significant new avenues towards a fuller understanding of the importance of mythology and folklore. *Folklore and Transformative Reflections* comprises 21 selected research papers on the creative writings by contemporary Indian writers. The essays in this volume seek to find connection between philosophic systems of the religious tradition and the beliefs, myths and rituals that occupy the lives of people belonging to those traditions. The present study also aims to provide a wealth of information on contemporary regional writings in India. I most humbly feel that the results of the research by this team would prove interesting and fruitful for the literary fraternity. This work is designed as a springboard for new research, and it is hoped that it would be a valuable addition in the area of the study of myth and folklore in literature

I am indebted to many for helping me with this project. I express my sincere thanks to all the contributors for so enthusiastically participating in this project. When the idea of book on this theme was floated among friends, their responses were encouraging and their submission was timely. I express my gratitude to Sudarshan Kcherry, Managing Director of Authorspress for his warm interest in this work and the encouragement he offered towards its publication. I thank the entire team of Authorspress for so meticulously transforming the concept into a finished product. My thanks to Prabhat, Eira and Tweisha—I cannot imagine having a more generous and supportive family, whose unconditional love has been, and will always be, that which sustains me.

Lata Mishra

Contributors

Debashis Baruah, Assistant Professor, Department of English, Furkating College, Furkating, Golaghat, Assam

Raj Kumar Mishra, D Phil, Department of English, Allahabad University, Uttar Pradesh.

Nitin Jarandikar, Assistant Professor, Radhanagari Mahavidyalaya, Radhanagari, District Kolhapur, Maharashtra.

S. Lavanya, Assistant Professor of English, PSGR Krishnammal College for Women, Coimbatore, Tamil Nadu.

L. Judith Sophia, Assistant Professor of English, Scott Christian College, Nagercoil, Tamil Nadu.

Krishna Singh, Associate Professor, Department of English, Government P.G. College Shahdol, Madhya Pradesh.

Sangeeta Das, Associate Professor, English Department, D.G. P.G. College, Kanpur, Uttar Pradesh.

O. P. Budholia, Professor, Department of English, Govt. KRG Autonomous PG college, Gwalior, Madhya Pradesh.

Margaret L. Pachuau, Associate Professor, Department of English, Mizoram University, Mizoram.

A.J. Sebastian sdb, Associate Professor, Department of English, Nagaland University, Kohima, Nagaland.

P.V.L. Sailaja, Research Scholar, Department of Humanities & Social Sciences, AUCE, Visakhapatnam, Andhra Pradesh.

T. Sasikanth Reddy, Academic Consultant, Yogi Vemana University, College of Engg, Proddatur Town, Kadappa Dist., Andhra Pradesh.

Supriya Agarwal, Head, Department of English, Central University of Rajasthan, Ajmer, Rajasthan.

A. Sujatha, Professor, Department of English, King College of Technology, Namakkal, Tamil Nadu.

Ankur Konar, Department of English, Burdwan Raj College, Burdwan, West Bengal.

Durgesh B. Ravande, Assistant Professor, Department of English, KKM College, Manwath, District Parbhani, Maharashtra.

Nigamananda Das, Assistant Professor, Department of English, Nagaland University, Kohima, Nagaland.

Abhinandan Malas, Department of English, Ramananda College, Bishnupur, Bankura, West Bengal.

Taniya Chakraborty, Institute Research Scholar, Department of Humanities and Social Sciences, National Institute of Technology, Durgapur, West Bengal.

Joydeep Banerjee, Assistant Professor, Department of Humanities and Social Sciences, National Institute of Technology, Durgapur, West Bengal.

Lata Mishra, Department of English Studies and Research Govt. K.R.G. (P.G.) Autonomous College Gwalior, Madhya Pradesh.

Contents

1

Ecological and Ecomystical World in Plays in English from Northeast India

Debashis Baruah

The states of Northeast India have quite a good number of plays written in their own respective vernacular languages. But the works of some of the Manipuri and Assamese playwrights have been translated into English, and these have shown how successfully this literary genre has been explored by these playwrights. These plays exhibit local colours, local sense and sentiment, deal with some of the core issues of the region, and at the same time, they have a universal appeal. The world of these playwrights, no doubt, is the very world around them; but ecology, myths and legends, tradition and mysticism form a vital part of their world. This reminds of their rootedness to their tradition and culture, and even being a part of the corpus of Indian drama, these also make them essentially Northeastern Indian playwrights. They are recognized with an identity of their own because of their legitimate, powerful voice.

Manipur has a rich theatre tradition. After its interaction with the British Indian Empire in the nineteenth century, people were exposed to western drama. The introduction of western education in Manipur during the last quarter of the nineteenth century also influenced the advent of a new group of playwrights into the scenario—playwrights such as Lairenmayum Ibungohal Singh (1895-1966), Lamabam Kamal (1900-1934), Sorokhaibam

Lalit Singh (1983-1955), Arambam Dorendrajit Singh (1907-1944), Ashangbam Minaketan (1906-1995), Hijam Angahal (1892-1943), etc. But it is Ratan Thiyam in whose hand Manipuri theatre has achieved a new dimension. He is a playwright of high calibre, a director, actor, poet, novelist, musician as well as a painter. His is a respected name in the realm of Indian drama, whose plays have been staged all over the world. He set up the Chorus Repertory Theatre in 1976 that has immensely contributed to the development of Manipuri theatre.

Ratan Thiyam explores through the vibrant world of Manipuri tradition and culture. He rediscovers the folklore, myths and legends of Manipur and bestows on them a contemporary meaning. Ecological concerns are strongly voiced in his plays. The plays of Ratan Thiyam "present a remarkable juxtaposition of traditionalism and the demands that a remorseless technological world takes on all of us. And through presentation of opposites and conflicts, he puts across the clear message that unless mankind resists war, halts the rat race of a frenetic existence and reverses the destruction of the only planet that we have, there is only doom in store for us.... His lament of the diverse ways in which we have destroyed or perverted the world of today is heard against the backdrop of angst presences in the mythical world of Manipuri deities and damsel, of mothers and wise men. In the ultimate analysis, his plays represent the victory of abiding traditional values over the present world of wars, conflicts, violence, greed and inequity" (Bezboruah 2008:1). Thiyam voicing his concern for the environment, says, "The human race has come a long way, especially due to technological advancements, but in the course of our development, we have somehow lost touch with our emotions. The more we become advanced, the more our society is forgetting its traditions, roots and the importance of human relationship." (2008:111-12)

The plays in Thiyam's *Manipur Trilogy* are *Wahoudok* (Prologue), *Hey Nungshibi Prithivi* (My Earth, My Love) and

Chinglon Mapan Tampak Ama (Nine Hills, One Valley). *Wahoudok* is a play with four scenes that tells, the Metei traditional myths regarding the creation of the universe. At the beginning of the creation there was a vacuum full of darkness. Then the Almighty cried "Hoong". 'Hoong' is a term used for invoking gods at the start of incantation; it is also used as an explanatory word meaning 'No'. As soon as the lord cried 'Hoong', suddenly a halo of seven colours appeared and there was light everywhere like it happened also in the *Bible* as God said, "Let there be light", and there was light. (Genesis: Chapter I). He went on creating the celestial bodies, animals and plants. Then following the advice of Mother Goddess, the sons of God created human beings in the image of their Father, the Almighty God, like that in the *Bible*, "God created man in his own image"(ibidem) . Thus human civilization flourished on earth and they went on enjoying the bounty of nature and the earth was a perfect paradise for human beings.

In course of time human population increased that put pressure on food and natural resources. Human beings started fighting one another for a share of the ever-diminishing resources in order to survive. Scientific and technological development failed miserably in liberating human beings from such a disaster. This war for survival eventually brought political and economic crisis that led to a crisis in tradition and culture. The earth was no more a paradise, rather, it became an entity under constant threat of extinction. People started introspecting. They went back to the history of human civilization for a solution in order to face these challenges before them. The worried, helpless people called upon their forbears, the seven wise men and the seven nymphs who had helped in creating human beings and who were lost in oblivion by that time. They prayed their forbears to save them from this disastrous condition. This is the story in brief in *Wahoudok* told in four episodes: The birth of the universe, the creation of living beings, the outset of human civilization and the modern times. The play tries to justify the need of practising traditional values as it is tradition, culture and age-old values that enable human beings to fight against the hazards of so-called modernization. Speaking on the importance of tradition, Thiyam says in an interview with Kavita Nagpal and Geeti Sen, "it is by the use of tradition that you try to drive away the civil factors." (Sen 2006: 242).

The ecology of our planet has been talked about in *Wahoudok* time and again. People have been reminded of the beauty and bounty of Nature quite a number of times. The Narrator in the play says, "See, how beautiful is the earth/Green, black. Saffron and white colored / Ranges of hills" (Thiyam 2008: 41). He speaks of the entire ecology of the earth. He speaks about the oceans, the green forests, the varied flora and fauna of earth. But this beautiful earth is now under threat. Human beings' exploitation has brought on ecological imbalance. "In the race of civilization, in the passage of time, grudge among nations have become very frequent. Killing and wanton murder arresting and kidnapping would happen more frequently, news of wars and devastations would reverberate in all the four directions and eight corners" (ibidem 38-39). But this should be stopped in order to create a peaceful planet is which all creatures can live peacefully. The ecology of the earth is to be maintained as "there is no paradise better than the earth." (ibidem 42)

The ecomystical tone is well heard in this play. The varied coloured hills, the clouds, different kinds of trees, flowers, fruits, and different species of animals, birds and insects are mentioned. All these, along with human beings are integral part of the ecological web. Mutual love, respect and dependence is must in order to maintain the ecological balance. This is what eco-mysticism tells us. It is the way of living ecologically like a mystic's way of life. Spiritual Ecology advocates the growth of an ethical sense that enables human beings feel an empathy with nature, to observe closely its mysteries and to act for its preservation. *Wahoudok* is a manifestation of this ecomystical spirit.

The second play in Thiyam's trilogy is *Hey Nungshibi Prithivi* (My Earth, My Love). It also powerfully voices ecological concerns. The play addresses a very important global issue like terrorism and shows how it can lead to environmental degradation. It has also references to Manipur suggesting Thiryam's sense of belonging to his native land. The play unfolds the dark pages of the history of human kind. Human history has been a witness of a number of horrendous events. It has witnessed hundreds and thousands of people died in the concentration camps during the Nazi regime in Germany and the revenge of the Russians when they raped fifty thousand German women, the Japanese attack of the Pearl Harbour and the American retaliation by atomic bombarding in Hiroshima and Nagasaki, the genocide during the Khmer Róuge regime in Kampuchea, the terrorist attack and devastation of the twin towers of World Trade Centre in Ground Zero. Besides all these, human history has also witnessed the devastation of Manipur by the Burmese. The play introduces the characters of seven celestial nymphs taken from Manipuri myths and legends, representing the peace-loving citizens of the world in general. They pray to the Almighty to restore harmony and peace in the world.

Ecomystrical ideas have been well exploded by Thiyam in this play. Wars, battles and armed exercises of nations for attaining superiority have polluted the planet apart from doing manifold harms to human civilization. They have been posing a threat to the very existence of the earth. "Do you hear, the Emperor called 'War' has vowed to devastate the Earth? Wake up, open your eyes" (ibidem 69). The devastation created by human beings has destroyed nature and the ecological balance: ".... one 'Earth' devoid of morning and day, with the sky covered by the vultures, turned by human beings, is created. In the garden of heaps of dead bodies, one is searching for varieties of flowers . . ." (ibidem). But in order to live in a perfectly ecological way, a new ethic is to be developed, in which anthropocentrism should give way to ecocentrism. This is the primary concept of ecomysticism and this is what Thiyam tries to express in this play: "The nature of human beings, to think and act for their benefit only, has crippled me...." (ibidem 78)

My Earth, My Love can also be studied from an ecofeminist viewpoint. Here women and nature are presented as synonymous. The wars and other man-made devastations in the history of human civilization have totally a negative impact on the ecology of the planet. Nature has been polluted and exploited by these devastations. Likewise, women are also made to suffer. In fact, they are the worst sufferers. One of the women characters speak of this pathetic condition of women throughout the long history of human civilization, which is dominantly patriarchal. The character's speech can also be seen as the voice of Nature:

> War, you have made us prostitutes.
> War, you have made us prisoners.
> War, you have made us bonded slaves.
> ... ...
> women and children are fed to war.........
> The epic of the Earth and voluminous Chapters of thousands of pages would not be sufficient to describe the woes and sufferings of women alone.
>
> (ibidem 73)

The very process of creation is under threat. The future of civilization is bleak as both women and nature, that sustain life, are polluted:

> Oh! I'm at a loss.
> Submerged in my blood,
> Growing in my womb
> ....
> It's a leftover of some inhuman and Characterless one.
>
> (ibidem 74)

The last play in Thiyam's trilogy entitled *Chinglon Mapan Tampak Ama* (Nine Hills, One Valley) has a powerful dramatic voice that also strongly expresses ecological concerns. Here, in this play a mystical valley is encircled by ranges of hills, which is supposed to be paradise once. But during the passage of time this valley has been robbed of its glory and tradition due to unfortunate turn of events. Genocide, political instability, unemployment, extortion, corruption—all these have become day- to- day affair in this land that is posing a great crisis before it. The common people are at a loss whose tradition and rich cultural heritage are at stake. The Seven Wise Men, who have been lost in oblivion so far and who are supposed to save the people and the land from this present crisis, call upon the celestial nymphs, the mothers, to help them write a new book of wisdom that may help the people to go back to their roots in order to rediscover themselves. After completing the book that contains the wisdom of freedom, peace, religion, politics, human rights, traditional culture, etc., the Seven Wise Men disappear leaving behind this book to the younger generation. Towards the end of the play mothers sing lullabies to their children stating the glorious history of the land and all these past happenings. The play ends with lamps lightened on the hill tops and in the valley to enlighten and remind the people of their glorious past. The burning lamps also enlighten the people with a desire to bring back those peaceful days once again.

Thiyam in his other plays explores Manipuri myths, legends, tradition and culture as is done in this play. In the 'Prologue' the rites and rituals performed by the Seven Old Women, the sentinels of Manipuri cultural tradition, show Thiyam's use of his native tradition. The 'Chant' at the very beginning of the play is reflective of the myths and legends of Manipur. Throughout the play Manipuri folk culture has been intelligently exploited and explored though that makes the play a richly colourful one. The playwright is very much concerned of the ecological degradation of the land. He has been referring to this crisis in the play time and again: "...Peepul tree was on fire; dead bodies were floating in a row in the river ..."(ibidem 87). People are proud and in praise of their native land which was once enriched with the bounties of nature, they say:

> Ah! Much adored oval-shaped land
> Where golden rice plants sway forming
> undulating waves,
> a land encircled by nine ranges of hills
> like a necklace studded with gems,
> O beloved golden motherland,
> the best of all.
>
> (ibidem 94)

But that beautiful land is now chaotic. The ecological balance has been disturbed by untoward events. It has become a cursed land where "people's minds are divided, all are irritated" (ibidem 88) or where "The sound I hear is that of a mournful voice, children were swimming in the river of blood, with no one to save them, they were calling for their mothers before being drowned" (ibidem). Due to these unfortunate happenings "the land is heading for utter chaos that will result in war."(ibidem)

The play advocates a revival of traditional values, cultural heritage and ancient wisdom in order to resist the evil forces. This quest of the people in search of their roots will enable them to rediscover themselves in a chaotic situation where people are facing identify crisis. "Identify crisis, a sense of alienation are some of the dominant features of contemporary politics in the Northeast. Racial autonomy, cultural and linguistic conflicts, the problem of insurgency have been ravaging the region. All these find artistic expression in the works of the writers writing in English from region. There is a conscious urge, in their works, of going back to their roots and it is used as a means of asserting an identity of their own" (Baruah 2010:63). This is what is reflected in this play by Ratan Thiyam. The playwright is also concerned of the incidents of terror and war in the global scenario those have been leaving a devastating effect on human civilization. The play has references to a number of such terrorist incidents happened in different parts of the globe such as Dar-es-salam, the United States, Afghanistan, Iraq, Cuba, Tunisia, Karachi, Indonesia, Russia, Morocco, Spain, Istanbul, Saudi Arabia, London, etc. All these violent events have a long lasting devastating effect that has ravaged human civilization as well as has destroyed the ecological equilibrium of the globe. In the same interview with Kavita Nagpal and Geeti Sen Thiyam says that even sitting in Manipur he thinks about Indo-Pak relationship, about the Gaza Strip, about Israel, Palestine, Afghanistan or about a bomb blast in Bali (Sen 2006: 230). This concern, both local and global, of Thiyam as a playwright, heightens the effect of his plays. He is voicing the sentiment of the common people:

> With prayer to the Almighty
> let's make a beautiful new ideal world,
> manured with goodness and love,
> where gentleness and peace prevail.
>
> (Thiyam 103)

In order to create such a world human beings must develop an ethic of living together with each and every objects of nature with complete harmony. They have to realize the mysteries of nature. The playwright recreates the mystical world of nature with the help of some touching images:

> Dusk has fallen, the crimson sun
> has set behind the hills.
>
> (ibidem 106)
>
> Or
>
> Look, manifesting as the history of many eons,
> the peace of many ages,
> the hilltops are standing.
>
> (ibidem)

Or

Night dew has turned into tears
Of bamboos and trees...

(ibidem)

An understanding of this mystical world of nature would make human beings feel an empathy towards nature, inspire them to live life in a perfectly ecological way by letting "the dwellers of hills and valley co-exist" (ibidem 107). This ecomystical fervour is dominant throughout this play. The play may also be studied from an ecofeminist standpoint. Throughout the play women and the environment have been treated synonymously. They both are the innocent victims of terrorism and war waged by the patriarchal society all around the globe. In order to recreate a world of peace and harmony nature as well as women, are to be restored. And in the play finally it is the women, the mothers, the sentinels of tradition who play a pivotal role in restoring an order in the society. This is also suggestive of human civilization's journey towards nature to restore an ecological equilibrium.

Another major Manipuri playwright is G.C. Tongbra who tries to expose the anomalous condition in the society and envisions a better life through his plays. He, as a playwright, believes that to sustain life is the fundamental question of human beings and challenges the issues of morality, law or justice as impediments to the life of the exploited class of the society. C. Tongbra's *Taj Mahal* (1972), said to be his masterpiece, revolves round the lives of some downtrodden people. Kebal a blind beggar, Ranimata, his daughter, Yadav, a hotel boy and Rajmohan, a bus handyman—all are slum-dwellers. All of them have dreams in their eyes of living a dignified life like human beings in the true sense, but they cannot afford to live such a life. Both Yadav and Rajmaohan have fascinations for Ranimata and they disclose this time and again. Rajmohan is a thief who, getting a chance, snatches valuables from rich people. Chitragupta, an artist with somewhat a peculiar temperament lives in a Kala Mandal. He dreams of breaking the Taj Mahal into small portions and hopes to distribute those portions to the poor people who are homeless. Rajmohan and Ranimata go to him and request him to make them Shahjahan and Mumtaz with the help of his artistic power, even for few moments. Rajmohan murders Sanarei, a rich woman and loots all her valuable possessions and gives these to Ranimata. In the Kala Mandal while Rajmohan and Ranimata are playing Shahjahan and Mumtaz and thus feeling the taste of a royal, majestic life, police comes and arrests Rajmohan for the crime he had committed. Eventually, Yadav takes charge of Ranimata at the request of Rajmohan who is to be hanged. Rajmohan says that Shahjahan inherited immense riches from his forefathers, who were emperors of a vast and rich empire. Likewise, ordinary people like them inherit poverty, grief, struggle, hunger, etc. Shahjahan, being an inheritor of immense riches could build the Taj Mahal. But they cannot afford to build a monument like the Taj even if they want to. But it is significant that the Taj Mahal was, in the real sense, built by the blood and sacrifice of the labourers, the forefathers of the ordinary people like them. Yadav and Ranimata build two pillars in front of the Temple of Art in the memory of Rajmohan. They also make a bell hanging between the pillars that reminds of the hanging body of Rajmohan.

Ecofeministic ideas can be marked in the play. Ranimata, one of the female characters is the prototype of the socially downtrodden class of women; she is a slum-dweller, a beggar who is utterly dissatisfied with her present condition of life: "The creator of this world must be surely an evil-hearted, prejudiced character" (Tongbra 2000:41). She is in love with Rajmohan, a vagabond, and aspires to live a prosperous life even momentarily as she believes that she and her fiancé have the right to dream as they are also human beings: "....We both destitutes are still human beings" (ibidem 53). But after Rajmohan is pronounced death sentence by the court of law, it is Yadav who takes charge of Ranimata. She does not have a choice of her own. It is as if mandatory for her to take a support from a male as she is insecure being a woman. She is a daughter of someone (Kebal's), a beloved of someone (Rajmohan's) and a wife of someone (Yadav's), but she does not have an identity of her own. This silencing of the voice of Ranimata by the social set up, which is essentially patriarchal, is, in a sense, the silencing of the voice of the women folk as well as of nature. The play has a reference also to Rajmohan's mother by Rajmohan himself: "I did not recognize my mother ... I had many fathers" (ibidem 54). This is also very much expressive of ecofeministic fervour.

Bus Stop is a play written by another important playwright of Manipur, Athokpam Tomchau. The play begins with a woman waiting for a bus. A woman is waiting for a bus to go to the city. Her dramatist husband is busy writing a play without paying any attention to her. They don't have a cordial relationship between them and she decides to part with him and leaves for the bus-stop. A traveller appears at the bus-stop and they go on talking on various topics in order to pass the time. Their conversation is a commentary on the modern way of living—a selfish, monotonous and a meaningless kind of life. A gentleman comes to the bus-stop and he is killed by a man just before their eyes. But neither the woman nor the traveller wants to engage themselves in a problematic situation and do not help the dying person. Instead, they bet on whether the person is dead or alive. But just for a moment the woman is awakened by her 'feminine' qualities and wants to help the person. But again she becomes selfish reflecting herself as a typical modern human being. They all leave the dying person without extending any help. The husband, who is a dramatist, who speaks of the downtrodden in his plays, also does not want to show his responsibility as a human being and leaves the helpless person. The dying person knows he is going to die but is uncertain of himself. He wants to die. The play portrays the modern predicament that is full of cut-throat policies, meaningless rat races, rampant corruption in all levels and so on. These have been creating confusion all around and not only human beings, but the entire ecosystem also is disturbed:

> I have come from that place
> Tension is very high there,
> There is a drama of skeletal phantoms
> In the river of blood.
>
> (Tomchau 2000: 72)

The ecological crisis posed by the changing values in the name of modernization is well depicted:

> It is the end of the earth, the end; There is
> war between the progenies of Darwin, the
> situation is worsened! It is terrible! What
> Shall we do now if the flames of war engulf us?
>
> (ibidem 72)

A note of ecomysticism is heard when living peacefully together with environment is emphasized in the play:

> . ...Light up the pine torches, pick up the fallen
> grains one flesh of lightening and you'll see
> stray coins on the flour. This mud house might
> fall when it so desires. But do not stop decorating
> the same, with new ornaments.
>
> (ibidem 73)

The play reiterates the need to develop a new environment ethics that can restore peace and harmony:

> The condition of your environment has
> charmed you, it protects, promotes, threatens
> And destroy; ....
> Taking a stand within the silent zone of
> Your heart just stands forth with a plan.
>
> (ibidem 76)

The woman in the play feels sympathy for the dying man even for a moment. It is suggestive of the 'feminine tenderness' both in women and in nature because both of them sustain life on earth. This can be interpreted in ecofeministic terms.

Leipaklei (A Tender Earth–Flower, 1988) is another notable Manipuri play written by Arambam Somorendra (1935-), a notable playwright of the post-War era, who attacks the hollow pretensions of the middle class and envisages a better society where human beings can live an unburdened life. *Leipaklei* is the story of a helpless destitute woman called Leipaklei. She has been in intense love with Ibotomba, but under some untoward circumstances she has to marry Chandrababu, who has gone to Macockchung to live with another woman abandoning Leipaklei. Leipaklei with her little girl has to live a life of misery and hardship. Thoiba, a rich but amorous contractor visits Leipaklei every now and then and proposes her to marry him which she strongly refuses all the time. She only thinks about Ibotomba, her only and real love.

Finally, Ibotomba arrives all of a sudden, after being a prisoner of war for many years and Leipaklei gets a new meaning of life. Being a woman, Leipaklei is treated by the male-dominated society just as an object—an object to be exploited, enjoyed and used for one's own interest without giving her an option of her own. Leipaklei is doubly burdened as she is a woman and also a poor woman. Above all, her loneliness as a poor woman makes her a soft target of the male gaze.

The helplessness of such wretched women find expression while Leipaklei says: "I am a woman and cannot challenge you. I live a very poor life" (Somorendra 2000: 91). Ecofeministic ideas may be seen in the objectifying of women as an entity who does not have a meaning without a man: "You cannot live alone, mind you. Women are meant for men" (ibidem 90), or "A woman belongs to a man" (ibidem 107).

Exploitation, domination, poverty are some of the major problems faced by women in any society. The patriarchal social set up has methodically placed women at the periphery. They have been reduced to such a condition where they are even unable to voice their sentiments. The pathetic condition of the dominated section finds expression in the following lines uttered by Leipaklei: "It is such a difficulty to stay with this small child alone. It is such a poor life. There is no other help except my own personal effort. In the meantime, men do not leave me in peace because I am a woman. I have suffered greatly under their hungry looks. I could not show my mettle as I live alone in poverty…." (ibidem 105)

Myriad views of ecology have also been presented through this play. The description of the natural objects is also a description of the ecology of the region: "… The fields are all green, … look at the colour of the sky, the patches of white clouds, are not they beautiful? The air is also so fresh…" (ibidem 97). Nature has an important role in moulding human behaviour. It is because of the age-old relationship between human beings and nature. This notion of the human- nature bond has also an echo in the play: "… with the beautiful aspect of nature in front of them I thought all people would seem good" (ibidem 97). The mysterious aspect of nature has also been presented:"Nature also has different aspects …" (ibidem 97). Ecofeminist and ecomystical ideas are thus artistically expressed in the play.

A Soul, Still Wishing to Stay Alive is another play from Manipur written by Wairokpam Kamni Singh (1948-), who is concerned about the loss of human values in the modern society. The play revolves around the dead body of a young boy who naturally had hopes and aspirations in life. His mother breaks down at the untimely death of her son, vultures are gathered near the body to have their own share of it. Bones and skeletons, the lamenting voices—all are personified and presented symbolically. Even the soul of the dead boy that still wishes to stay alive, has a symbolic presence. The play is a commentary on the contemporary time where the age-old human values have been degenerated, where human beings become hostile to one another.

Every individual is as if in a war with him/herself, with another individual, or with nature as a whole: "Man hunted man like a beast of prey, and he who still wants to stay alive, met his end at the hands of a hunter" (Singh 2005:46). The blood—thirsty nature of human beings in this degenerated modern times can also be marked from such images like:

> The droplets of blood sticking on the bones,
> let's suck even those completely,
> let's suck those completely dry.
>
> (ibidem 51)

Human beings are mechanized. They become so insensitive that even death of a fellow human being cannot arouse pity in them. Their only concern is to get a "profit from the dead" (ibidem 46). In such an insensitive, mechanized society women have to suffer more. The desolate condition of women in modern times is echoed in the following lines:

> My own mother,
> survives alone, a true widow.
> Whenever anyone among you hungers for fresh human flesh,
> don't divide her, don't devour her.
> She has no one to call her own,
> She lives, because she's born human.
>
> (ibidem 49)

Because of her wretched condition and the treatment meted out to her, the mother here can also be synonymous to Mother Nature. Hanuba, the old vulture says that it was born a human, then turned into a dog, and then, in present times, turned into a vulture. This metamorphosis has great symbolic significance suggesting the degeneration of life of that entity who is dissatisfied of its present living: "born a human, I am no longer content to live." (ibidem 56)

Echoes of ecomysticism are recurrently heard in this play. There are suggestions that in order to make an end to this overall degeneration in modern living, and to revive the good old days of the past, going back to nature as a solace is a must. Human beings can peacefully survive on this earth only by identifying themselves with nature: "Let my soul enter the immobile trees and the bamboo, grass and reeds" (ibidem 59). Human beings must feel empathy for nature and consider nature as a part of their selves:

> As we, the living beings suffer, the immobile trees and bamboo, grass and reeds also have limitless miseries.
>
> Only when you are born as one of them,
>
> will you come to know their suffering and discontents.
>
> Will you be able to feel their sufferings and discontents.
>
> (ibidem 60)

Nature is not a passive object only to be explored, exploited and consumed for the benefit of human beings. Instead, nature is a dynamic entity and is to be revered, preserved and taken care of:"All the living beings in this world, whether mobile or immobile, have to accept the inescapable duty of life. It's the law of nature" (ibidem 60). Such ecomystical ideas embodied in the play enshrine Deep, Shallow as well as spiritual ecology.

Ganesh Gogoi (1907-1937) was an eminent Assamese poet and playwright. His *Sakunir Protisodh* (Revenge of Shakuni) is a remarkable play in the history of Assamese drama for its theatrical consciousness as well as unique treatment of the subject matter. Its story is taken from the *Mahabharata*, the great Indian epic and its protagonist is Shakuni, the maternal uncle of the 'Kauravas'. Shakuni has been instigating the 'Kauravas' against the 'Pandavas', their cousins. It is he, who, in a treacherous way, aided the 'Kauravas' to defeat the 'Pandavas' in the great game of chess that eventually led to the battle of Kurukshetra. But Shakuni had a specific purpose. In reality, he wanted the defect of the 'Kauravas' as he had a great revenge to take against them. Shakuni, along with his father and his ninety nine elder brothers were once put to prison by Dhritarashtra. His father along with his ninety nine brothers starved themselves by feeding Shakuni with their share of food. They wanted Shakuni to survive so that he could avenge the injustice showed to them by Dhritarashtra. So Shakuni took the revenge by letting the 'Kauravas' defeated and killed by the 'Pandavas' in the battle of Kurukshetra.

Revenge of Shakuni ends with the death of Shakuni who dies a happy and a fulfilled man. The play can be studied from ecofeministic ideologies. As the story is taken from the *Mahabharata*, it is interesting to note that recent concept of ecofeminism dates back even to the age of the epics. Ecofeminism believes that nature as woman/mother has been exploited and treated as a passive object by the patriarchal society. The ecofeminists are of the opinion that the notion of womanhood is a social construct and women have been without a 'space' in all ages of human history. A close study of the play *Revenge of Shakuni* opens up many such issues that strengthen this claim of the ecofeminists.

In the play there are three female characters, viz., Gandhari, queen of Hastinapur and wife of King Dhritarashtra, Padmaa, wife of Karna and Draupadi, wife of the 'Pandavas'. That they are marginalized in many occasions can be seen even in the *Mahabharata*. Draupadi had married to the five brothers of the 'Pandavas' where her consent was never asked for; but she was a wise lady who surely had a say of her own. The wisdom of Draupadi can be marked in one occasion in the play where she is counseling and encouraging a dejected Arjuna with her wise words:"This accidental defeat can't demoralize our force. It rightly prevails; if the judgement of right and wrong is the prevailing order, then the greedy Duryodhana will definitely meet with a faithful end." (Gogoi 2006: 134)

Like Draupadi, Padmaa, wife of Karna, the illegitimate elder brother of the 'Pandavas' and the great general of the 'Kauravas' has been silenced and kept in the periphery, far from the centre of action. But she was also an intelligent lady whose opinions and observations could have mattered a lot during the whole course of action in the battle of Kurukshetra. She is a mute spectator of events and is presented with just one identity, the identity of being the wife of Karna: "You're my husband, my best guru and my lord supreme" (ibidem 115). This is reflective of the concept of womanhood as constructed by the traditional patriarchy. Her 'feminine' quality also comes out when she comes to know how Kunti, Karna's mother abandoned Karna immediately after his birth:"Oh God! How cruel a mother can be to sacrifice motherhood for femininity... " (ibidem 117). But it is the women who suffer the most. Their sensitivity aggravates their sufferings. Anything happened in the world of nature might be a premonition of any happening in the world of human beings, and, significantly, this could even be perceived by a woman. During the battle of Kurukshetra, Draupadi has a mental disturbance and this trauma has been expressed with the help of images from the world of nature:

> Why do I feel something ominous?
> My heart is trembling
> Why is the melody doleful?
> Why is melancholy echoing all around?
> Why is the air heavy with
> a strange, doleful tune?
> The autumn dew
> that sits on plantain leaves
> Instead of glinting—
> why do they appear as tears?
>
> (ibidem 134)

Gandhari, mother of the 'Pandavas' has also been going through such mental traumas. Being a woman and a mother she sustains life, but becomes mentally devastated after loosing her sons in the battle. It is Gandhari the mother who has a wise counseling to Duryodhana, her elder son to stop the war, to live together with the 'Pandavas' peacefully: "Then stop this fight. I lost everything. Now I'm left with you and Dushasana only. Arrest further misfortunes befalling the race. Stop this war son; stop this." (ibidem 122)

She is voicing here the sentiments of a woman as well as a mother. But she is never listened to with serious attention neither by her husband Dhritarashtra nor by her son Duryodhana, the representatives of the patriarchy. But it is she who suffers the most: "... The agony of a bereaved mother is beyond words to make you feel what it is. I groomed one hundred lads in mirth and merriment. I am in bereavement of ninety-eight of them at their prime. They filled my heart with joy, which is now deserting it. How much more I have to bear?" (ibidem 123). Gandhari is sad, frustrated and upset. Her mental agony is externalized when, in a course of discussion, she says to her husband: "Who can stand unperturbed at the untimely sad demise of my hundred sons except the two? To that stonehearted father what penalty can a lady inflict, Maharaja?"(ibidem). This may be seen as a voice of protest against male arrogance or domination.

Arun Sarma (1931-) is one of the major Assamese playwrights of the post-Independence era who has a distinct voice as a dramatist in the scenario of Indian theatre. His famous plays like *Ahar*, *Nibaran Bhattacharya* and *The Wolf Boy* have been translated into many Indian languages and they have been included in the volume of hundred best Indian plays complied by Sahitya Akademi. His *The Wolf Boy* is a typical modern play presenting doubts, conflicts and contradictions in the backdrop of a complex set up.

Prof. Ashok Choudhary, a genetic scientist goes to Ramsang forest in search of an endangered tribe known as the 'Wolf Men', a human species that has acquired some of the wolf-like qualities because of its long-term association with the wolves. Prof.

Choudhary recovers a child of that species whose parents have been killed by the wolves and brings it along with him. He christens this child as Romu and brings it up with utmost care and love like his own daughter Reema. Romu, at the beginning, behaves like an animal in his manner of talking, eating and other day-to-day behaviour but gradually adopts human nature owing to Prof. Choudhary's and Reem's continuous effort. Professor gets Romu admitted into a very prestigious school along with Reema but has to withdraw him because of public pressure. As people consider Romu as 'non-human' and make it a prestige issue in sending their wards to the same school in which Romu also studies. Prof. Choudhary offers Romu education himself in their home itself, and in due course of time, Romu becomes a great genetic scientist himself.

Dilip, son of Nripati Baruah, a politician and a friend of Prof. Choudhary, is an M. Sc. who assists Romu in a research project as per the advice of Prof. Choudhary. Romu develops a fascination for Reema but her marriage is finally fixed with Dilip. The research project becomes successful that discovers newer things in genetic science only because of Romu's hard work. But Nripati Baruah, by dint of his political power, arranges a prestigious award for his son Dilip for this discovery completely depriving Romu of any recognition. Citing 'technical reasons' for not considering Ramu's name for the award, Mr. Baruah speaks of Romu's 'non-human' origin, his lack of a formal education, etc. He also arranges a scholarship for Dilip for pursuing higher studies in the USA. Prof. Choudhary also feels helpless but does not say anything considering the future of his daughter. Thus all of them snatch from Romu the things he actually deserves showing that they are 'wolf men' in the real sense. Finally, Romu takes out a piece of stone, the very piece of stone he had taken with him when he came to this house for the first time. He says that the piece of stone is his very identity that keeps on reminding him of his background and tradition.

The play envisages a human–animal association. The possibilities in such interactions have been explored. Romu, the representative of the species called the 'Wolf Men' has acquired wolf–like qualities because of his long term association with the wolves in the jungle. That same Romu, after his stay in the human world adopts human behaviour again. This is suggestive of the various interactions between the human world and the world of nature. The 'place' of nature and the 'nature' of place interacts in this situation when wilderness is accommodated in the human world. It surely calls for a new ethic that has a larger 'space'. But the doubts, conflicts and reluctance of the human world to accommodate the wilderness at the very centre can be seen in many occasions during the course of the play. People complain Prof. Ashok Choudhary against enrolling Romu in the same school where their 'human' children are also admitted: "But Ashok, a lot of letters have been received by the Principal of Great Heart School, and a number of people have also complained verbally that they object to this boy being allowed to study with their children. That is the issue raised by the respectable guardians of the town. So it would be best if the boy is taken out of the school...." (Sarma 2005: 76)

That Romu has been treated as the 'other' is seen in other such occasions. He deeply loves Reema but it is Dilip, the 'human' who gets her, he discovers revolutionary things in the field of genetic science, but again it is Dilip, the 'human' who gets the award and a scholarship. Romu's taking out of that piece of stone which he brought with him from the jungle, is significant. If may be a token of his protest against the so-called human world or may be assertion of an identity.

Ecocritical principles may be adopted in studying the play. It expresses the agony of the rootless people. They have been displaced, in many cases, for the interest of the powerful section of the society. But there is little chance of their rehabilitation. They are marginalized and their voice remains unheard. At the end of the play there is a note by the author that speaks of these things. It says, "In the central theme of this play, the wolf boy represents the plight of minority communities. When an uprooted community also happens to be a minority, its very existence suffers from grave disadvantages. A community may get severed from its roots because of natural calamities, or man-made political and economic crisis. History has established a sad fact about displaced people:their rehabilitation is a difficult process.... This play is about the deprivations of rootless people and more" (ibidem 114). "Ecological humanism (eco-humanism) is a theoretical coinage to humanize ecology and to give humanist/human dimensions to ecology. Ecology in its multiple manifestations essentially refers to the physical macro nature and the human spiritual world including all moral and ethical values that govern the human activities" (Das 2011:181). The matrix of ecology, ecofeminism and ecomysticism in the plays from northeast India is very much apparent. The ecological world in the plays of this region is enriched with exploration through ecology enacting the very idea of ecomysticism, the idea of living together peacefully and maintaining a balance in the entire ecosystem.

Works Cited

Baruah, Debashis. (2010) "Insurgency, Peace and Quest for Identity:A Study of Contemporary Writing in English from India's Northeast": *Peace, Conflict And North East India.* ed. Lachit Baruah & Ajanta Rajkhowa. Guwahati: Purbanchal Prakash, 62-71.

Bezboruah, Dhirendra Nath. (2008)."Foreword": *Manipur Trilogy.* Guwahati: Wordsmith, 1-2.

Das, Nigamananda. (2011). "The Art of Ratan Thiyam": *Matrix of Redemption: Contemporary Multi-Ethnic English Literature from North East India.* ed. Nigamananda Das. New Delhi: Adhyayan Publishers, 180-186.

Gogoi, Ganesh. (2006). "Revenge of Shakuni": *Indian Literature,* Vol. 213, Jan-Feb. New Delhi: Sahitya Akademi, 111-148.

Sarma, Arun. (2005). "The Wolf Boy": *Fresh Fictions.* ed. Geete Dharmarajan. New Delhi: Katha, 62-114.

Sen, Geeti. (2006). "Re-inventing Tradition in Performance": *Where the Sun Rises When Shadows Fall: The Northeast.* New Delhi: India International Centre, 227-242.

Singh, Wairokpam Kamni. (2005)."A Soul, Still Wishing to Stay Alive": *Fresh Fictions*. ed. Geeta Dharmarajan. New Delhi: Katha, 37-61.

Somorendra, Arambam. (2000). "Leipaklei": *Indian Literature*, vol. 196, Mar-Apr. New Delhi: Sahitya Akademi, 81-109.

Thiyam, Ratan. (2008). *Manipur Trilogy*. Guwahati: Wordsmith.

Tomchau, Athokpam. (2000). "Bus Stop":*Indian Literature*, Vol. 196, Mar-Apr. New Delhi: Sahitya Akademi, 40-67.

Tongbra, G. C. (2000). "Taj Mahal": *Indian Literature*, vol. 196, Mar-Apr. New Delhi: Sahitya Akademi, 68-80.

2

Home Myths in Ramanujan's Diaspora Consciousness

Raj Kumar Mishra

Attipat Krishnaswami Ramanujan (1929-1993), a poet of Indian origin, worked and heaved his last breath in America. Although he left India when he was just 30 years old, he could not forget his Indian heritage and sensibility which at last resulted in desire for home. His attempt to celebrate family, family relations, rituals, religion made critics and scholars to include him among Indian leading poets. In fact he ultimately found his roots through the medium of poems. The aesthetics of 'cultural nationalism' enabled Ramanujan to get over the problem of relatedness or rootedness by encompassing history, myth, folklore, language, religion etc.

After the Second World War and with the end of European colonies from the most of the countries, it was being earnestly felt among survived communities that they should work for cultural identification not only for themselves but nation also. During the colonial period, European value systems were imposed on the colonized, oppressed communities. These value systems threatened from the very root of the indigenous art, culture, and organization. But with 'postcolonialism', native survivals and various ethnic groups living across the borders who anyhow survived/preserved their culture and identity did their best to assert them. As such, 'cultural nationalism' became a reliable strategy of self-(nation included) affirmation. The colonials tried all the way to inculcate the sense of inferiority among natives that their art and culture are of no use. In fact, after political freedom and national sovereignty, it was necessary to mend identity and culture and get over the problem of identity crisis. As we all know, the colonials badly disjointed and dislocated everything. Cultural consolidation programme was of course to ferret out roots. The aesthetic of cultural nationalism is a mode of self-affirmation. This draws images and symbols from the various components of culture and history. To decolonize the once colonized mind, creative writers thoughtfully exhausted national history, legends, myths, folklore, music, religion, language etc.

In his writings, India alongside its culture, history, and religion are never missing. Family metaphor occupies central space in his poetry with which he thinks, so writes a noted Indo-Anglian poet, R. Parthasarathy (Parthasarathy 95). He is a well-famed poet of Indian diaspora. Diasporics migrate to a 'new world' not only physically and geographically but with their 'cultural artifacts' and native consciousness also. Diaspora studies is primarily a narrative of displacement comprising feelings of homelessness, alienation, memory or remembrances, and romantic longings for eventual return caused either by voluntary displacement or involuntary. According to James Procter, '"diaspora" can appear both as naming a geographical phenomenon—the traversal of physical terrain by an individual or a group—as well as a theoretical concept:a way of thinking, or of representing the world (McLeod 151). The latter part of the definition is more interesting and implies of course the diasporisation of the world. Leela Gandhi writes:

> ...postcolonialism is generally concerned with the idea of cultural dislocation.... While diaspora... is generally invoked as a theoretical device for the interrogation of ethnic identity and cultural nationalism... diasporic thought betrays its poststructuralist origins by contesting all claims to the stability of meaning and identity. In its postcolonial incarnation, such thought reviews the colonial encounter for its disruption of native/domestic space.
>
> (Gandhi 131-132)

Diaspora literature more often than not involves a history of displacement, remembrances of the homeland (from where the dispersal occurred), feelings of alienation in the adopted country, and romantic desire for return (which is possibly impossible). Basically, 'diaspora' is a minority community living in exile. Due to social exclusion, seclusion and marginalization, diasporics retain the country they were once part of in their consciousness as a marker of distinctiveness and difference. Even empirically, the majority of diasporics worldwide constitute minority groups in their host countries and therefore remain unprivileged and embattled. It primarily refers to the permanently displaced and relocated groups having or sharing common national and/or ethnic identity. In fact, diasporics made cultural scholars and theorists to revisit centre-periphery relationships and identities. They even threatened the supremacy of nation-states.

The term 'diaspora' immediately conjures up the image of a journey. But this journey is altogether a different one. Diasporic journeys are about settling down and putting roots or 'staying put' elsewhere (Brah 182). Home is central to the thinking of Avtar Brah about diaspora. She writes in her *Cartographies of Diaspora*, "Home is a mythic place of desire in the diasporic imagination. In this sense it is a place of no-return, even if it is possible to visit the geographical territory that is seen as the place of 'origin.'"(Brah 192). This tendency is what she calls 'homing desire'. Brah and Phoenix in an essay "Ain't I a Woman? Revisiting Intersectionality" write of 'diaspora space' (already introduced in *Cartographies of Diaspora*) which according to them, is a unison of 'border', 'home politics', and 'diaspora'. They write: "The intersection of these terms is understood through the concept of 'diaspora space' which covers the entanglements of genealogies of dispersal with those of 'staying put'. They further argue that "the concept of 'diaspora space' embraces the intersection of 'difference' in its variable forms, placing emphasis upon emotional and psychic dynamics as much as socio-economic, political, and cultural differences"(Brah and Phoenix

83). To say simply, by 'diaspora space' they mean the journey from the point of deterritoralisation to reterritorialisation alongside all 'emotional and psychic', social, cultural, political, and economic uniqueness. Actually 'diaspora space' is a kind of crucible wherein creolisation or hybridisation of identities happens undermining any notion of fixity based on skin, colour, birth, country, or affiliation/heritage.

James Clifford in his essay simply titled *Diasporas* (1994) is mainly concerned with 'experiences of displacement' and imagining process of home being away from original home, and with the question as to how these are addressed in diaspora discourses. The poetics of diaspora, according to him "is increasingly invoked by displaced people who feel (maintain, revive, invent) a connection with a prior home." According to him, diasporics commonly share "a history of dispersal, myths/ memories of the homeland, alienation in the host (bad host?) country, desire for eventual return, ongoing support of the homeland, and a collective identity importantly defined by this relationship" (Clifford 305). According to him, "Diaspora consciousness lives loss and hope as a defining tension" (Clifford 312). Rajeev S. Patke similarly opines that diasporics combine loss and gain, the elegiac and the recuperation, by depicting the self as the bearer of a legacy which belongs neither to a past that is mourned in the memory nor to a future that is celebrated in augury, but to the acts of mind in which pastness and futurity have their being, negatively shaped by the feelings and experiences of discrimination and social exclusion, and positively through identification with world historical, cultural/political forces, such as Africa or China.

In all diasporic life, 'roots', 'routes', 'home', and 'dispersion' are placed in "creative tension, inscribing a homing desire while simultaneously critiquing discourses of fixed origin"(Brah 193, Mishra 75). Diasporic imaginary is closely connected to the idea of homing desire (Mishra 5). Vijay Mishra in his book *The*

Literature of the Indian Diaspora: Theorising the Diasporic Imaginary (2007) expresses his unwillingness to call all people moving away from their land of origin as diasporic people. No doubt, around ten million people are mobile but all of them cannot be designated as diaspora.

Once in the 1980's *The Statesman* claimed that Indians are ubiquitous. It does not mean that all are diasporic. According to Vijay Mishra, only those are diasporic who could not even today forget the hangover (trauma) of the moment of dispersal. Although they are rich enough yet they could not adjust with their hostland emotionally, and nor could return to their land of origin. Actually, Vijay Mishra reserves the term 'diaspora' only for unhappier breed, whose progress and prosperity could not compensate for the pain they once suffered and continue to suffer due to social exclusion and marginalization. They still long for that which is no longer existing in real terms. Other than the unhappier breed, they are immigrants, transnationals or global people. As he writes:

> All diasporas are unhappy, but every diaspora is unhappy in its own way. Diasporas refer to people who do not feel comfortable with their non-hyphenated identities as indicated on their passport. Diasporas are people who would want to explore the meaning of the hyphen, but perhaps not press the hyphen too far for fear that this would lead to massive communal schizophrenia. They are precariously lodged within an episteme of real or imagined displacements, self-imposed sense of exile; they are haunted by spectres, by ghosts arising from within that encourage irredentist or separatist movements. Diasporas are both celebrated (by late postmodernity) and maligned (by early modernity)
>
> (Mishra 1)

Actually Vijay Mishra is more interested in recovering the bitter experiences during the horrible, dehumanizing, and life-threatening journeys across the 'black atlantic'; slaves and indentured labourers savoured, as represented and depicted in various writings of Indian diaspora. The 'diasporic imaginary' is another concept of Vijay Mishra. He defines it as "any ethnic enclave in a nation-state that *defines* itself, consciously, unconsciously or through self-evident or implied political coercion, as a group that lives in displacement." The term 'imaginary', he uses in Lacanian sense, meaning a desire, wish or image that diasporas prefer to be identified with (Mishra 14). About transnational social, cultural, political, economic, and literary actors or players, Schiller et al writes:

> Transmigrants develop and maintain multiple relations — familial, economic, social, organizational, religious, and political that span borders. Transmigrants take actions, make decisions, and feel concerns, and develop identities within social networks that connect them to two or more societies simultaneously.
>
> (Schiller et al. 1-2)

II

Ramanujan's sense of identity crisis and physical absence made his identification with home or family inevitable and inescapable. Actually his strained feelings acquire redressal outlet in his poems. Niranjan Mohanty is of the opinion that like many other diasporic writers, Ramanujan's return on the mental level "decisively resolves the poet's problem of identity, sanctions a kind of security, orchestrates a kind of solace for not being altogether faceless, illustrates a type of rootedness or relatedness, weaves an experiential web which is authentic"(Mohanty 50). Ramanujan emerges as a home-haunted poet in several of his poems. "Snakes", "Of Mothers, among other things", "Love Poem for a Wife, 1", "Small-Scale Reflections on a Great House", "History", "Obituary", "Death and the Good Citizen", "Extended Family", "Farewell" etc. have been selected to verify his home-haunting melody. Home, family, and family relations are intertwined in these poems. Nobody can generally do away with the reminiscences of the immediate-left-home. It is altogether impossible to wipe all traces of lost-home away.

"Snakes" is one of the earliest home-poems. Ramanujan bizarrely associates snakes with family. In the first stanza he tells how, when and where he used to be reminded and feared of snakes. But "it does not happen/ when I walk through the woods." It happens while walking through 'museums of quartz' or libraries. The snakes often take refuge in museums, book-shelves, glass-shelves, etc. The poet says that he is reminded of snakes whenever he sees books of yellow vein or yellow amber or books with golden spine, and shelves arranged in geometric lines. In the second stanza the hissing sound of the revolving snakes is compared to the little dust clouds arose while walking along a dusty road. The dust and the snakes both by their nature encircle one's feet. The hoods snakes display take after the etched black lorgnettes. It looks ridiculous or absurd all the same. Then the snakes are likened to some 'terrible aunt'. The aunt is proud of her tiles (silk hat). Both aunt and snakes shed their scales (layers of skin) with the warming of moon. In the third stanza, the poet recounts a real incident. One day a snake charmer brings 'a basketful of ritual cobras' to the poet's home. Their bodies are wheatish in colour with ripples (rings) all over. They move on the floor 'writing a sibilant alphabet of panic' here and there. Then the poet's mother 'gives milk in saucers'. As they suck the milk 'the black-line design/etched on the brass of the saucer' reappears. The snake charmer then wears them on his neck to impress and attract 'father's smiling/money. But I scream.' In the fourth stanza, the poet tells that he has a sister who has knee-long hair. He notices her making plates in her hair and adorns with tassels (ribbons) pins. Her braids immediately remind poet of snakes and look like the scales on the body. Both glisten. He is very much frightened of her long braids and waits impatiently it to be trimmed and tied neatly. He writes:

> My night full of ghosts from a sadness
> in a play, my left foot listens to my right footfall,
> a clockwork clicking in the silence
> within my walking.
>
> (*CP* 5)

In the last stanza the poet narrates a story when the poet was walking through a forest suddenly he felt as if he were walking on a wet land, and there a snake writhing in pain. Its body was 'green white measured by bluish nodes' looking like 'a water-bleached lotus stalk plucked lately'. He is so terrified that he tramples it to death. Now he is confident and fearless. He says:

> Now
> Frogs can hop upon this sausage rope,
> flies in the sun will mob the look in his eyes,
> . . . .
> and I can walk through the woods.
>
> (*CP* 5)

In the poem "Of Mothers among other things" he depicts abiding relationship between him and mother. Mother is the centre. The poet is reminded of his mother's glistening youthful days (silk and white petal) when she used to pamper herself with jewelleries. It coincides with the smell of 'twisted black bone tree'. This also reminds the poet of his mother's delicate motherly affection for her baby as she runs back from 'rain to the crying cradles'. The last three stanzas are rich in imagery. The rainfall is tacking against trees as if a tailor was sewing worn-out clothes with broken threads; but her hands are like that of 'a wet eagle's two black pink-crinkled feet', one of her fingers (talon) is crippled or disabled; her sarees look like an unfastened feather. It means that she is now weak and thin. In the last stanza the poet feels struck dumb when he sees 'her four still sensible flex fingers' inclined 'to pick a grain of rice from the kitchen floor'. This was the sincerity at the domestic chars of his mother. She is still mentally agile though physically weakened.

"Love Poem for a Wife 1" is based on the poet's relationship with his wife. The first seven lines bring out his sense of estrangement from his wife. The reason for this, according to him is 'unshared childhood'. As a result the couple cannot know each other's likes and dislikes and temperament. Also they cannot know about their parents. The second seven lines inform that the wife and husband both recall their past a little nostalgically and look upon each other's indulgences enviously. The recognition of each other comes slowly as the third stanza tells:

of the seven crazy aunts
You begin to recognize me
as I pass from ghost to real
and back again in the albums
of family rumours, in brother,
anecdotes of how noisily
father bathed,

(*CP* 65)

She can form some idea of his parents by looking at the family albums or by listening to his brother's anecdotes. She looks strangely at a 'sepia wedding/ picture of father in a turban' and at 'mother standing on her bare feet', wearing 'silver rings on her second toes.' She cherishes peculiar ideas about his entire career without realizing its unique charms or successes. Her father has now grown old and lost his temper and memory. He is now so weak and careless that he doesn't even bother about her visiting, about meeting 'nice Muslim friend' at odd hours. Then is mentioned her fight with brother James about the location of the bathroom. While they quarrel over, the poet sits along with his sister-in-law in the adjoining room without making any movement. She goes on quarrelling with her brother, they draw sketches of the bathroom from memory, from newspapers to the backs of envelopes. This is all about the ninth stanza. She suddenly becomes more assertive and wagers the family belongings and the husband's earnings over the question of what uncle in Kuwait will say about the disputed bathroom and the well and tree standing nearby.

In the eleventh stanza the poet starts speculating about the rightness of the Egyptians in marrying their own sisters to 'continue the incests/ of childhood'. The poet wants to drive home the point that his wife would have found a fitter life-partner in her brother, for both of them are of the same temperament and are prone to fight over petty things. In the next stanza the poet suggests another possibility. He and his wife should have lived more happily had they been betrothed before their birth. The marriage before birth, as the well-meaning Hindus did long ago, could have cemented their relationship and would have saved the labour of horoscopists.

"Love Poem for a Wife 1" is an evocation of the poet's family life. His sense of frustration caused by the marriage of an ultra-modern lady is quite evident here. He actually desires to overcome his alienation from his wife, but emotional and cultural gaps come before him.

The poem "Small-Scale Reflections on a Great House" celebrates the possessiveness of the poet's ancestral 'great house' and his failure to do away with its hold. He writes:

> Sometimes I think that nothing
> that ever comes into this house
> goes out. Things come in every day
> to lose themselves among other things
> lost long ago among
> other things lost long ago.
>
> (*CP* 96)

As the poet has left this 'great house' long ago, he recalls each and everything. He catalogues all those things that come from outside and stay back for good, and those things that go outside temporarily but later on return. And the third section registers those items which never stay out. The stray cows, library books, plates came from the family in vicinity, servants, phonographs, sons-in-law never go out of this 'great house'. Bales of cotton are exported to the foreign cities like Manchester but return being processed and refined 'and often with long bills attached' therewith. Letters return having been directed wrongly. Ideas go out but come back as rumours. The married-off daughters, the runaway sons and nephews engaged in some war or fight never stay away for long. This is the face value of the text. But to my mind the 'great house' of the poet's ancestry symbolizes all-assimilating, all-embracing, and all-enamouring potential of India and Indian culture. The poet, of course feels handicapped before such 'great house'.

"History" is another family saga. It is occasioned on the day before the poet's great aunt died. In it the poet records the selfish history of family members. According to him, history underwent changes and with the progress of time selfishness gained ground in the family firmly. On the day the great-aunt died, the poet tells that his 'petite little aunt' was altogether indifferent. She was 'looking for something, half/ her body under the cot, / may be a rolling pin/ her little son had brought for play/ from under the richer mob/ of cooking and washing relatives.' But it was overly condemnable condition the day before great-aunt died. The little dark aunt has two daughters, one dark and one fair. What happened then the poet tells:

> alternatively picked their mother's body clean
> before it was cold
> or the eyes were shut,
> of diamond ear-rings,
> bangles, anklets, the pin
> in her hair,
> the toe-rings from her wedding
> the previous century,
> all except the gold
> in her teeth and the silver g-string

they didn't know she wore
her napkins on
to the great disgust
of the orthodox widows
who washed her body
at the end,

(*CP* 108)

Finally the dark and stony face of the poet's aunt became eloquent. Here the tone of the poem is serious and sullen yet Ramanujan does not forget incorporating Parvati, the wife of Shiva:

And my little dark aunt was there
nose eyes and knee-bend cut
fresh from stone for a Parvati statue—

(*CP* 107)

"Obituary" is another home-poem. The poet tells that on the occasion of his father's death the father has left a table covered with dust and old newspapers, debts, daughters to be married away, a bedwetting grandson, and a dilapidating, crumbling house. As he writes:

a house that leaned
slowly thhrough our growing
years on a bent coconut
tree in the yard.

(*CP* 111)

This all signify that the family is on the verge of going without food and shelter. The house is about to be ruined. The next few stanzas detail about the father's cremation and his ashes to be immersed into the holy Sangam (confluence of three rivers); and a memorial having 'his full name and two dates' (death-date and birth-date). Actually the poet seems disapproving of his father. His death caused by cordial wrest was reported in some daily newspaper in Madras which was in turn sold off to the hawker's hand and in turn to groceries 'where I buy salt, coriander and jaggery' in 'newspaper cones/ that I usually read for and later in hope of finding these obituary.' It was all simple not causing much trouble but his death brought:

> a changed mother
> and more than
> one annual ritual.
>
> (*CP* 112)

In "Death and the Good Citizen" Ramanujan expresses his desire to be cremated as per his native culture and nature amidst mantric recitations. The people of his clan "will cremate me in Sanskrit and sandlewood/ have me sterilised/to a scatter of ashes'. Other than his native culture, he says:

> My tissue will never graft,
> will never know newsprint,
> never grow in a culture,
> or be mould and compost
> for jasmine, eggplant
> and the unearthly perfection
> of municipal oranges.
>
> (*CP* 136)

This affirms explicitly that Ramanujan is bound with India and its culture.

III

Hinduism is another indelible ink in the fountain pen of Ramanujan. It occupies central space and lies at the heart of India and Indian people. India is the home of religion and tradition.

Ramanujan like many other Hindus had learnt indigenous myths and folktales. Myth refers to any story, true or false, among hereditary stories which serve some specific purposes. These are traditional stories which still have influence on Hindus, if a story engages beings of supernatural stature and do not be part of systematic mythology "a system of hereditary stories of ancient origin" (Abrams 170). Such stories are called generally folktales. In Indian belief and practice, the human body is made up of five elements *(panchbhutani)*—air, water, fire, sky, and earth. After the death of the body (as soul is immortal and not subjected to death and decay), all these elements naturally return to their respective elements. In the poem "Towards Simplicity" Ramanujan writes that 'corpuscle, skin, cell, and membrane' all have certain life and are bound with one another in an intricate manner. Each element runs towards its perfection that is death. As such the life-death cycle runs infinitely. He writes:

> Millions grow lean and fall away
> in the hourly autumn of the body. Stories of
> But fertile in fall, ending as others begin,
> to the naivete of death they run.
>
> (*CP* 37)

In "A Hindu to His Body" Ramanuajan seeks to drive home the fact that to a Hindu, body and soul are both equally important. A little fancifully the poet calls the body 'Dear pursuing presence', 'dear body'. That is why the body requests the soul not to leave it behind. He knows that often after the see-off of immortal soul, the body will return into nature. He writes:

> When you leave all else,
> my garrulous face, my unkissed
> alien mind, when you muffle
> and put away my pulse
> to rise in the sap of trees

let me go with you and feel the weight
of honey-hives in my branching
and the burlap weave of weaver-birds
in my hair.

(*CP* 40)

In Hindu philosophy, every creature has a perishable body and an immortal soul. The soul is immortal. And therefore every creature, big or small, deserves equal importance. The essence of Hindu philosophy is tolerance, sympathy, and sensibility or sensitivity. On should ever have mercy on others. Ramanuajan being born in a south Indian brahmin family is deeply rooted in Hinduism. He doesn't like to hurt a fly or a spider either because he thinks that these creatures might be one of his ancestors. He affirms:

Maybe it's once again my
. . . . . .
great swinging grandmother,
and that other (playing at
patience centered in his web)
my one true ancestor,

(*CP* 62)

No place is approved for suicide in Hindu philosophy. Every Hindu knows that suicide is not a problem-solving approach to life. It is a kind of crime. Those who commit suicide are cowards. Perhaps this belief inspired the poet to muse upon two-three reasons against suicide in the poem "One, Two, Maybe Three, Arguments against Suicide". He ironically calls one dear departing saint who commits suicide. He focuses on the horror of the sight of the suicide:

you see red, you faint, at the sight
of blood. And there's always the danger

you may be understood, as never
before, misconstrued by some
casual stranger.

(*CP* 71)

In Hindu belief, one who commits suicide makes his/her soul restless and sends soul to hell which is not the aim of life. In Hindu thinking attainment of liberation or *moksha* is the highest end of life. Now the poet looks at the later situation of suicide:

now, yet live on forever in spite
of what those doctors certify:
your self now a mere odourless soul,
a see-through man-shaped hole
in the air, a late lamenting ghost
looking in vain for an empty seat
at the full house of your posthumous
fame where you can see but not hear
the rain of applause, the jungle
of medals on the breast of your happy
unhappy widow.

(*CP* 71-72)

Very often untemporised desires and emotions result in suicide. Since desires are endless, one should keep one's physical desires cool and calm but not altogether. Here the poet stealthily weaves out the Kamadeva myth into the texture of the third section of the poem. He writes:

Remember what the wise callous hindus
said when the love-god burned:keep your cool,
make for love's sake no noble gesture.
All symbol, no limbs, a nobody all soul,
O Kama, only you can have no use

for the *Kamasutra.*
Ashes have no posture.

(*CP* 72)

In "The Hindoo: he reads his GITA and is calm at all events" the poet inveigles against those Hindus who claim good mastery in the teachings of the *Gita*. The *Gita* stresses fortitude and 'calm of mind, all passions spent', sympathy, mercy, tolerance etc. But Hindus often misconstrue the essence of the *Gita* which is a blunder. The persona claims that he doesn't bother at all about good and evil things. He just passes by events even when help or support is expected. The poet writes:

...Knives, bombs, scandal,
and cowdung fall on women in wedding lace:
I say nothing, I take care not to gloat.

(*CP* 79)

Moreover, the personae 'look at wounds calmly'. Though the *Gita* teaches one to take the world as a family, Hindus have forgotten instead their claims. Here the poet doesn't slander the sacred Hindu scriptures. He jeers at Hindus, not Hinduism. He wants Hindus to be consistent with the Hindu philosophy. Finally in "THE HINDOO: the only risk" the poet arrives at the conclusion that Hindus who keep incomplete knowledge of sacred texts are given to selfishness and heartlessness. These Hindus do not follow the essence of Hinduism. They need a squiare meal every day and have nothing to do with spirit of the *Gita*. This is another casualty of Hindus.

As I mentioned earlier, Ramanujan sporadically weaves out Hindu mythologies in his poems. In the poem "Compensations" he depicts the situation and condition of soldiers who suffered massive blows of war bells, aftermath of the wars. He depicts them as engaged in several activities. But towards the closing of the poem the poet takes recourse to the Hindu myth of Tandava (deadly dance of God Shiva). It is believed among the Hindus that Lord Shiva performed the Tandava whenever He wished to herald a new generation (Yuga). Ramanujan alongside all Hindus believes that the Tandava marks the greatest destruction. He writes:

> surpassed only by the last
> miracle of grace, the three-eyed
> whirlwind of arms, dancing on
> a single leg though he can dance
> on many, kind returning god
> of Indian deluges,
>
> (*CP* 110)

According to Ramanujan Lord Shiva at every time of the Tandava brought a new era but in its wake leaving traces of destruction like famine, war, and riot. This is the compensatory work. Since Lord Shiva sooner or later will destroy the entire world, the periodic wars, blood-shed and many other lethal human works become useless. The poet criticizes the wars for power and dominion sake.

In "Prayer to Lord Murugan" the poet laments the loss of faith among people. People are not worshipping this 'ancient Dravidian god of fertility, joy, youth, beauty, war, and love' (*CP* 113) sincerely and faithfully. This reminds me of Mathew Arnold's attitude expressed in "Dover Beach". Actually people are becoming corrupt very fast and selfish, and therefore spiritually inclined people feel estranged:

> Lord of headlines,
> help us read
> the small print.
> Lord of the sixth sense,
> give us back
> our five senses.
>
> (*CP* 116)

In "Mythologies I" the poet reworks the Putana and Krishna myth. According to this myth, Kansa, the uncle of the baby Lord Krishna, sent Putana (a female demon with poisoned breasts) to kill the baby by offering her poison-coated breasts but the baby happily suckled at her nipples and blessed her:

> She changed, undone by grace,
> From deadly mother to happy demon,
> Found life in death
>
> (*CP* 221)

Every Hindu prays to God for salvation and resurrection. He invokes God to:

> Drink my venom.
> Renew my breath.
>
> (*CP* 221)

In "Mythologies II" Ramanujan similarly reworks the Lord Vishnu and Hiranyakashapu myth. Kashyapu was a great atheist but an extraordinary devotee of Lord Vishnu. This clever devotee asked for a perfect boon:

> not be slain by demon, god, or by
> beast, not by day nor by night,
> by no manufactured weapon, not out
> of doors nor inside, not in the sky
> nor on earth.
>
> (*CP* 226)

But Lord Vishnu had 'to disembowel his pride'. He appeared in the shape of half-man-half-lion amidst twilight (neither day nor light) and killed Kashyapu cleverly. The poet calls Lord Vishnu 'midnight sun', 'connoisseur of negatives and assassin of certitudes'. He calls upon him:

...slay now my faith in doubt.
End my commerce with bat and night-
owl. Adjust my single eye, rainbow bubble,
so I too may see all things double.

(*CP* 226)

In "Mythologies III " the poet talks of a lately wedded couple. The bride advises her bridegroom not to touch her at the time of worship to Lord Shiva. She even tells him that he might lose her if he touches three times. The bridegroom is unmindful of her warnings. He doesn't even hear his bride's 'Om, Om! / she seemed to intone in bed with every breath'. But:

And all he could think of was her round breast,
Her musk, her darling naval and the rest.

(*CP* 228)

Here thc husband is inclined to have sexual fulfilment but she is engaged in offering prayers to Lord Shiva. Both are polaes apart temperamentally. But the poet, to convey and show this gap, took recourse to Lord Shiva and Parvati.

It is well known that Ramanujan devoted much of his time in folk mythologies, traditions, and the *Upanishads*. In the poem "The Watchers", taking cue from the *Mundaka Upanishad* he discusses various layers of consciousness (psyche) as watchmen engaged in the body where they remain gently watching and enjoying the earthly puppet's tale:

Lighter than light, blowing like air
through keyholes, they watch without questions,
the watchers,
they watch even the questions, as I live
over and over with cancelled stamps,
in verandas,

(*CP* 137)

And moreover, these layers of psyche compel nothing, and nowhere occupy the central position. They can just watch whatever is happening inside and outside:

> impotence
> their supreme virtue, they move only
> their eyes, and all things seem to find their form.
> Mere seers,
> they make the scene.
>
> (*CP* 137)

Ramanujan, well steeped in Indian legendary tradition, narrates a story about five brahmins in "No Fifth Man". These brahmins 'went abroad to learn all the sixty four arts', to show off their mastery in all arts by bringing back a tiger into life. In the process all four brothers lost their lives but the last brahmin was rich in common sense anyhow and managed to save his life. The poet writes:

> The fifth man, the coward,
> cried, 'Wait, wait
> just one second',
> and climbed up a tree in a hurry
>
> (*CP* 244)

In this way the fifth brahmin could save his life but the rest were left with not even a bone.

IV

In Ramanujan's poetic pilgrimage Mysore and Chicago both coalesce and proceed along. His 'from-to' consciousness gets eloquent in most of the poems. The focus on Indian culture is the key region of treatment but often he relates it to its Western counterpart. S.S. Dulai says, "His poetry is borne out of the dialectical interplay between his Indian and American experience on the one hand and that between his sense of his own self and all experience on the other"(Dulai 151). In "Small-Scale Reflections on a Great House", 'great house' is more than the poet's ancestral house. It may mean India or Indian culture where:

> Things come in everyday
> to lose themselves among other things
>
> (*CP* 96)

Identity and culture are not to be into a particular container. They are social victims. They either modify or get modified. The sons-in-law who forget their mothers enjoying foreign lands 'stay to check accounts or teach arithmetic to nieces'. That is, the alien and alien cultures have contributed a lot in terms of technology and knowledge. Ramanujan's transnational awareness gets words in the following excerpts:

> And also, anything that goes out
> will come back, processed and often
> with long bills attached,
> like the hooped bales of cotton
> shipped off to invisible Manchesters
> and brought back milled and folded
> for a price, cloth for days'
> middle-class loens, and muslin
> for our richer nights.
>
> (*CP* 97)

This is multicultural nature of India which undermines Western notions of fixity and stability in everything. Later on, he writes:

> Nothing stays out:daughters
> get married to short-lived idiots;
> sons who run away come back.
>
> (*CP* 98)

The implication is that everything seeks in the long run to be identified with its roots. Daughters who have been married off to some idiots return finding them incompatible or they have been turned out due to some racial differences as it is often practised in the West.

"Astronomer" is another poem dwelling on the theme of transculturation and hybridity. Ramanujan himself reveals the fact that the poem is about his father Srinivas Ramanujan who was a renowned mathematician. All the same, he was:

> Sky-man in a manhole
> with astronomy for dream,
> astrology for nightmare;
>
> (*CP* 134)

His father was also a Sanskrit scholar and astrologer. He had equal mastery in astrology, astronomy, and mathematics. The poet and his generation were always flummoxed by his father's acumen. Actually he was an epitome of English, American and Indian awareness.

In "Death and the Good Citizen" Ramanujan's awareness about death rites in different cultures finds expression. In East, burning pyres are prepared to burn the body accompanied by Sanskrit mantras, and the ashes are to be scattered into the holy Sangam (confluence of rivers). As he writes:

> they'll cremate
> me in Sanskrit and sandalwood,
> have me sterilized
> to a scatter of ash.
> But in the West-
> they'll lay me out in a funeral
> parlour, embalm me in pesticide,
> bury me in a steel trap, lock

me out of nature
till I'm oxidized by left-
over air, withered by my own
vapours into grin and bone.

(*CP* 136)

No doubt in this poem Ramanujan explores the possibilities about his death rites. But like all diasporics as multiculturalists having sufficient tolerance towards Western patterns writes:

My tissue will never graft,
will never know newsprint,
never grow in a culture,
or be mould and compost
for jasmine, eggplant
and the unearthly perfection
of municipal oranges.

(*CP* 136)

According to him, biodegradation of the body is the proper process.

In 'Extended Family" the poet finds himself as a marriage bed of Westrtern and Eastern cultures:

Yet like grandfather
I bathe before the village crow
the dry chlorine water
my only Ganges
the naked Chicago bulb
a cousin of the Vedic sun.

(*CP* 169)

Here the Chicago bulb is conflated with the Vedic sun.

Like his mother he used to listen to 'faint morning song (though here it sounds / Japanese). As such Ramanujan is quite conscious about multicultural and transcultural location.

In "The Difference" the poet hints at his multicultural make-up:

> But I, a community of one,
> mould
> myself both clay and metal
> body shape and lips;
>
> (*CP* 172)

The implication is that Ramanujan is proud of his multicultural upbringing.

In "Waterfalls in a Bank" Ramanujan explicitly gives vent to his transcultural position and location:

> As I transact with the past as with another
> country with its customs, currency,
> stock exchanges, always
> at a loss when I count my change:water-
> falls of dying children, assam
> politics,
> and downtown Nairobi fall through me
> in Hyde Bank, as I rise among them,
> mud on my nose,
>
> (*CP* 189)

In "Looking for the Centre" Ramanujan in fact overlooks Euro-American notions of centrality, fixity, and stability:

> Looking for the centre these days
> Is like looking for the centre
> For missing Children
>
> (*CP* 184)

In "Chicago Zen" Ramanujan versified his transcultural position and its concept. His location in Chicago made him feel fractured and cracked:

> The traffic light turns orange
> on 57th and Dorchester, and you stumble,
> you fall into a vision of forest fires,
> enter a frothing Himalayan river,
> rapid, silent.
>
> (*CP* 186)

From here, to the poet 'returning is as tedious as to go over' (Macbeth). No means of transport can replant on the land of origin:

> Now you know what you always knew:
> the country cannot be reached
> by jet....
> Nor by any
> other means of transport,
>
> (*CP* 187)

If any possibility is left, it is only by talking to kiths and kins through electronic media:

> migrating with a clean valid passport,
> no, not even by transmigrating
> without any passport at all,
> but only by answering ordinary
> black telephones, questions
> walls and small children ask,
> and answering all calls of nature.
>
> (*CP* 187)

In "A Report", Ramanujan hints at the prevalent global discrepancies with regard to art, culture, and social life. He denounces these hurdles to developing pluricultural society:

> Hitler, housepainter who painted Warsaw
> red, rumored alive in Argentina,
> is dead; Stalin defaced; Lenin is a name
> for a telephone museum. Vietnam
> is a box office hit. Gandhi and King
> are black and white photographs smiling
> away in bidi shops.
>
> (*CP* 248)

Everywhere the upmanship endeavour has gained ground being unbothered by the increasing hiatus among the people. The poet is sighing and invokes the god of death and Ganges (goddess of sweet water) as he is incapable to do something for the degrading society except 'to dream of a blue Mysore house in Chicago' lest he should fall asunder.

Thus we can say that Ramanujan never forgot his dislocated position throughout his poetic journey to homeland. India and America stand side by side in his poems and in his consciousness. Without doubt, his sensibility got sharpened and enriched by his translocation. He quite successfully managed both experiences and celebrated in poems. In many of his poems he recounts and reworks Hindu myths, legends, religion, culture etc. with no fear, as we saw in a few of them like "Towards Simplicity", "The Hindoo: he doesn't hurt a fly or a spider either", "One, Two, Maybe Three, Arguments against Suicide", "The Hindoo: he reads his Gita and is calm at all events", "Compensations", "Prayers to Lord Murugan", "Death and the Good Citizen", "Mythologies I", "Mythologies II", "No Fifth Man", "A Hindu to His Body", "The Watchers" etc.

Since migration proved quite painful to him, hence home myths and folklores are nowhere missing. They are perfectly sprinkled over his poetic path. In fact, his diasporic situation turned him into a home-haunted multicultural, multi-vocalic bard of Indian origin. It stands for him loss, alienation and estrangement, finally culminating in 'homing desire'. No doubt his poems begin with his centre (self) but soon turn towards the periphery (that is, his parents, native culture, art, tradition, religion, myth, and ideas). This is his 'heteroglottic' approach. In Ramanujan's case, migration has negative colours, that is, loss of home, estrangement of relations alongside culture, art, tradition, religion and rituals. Ramanujan, by celebrating the Indian myth, folklore, culture, tradition, language etc., restored Indian identity and India.

Works Cited

Abrams, M.H. *A Glossary of Literary Terms* (7th ed.). Singapore: Thomson Asia Pte Ltd. 2003. Print.

Brah, Avtar. *Cartographies of Diaspora:Contesting Identities*. London and New York: Routledge, 1997. Print.

Brah and Phoenix. "Ain't I A Woman? Revisiting Intersectionality". *Journal of International Women's Studies* 5. 3 (2004): 75–86. Print.

Bhatnagar, M.K. Ed. *The Poetry of A.K. Ramanujan*. Delhi: Atlantic Publishers and Distributors, 2007. Print.

Clifford, James. "Diasporas". *Cultural Anthropology*. 9. 3(1994): 302-338. Print.

Dulai, S.S. "First and Only Sight:The Centre and Circles of A.K. Ramanujan's Poetry". *Journal of South Asian Literature*. 24(1-2)(1989): 149-175. Print.

Gandhi, Leela. *Postcolonial Theory:A Critical Introduction*. New Delhi: OUP, 2005. Print.

McLeod, James. *The Routledge Companion to Postcolonial Studies*. London and New York: Routledge, 2007. Print.

Mishra, Vijay. *The Literature of The Indian Diaspora:Theorising The Diasporic Imaginary*. New York: Routledge, 2007. Print.

Parthasarathy, R. *Ten Twentieth-Century Indian Poets*. New Delhi: Oxford University Press, 1976. Print.

Ramanujan, A.K. *Collected Poems*. New Delhi: OUP, 2009. Print. (All textual references are given parenthetically to this edition, referred as CP.)

Schiller, Nina G., et al. Transnationalism: a new analytic framework for understanding migration. *Annals of the New York Academy of Sciences* 645(1992): 1-24. Print.

3

Use of Myths and Legends in Kiran Nagarkar's *Ravan and Eddie* and *Cuckold*

Nitin Jarandikar

Kiran Nagarkar (b. 1942) is a significant Indian English novelist. He deals with the novel form with all its intricacies, and brings out the various dimensions of the human experience. It has been observed that while handling the tension and balance between the social and personal worlds of his protagonists, Kiran Nagarkar essentially writes in a realistic mode of presentation. However, his realistic presentation is a significant departure from the conventional 'realism'. He is well aware of the limitations of the conventional realism to delineate the anxieties and crises of the modern man. That's why he consciously makes experimentation with the narrative techniques, and in that way utilizes mythical and legendry resources.

Nagarkar's use of myths and legends in fiction can be seen particularly in his two novels, namely, *Ravan and Eddie* (1995) and *Cuckold* (1997). But again, his inclination to myths and legends has to be differentiated from that of James Joyce, W.B. Yeats or J.M. Synge from the Western tradition or Girish Karnad, or Salman Rushdie from the Indian tradition. In his novels myths and legends do not form the centrestage. On the contrary, Nagarkar uses these elements as a stepping stone and attempts to comprehend the predicament of the human persona. In the present article, the researcher intends to analyse in what way Nagarkar uses myths and legends in the novels namely, *Ravan and Eddie* and *Cuckold* to underline the anxieties and crises of the human persona.

I

In any literary world, the mythical ethos enters with a specificity of purpose and objective. The writer makes use of a myth from different positions. It is the contemporaneity of a myth that gives author a space to communicate his ideas. Sometimes like *Rape of the Lock* he uses myth to parody the world or like James Joyce's *Portrait of the Artist* as a young man he sees the mythical hero, Stephan Dedalus, representing the predicament of the artist in the modern world. The use of the mythical world thus provides the writer to focus his point of view by delineating different aspects of myth in his own time. It is incorporated in the narrative at different levels and in different modes to emphasise the major themes of novel. The following discussion helps to illustrate this point where Kiran Nagarkar in his novel *Ravan and Eddie* makes use of mythical worlds from two religious cultures and puts forth the complicated predicament of modern man living in a multi-cultural society.

The novel *Ravan and Eddie*, much applauded for its burlesque kind of humour, unfolds the life story of the protagonists with the same names who live in the Central Works Department's (CWD) chawl no. 17, Mazagaon, Bombay. The beginning of the novel very dramatically reveals the accidental fall of Ram, the thirteen-month-old baby and his miraculous escape from major injury, his renaming as Ravan and the birth of Eddie. The novel begins on the eve of Christmas immediately after India's independence, and ends when leaving their teen age, both Ravan and Eddie enter the world of adulthood. Thus, the novel encompasses roughly a span of 20 years. Nagarkar, as an onlooker, observes the surrounding world through the eyes of Ravan Pawar and Eddie Countinho. However, these two protagonists seldom confront vis-à-vis throughout the novel. There is a kind of unspoken rivalry growing between Ravan and Eddie. Certain situations make their rivalry more bitter. Nagarkar locates his protagonists in the specific entity of Mumbai chawls which represent in true sense the multicultural society.

As the title suggests the fictional world of *Ravan and Eddie* is dominated by the predicament of Ravan and Eddie as the individual characters. It is interesting to observe that, though the novel deals with the children, it does not depict the world of innocence. Like Ralph and Jack's rivalry, which becomes fatal in course of time in William Golding's novel *Lord of the Flies* (1954), there is a rivalry between Ravan and Eddie about which they are unaware. Nagarkar looks at the world through the eyes of Ravan and Eddie, but perceives that the world is very much intoxicated by the adult sentiments of rivalry.

The death of Victor Countinho, with which the novel begins, forms the bone of contention for the rivalry between Ravan and Eddie. At the beginning of the novel, it is seen that Victor Countinho, the father of yet to-be-born Eddie, is returning from his day-shift one evening. While returning, he sees Parvati Pawar standing with her thirteen-month-old son Ram. For Victor, Parvati is a fascinating figure. He is mesmerized by her physical beauty. He waves in the direction of Ram, rather Parvati, and within a moment, the baby bounces from her hands. Victor catches the baby, gets severe heart attack, collapses and dies. Violet, the wife of Victor, Calls Ram as "Cain. Murderer". At the time of Victor's funeral, Violet gives birth to Eddie. Parvati considers Ram's accident as an evil act, and after this incidence to remove the evil eye, 'nazar', decides to call Ram as Ravan. As the narrative proceeds, it is seen that Ravan's identity as a 'murderer' is intensified and he has been held guilty for the crimes which he hasn't committed.

Ravan's 'fall' and Parvati's renaming of Ram as Ravan with which the novel begins incorporates the complexities of Hindu-Christian mythical consciousness, and very significantly poses the problematic of identity confronted by Ravan Pawar, the protagonist of the novel. Ram, the erstwhile Ravan Pawar, inevitably reminds one of the epic hero of the *Ramayana*. The mythical figure of Ram has been depicted as the 'Maryada Purushottam', an epitome of principles and ideals. In the epic *Ramayana,* Rama and Ravana confront with each other in the forms of virtue versus vice. Quite naturally, Ram's metaphorical 'fall' at the beginning of the novel is denied by his inevitable renaming as Ravan. The writer reveals the intricacies of this 'duel' identity of the character in modern times. As a reader, we can perceive that this episode is mixed with another mythical reference – the biblical myth of the first 'sin' and the first 'crime'. The depiction of Ravan Pawar's character underlines these mixed references of myths from different cultures, and by that way Nagarkar projects the complexity of modern man living in a mixed society with mixed identity and multi-cultural milieu.

Christianity emphasizes 'moral evil' as the root of man's unhappiness. It insists on the loving fellowship with God as life's highest goal. It promises an immortality of glory and blessedness with God; and offers the forgiveness of sin and the renewal of the soul of man by the grace of God received by human faith. Christianity considers God as creator, judge, king, and man as debtor, culprit and subject. Christianity believes that all are under law, all have violated law, and hence all are under sin. Human life is sinful through and through. God punishes sin, but far greater is the truth that men can '*repent*' (emphasis added) and that all sins can be forgiven. This is how Christianity promises *redemption* (emphasis added) for mankind from his sense of sin and guilt.[1]

In the epic narratives, it is said that the fates of the mythical characters are governed by the divine design. However, the modern man's fate is mostly subject to the elements of 'chance' and 'coincidence'. Ravan's fall in the novel is purely accidental and even then coincidently he is trapped in the conscience of sin and guilt. In that light, Ravan's dilemma appears closer to the Christian theology. Ravan's problem is that he has been drifting towards the world of 'sin' and ' evil' for which he is not at all responsible. Parvati repeatedly says, "Ravan is beyond redemption". The ground is already set for Ravan's crisis in Nagarkar's earlier novel, *Seven Sixes Are forty Three* (1981).[2] In this novel, at one instance, Kushank, the protagonist of the novel, overhears a dialogue in a cinema theatre between an unseen father and a lady:

> "It's not too late, Marina, you can still repent, the invisible man advised. And then the woman's voice, helpless, "But how can I repent, Padre, when I don't feel guilty"?

Like Marina, Ravan fails to understand the possibility of 'redemption' since he hasn't committed any 'sin'. As a baby, Ravan falls from the balcony and Victor saves him at the cost of his life. Violet calls him "Cain. Murderer". Ravan carries this burden of 'murder' throughout the novel. When Ravan goes to invite Chandrakant Dixit, his friend, to join the Sabha of the RSS organization, Chandrakant's father slaps Ravan calling him "the murderer of Mahatma Gandhi" (*RE* 24).[3] Ravan cannot recall either of the events. But the stain of murder definitely darkens Ravan's life. His identity as a murderer is confirmed when Prakash Sonawane requests him to kill his father and coincidently the father dies. The appeals of Rajeev Borade, Sudhir Salukhe, or Ashok Sane, the school mates of Ravan to commit the crimes, assuming him to be a murderer, take Ravan to a deep chasm of sin and guilt. Towards the end of the novel, his friend Shobhan Sarang commits suicide, and everyone suspects Ravan. Ravan's crisis becomes graver.

Ravan Pawar is confronted with the identity crisis since he inherits the fate of Rama, the hero of the *Ramayana* and Adam, the hero of the *Genesis*. Besides he is even labelled as "Cain, murderer". Getting the name of Ravan complicates his situation and also hints at the fact that once fallen down, Ram can never remain Ram; he has to be a 'Ravan'. It's not merely a change in name; it incorporates the fatal entrapping of the modern man in the realm of 'sin' and 'guilt' where there is no possibility for any kind of 'redemption' . By providing the blend of myths from the different cultures to figure out the human being, Nagarkar tries to explore the predicament of human being in the modern multi-faceted world where the man has to perform the different roles. Should he locate himself to a race, to a family, to a nation or to the existing milieu is his dilemma. The complexity of connotations puts forth the complexity of human existence.

However, the narrative of Ravan and Eddie does not merely explore the problematic o f such complexity of human existence. By presenting the complex, complicated world of Ram turned into Ravan and Eddie the novel also inquires into the grand narratives of religions as institutions and their 'ideology' that plays dominant role in providing existence to the human being. In this way, Nagarkar presents the modern identity of Ravan who is in other ways associated with the evil forces in the epic *Ramayana*. In the altered circumstances, Nagarkar perceives the fuzzy boundaries between 'good' and 'evil' and expects their re-assessment in the modern contexts.

Ravan of the modern times is expected to bear the burden of sin, the sin for which he is not responsible. How can he 'hang the Albatross' around his neck, what is his penance and how can he can get the redemption is Ravan's crisis. Human life is sinful, and yet all sins can be forgiven, is true. But Nagarkar doubts that mere confession will not bring redemption since 'confession' itself has become a mere ritual. It has lost all its sanctity. Through the episode of Eddie's confession, Nagarkar mocks at the void ritual. In one instance it is seen that Eddie's clothes are torn while collecting a ticket for his favourite movie, Rock Around the Clock, but in the confession box he narrates the false stories to the father about the attack of Mawali Gang of Ravan. It is very ironic that Eddie names his imaginary gang as 'Do or Die Devils'. The Father announces the "unorthodox repentance" for Eddie's crime, the crime that he hasn't committed.

Thus, the novel, in a wider context, becomes a critique of the Christian dialectics of sin- repentance and redemption. But it is to be noted that Nagarkar believes not in any particular religious ideology. He believes in the presence of human life itself, which is forsaken by the divine power. Hence, he believes 'helplessness' being dejected by God is the ultimate reality. Nagarkar elaborates the helplessness of the human lot through a dream sequence where Ravan is seen flying high the kites (*RE* 318-322) . It cannot be a coincidence that Nagarkar names the kite, King Syed Ali, as the 'Butcher'. Syed Ali is a skilful kite-player. Everyone loves his 'pure and simple massacre'. Ravan has a strong desire to defeat Ali by cutting his kite. He dreams that he is successful in pulling down the kite of Syed Ali. The whole kite–episode has metaphorical implications and suggests the ardent human desire to conquer the uncertainties in human life.

With his 'insider–outsider' identity, Nagarkar looks at the Christian concept of 'sin' through Ravan. Likewise, he looks at the Hindu concept of 'sin' through Eddie for which he turns to Hindu myths. After becoming a member of the Sabha, Eddie receives the gift of a storybook. These are the stories from the *Ramayana* and the *Mahabharata*. Eddie is very much attracted by the colourful stories. He reads these stories secretly in his house. Eddie's confrontation, particularly, with the three stories – story of Shishupal, Karna and Abhimanyu – is very significant. All the three are the great warriors and their life stories end with their deaths. Eddie reads in the book, "Shishupal was an evil man who had committed every crime under the sun" (*RE* 116). He is allowed by Lord Krishna to commit a hundred sins. The moment Shishupal commits his ninety-ninth sin, Krishna appears, whose face is "strong, decisive and unforgiving" (*RE* 116) . Krishna kills Shishupal with his Sudarshan Chakra. Eddie thinks of the 'confession' of Shishupal:

> He could have gone down on his knees, wept and begged and apologized and sold himself and the next hundred generations of his children and their children as slaves . . . . . (*RE* 169)

But as per the Hindu tradition, 'confession' is not a way for 'liberation'. Shishupal has to die because he must undergo the unending cycle of life and death till he proves himself fit for 'liberation' or 'Mukti.' [4] Like Shishupal, Karna also commits the 'sin' of joining 'Asatya' – the untruth. As far as, the birth secret of Karna is concerned, he cannot be held responsible for the 'sin' of growing up as an outcaste. But he joins Duryodhana intentionally. And for this crime, death is the only penalty. But the absurdity of a life is that the consequences leading to ' death' cannot always be related to the 'sin'. Nagarkar projects this absurdity through the story of Abhimanyu. Abhimanyu knew 'the secret of penetrating a military maze' but was unable to negotiate it. Eddie can understand the death penalty for Shishupal and Karna, but he wonders about the death of Abhimanyu who hasn't committed any sin. In this way, through Eddie's re-reading of the stories from the Hindu mythology the novel emerges as a critique of the Hindu concept of 'sin' and ' salvation'.

This is how, by juxtaposing the Hindu–Christian myths, Nagarkar highlights the fatal entrapping of the modern man in the domain of sin and guilt from where there is no possibility of any kind of 'redemption'. For him the helpless human existence intensified by the pangs of loneliness is the only fate. He admits that the greater loneliness on the earth is 'the loneliness of being forgotten' which is more pathetic than "the loneliness of death, misunderstanding, distance, separation" (*RE* 248). Therefore, at one instance in the novel the narrator argues that the terrible pain for Jesus was not nailing down, but abandonment by the Father. That's why Jesus might have asked, "Father, Father, why hast thou forsaken me?" (*RE* 248). It is but natural that towards the end of the novel it is seen that Ravan is fatally attracted by the 'swirling' and 'unravelling' infinite danger of Eddie's gymnastic movements of a bamboo pole.

Their interlocking in 'the ritual of battle' indicates the unending phenomenon of guilt and crime, and their "perfect harmony, intersecting each other's orbits in a Pythagorean paradise" suggests the impossibility of any kind of escape from this conscience.

II

Kiran Nagarkar's Hindu–Christian perspective as revealed through the mythical dimension in the novel *Ravan and Eddie* is a rare phenomenon in Indian English fiction. Nagarkar continues his jostling with the notion of 'liberation' and 'salvation' in his next novel *Cuckold*. But this time his recourse is to the tradition of legend enriched by the folklores. The medieval age Indian history and its tradition of saint poetry is a rich heritage. Madhava, Nimbarka, Jnanesvara, Namdev, Eknath, Tukaram, Ramdas, Jaydeva, Chaitanya, Raidas, Kabir, Surdas, Tulsidas and many other poets are the proponents of the medieval age of Bhakti movement in India. Besides its philosophical speculations, the biographies of these poets have been cherished by the myriad folklores.

Saint Meera is one such prominent saint poet from this tradition. Historically speaking, except for her extraordinarily brilliant poetry, known as Padavali, there are very few documents that throw light on the life story of Meera.[5] However, along with her poems, saint Meera has been immortalised by the folk tradition. Meera's poetry reveals her quest to know the 'self' and the ardent desire to become one with divinity. History does speak of Meera's husband and his untimely death. With the help of her life story and the scanty references to her husband as cherished by the folk tradition particularly, Nagarkar in the novel *Cuckold*, fully exploits the space and constructs a marvellous narrative weaving around Meera and her husband. As Nagarkar says, "Meerabai's name is on almost every Indian lips" (*C* 609) [6] but the irony is that her husband, Bhoj Raj, the Maharaj Kumar, the eldest son of Rana Sanga and the would-be king of Mewar, has disappeared from the pages of history. Nagarkar fictionalizes the legendary figure of Bhoj Raj and through him looks at the history of Mewar. In the novel, he appears as the Maharaj Kumar which is not a name of the character but a title conferred on him.

Like *Seven Sixes* or *Ravan and Eddie*, *Cuckold* also begins in a dramatic way. As the Maharana is engaged in a war with Gujarat, the Maharaj Kumar is shouldering the responsibilities of his father. In the small-causes court, he confronts with an interesting case. One washerman accuses his wife on the charge of infidelity. Before going for further hearings, the Maharaj Kumar asks him to prove his virility in a courtesan's bed, and with that the court is adjourned. Interestingly, the same woman comes to the bedchamber of the Maharaj Kumar and surrenders herself to him. The opening scene of the novel projects the Maharaj Kumar as a prince who can manipulate his 'manly' identity. But this identity of the Maharaj Kumar intersects with the title of the novel. On the very first night of his married life, the Greeneyes, the princess of Merta and the wife of the Maharaj Kumar, announces to him that she has been betrothed. The Maharaj Kumar fails to conquer her as a husband. In one sense, the whole novel is the Maharaj Kumar's incessant struggle with his wife. As the narrative proceeds, the Greeneyes transforms into a Little Saint, her popularity rises day by day. On the other hand, in spite of his ambitious project of town planning and his victorious battles, the Maharaj Kumar becomes more and more unpopular. The rejection by the society as a prince, as a future king, and the rejection by the wife as a husband enfolds a torturous journey of the Maharaj Kumar.

Cuckold is written against the backdrop when the Nehruvian aura is almost extinguished. Highly original thinkers like Ram Manohar Lohiya or Jayaprakash Narayan are no more. The scenario in the 1980s and the 90s in India was of perplexity because of drastic social-cultural changes. The Dalit movement, the Socialist movement, the Feminist movement, the Little Magazine movement and all such 'positive and activist movements' of the 1960s and the 70s 'suffered a terrible attenuation' in the 80s and the 90s which created 'a tremendous ideological vacuum'. The period reveals a general sense of 'disorientation, of tentativeness and hesitation'.[7] It is perhaps this kind of 'collapse' that urges Nagarkar to return to the past.

Apart from its social domain, as the title indicates, the major crux of the novel is the Maharaj Kumar's personal world and that again is restricted to his relationship with his wife, the Greeneyes. The references to the Greeneyes explicitly convey that she is none other than Meera, the legendary saint-poet of medieval India. In spite of this fact, she has never been referred with this name throughout the novel. The image of the Maharaj Kumar as has been presented as a prince, a diplomat and a warrior counterbalances his image as a husband. On the first night of the wedding, the Greeneyes announces, "I'm spoken for...I'm betrothed to someone else" *(C* 46) which hurts the Maharaj Kumar, the embodiment of the male ego. Being a part of the royal family, he can easily manipulate his 'manliness'. It is no wonder that when Sunehria, who has been charged as an adultress by her husband in the open court, surrenders herself to the Maharaj Kumar, he accepts her without any hesitation. His wet-nurse, Kausalya, who has taught him the first lessons of the love-making, takes all the precautions of the Maharaj Kumar's bed chamber. It's very natural that his 'ego' is hurt by the rejection of the Greeneyes.

The very first reaction of the Maharaj Kumar after realizing that he has been cuckolded, is his doubt and suspicion about the 'third one': who must be 'he'? The thought torments him. He insults the Greeneyes to know his name. Kausalya witnesses the tensions between their relationships. She finds the Greeneyes writing something in secrecy in the absence of the Maharaj Kumar. She steals some of the papers and hands them over to the Maharaj Kumar. He reads them and comes across the open confession of her love through the lyrics. He becomes frenzied and wants to kill the 'third one'. He is now obsessed to know the identity of the Greeneyes's beloved. He interrogates her consistently: "Is it my younger brother, Ratan? Or my debonair paternal cousin, Rajendra? Or is it Vikramaditya...? Or is it the uncle of yours, the one you went back with to Merta, Rao Viramdeo. . .?" *(C* 89 -90). Unable to bear the humiliations, the

Greeneyes, finally, points her finger in the direction of the idol of Shri Krishna. The Maharaj Kumar considers it as an old trick of deceiving him. He once again scans the poems she has written and comes to know that she calls her lover with different names like Shyam or Giridhar. He suspects that all these different names could be "a pseudonym, a pet name or a private code name for a beloved" (*C* 102). Thus, he cannot believe in what she is saying. It only drifts afar the husband-wife relationship. Gradually, the Greeneyes's worship of Krishna becomes a 'public affair'. In the eyes of Vikramaditya, Karmavati and the other noble people, she emerges as a 'national scandal' and the Maharaj Kumar remains 'a weak and unassertive husband'.

The Maharaj Kumar's realization that he has been cuckolded by none other than the Blue God, the Flautist himself, is devastating. Though the Maharaj Kumar worships Shri Eklingji, the royal deity, it is the Blue God, Shri Krishna, whom he adores in a true sense. He has many heroes, some from his family tree and many from the *Ramayana* and the *Mahabharata*. But the real hero for him is Krishna himself. He believes that the God grows with him and there is not one Shri Krishna but at the very least three to four (*C* 106). He loves Bala Krishna as 'the ultimate brat' who is a 'mischievous, obstinate, disarming, cocky, exasperating, lovable and gregarious' (*C* 107). He deeply adores Krishna's diplomatic policies. The Maharaj Kumar's upbringing so far has been nurtured on the principles and lessons as taught by Krishna. But because of the Greeneyes, the same hero confronts before him as a rival, as an enemy. Thus, a common, typical story of an adultery that begins with a doubt and a suspicion, takes a new turn with an arrival of an Almighty God on the scene. The Maharaj Kumar realizes, "One can exorcise the devil, but how can one get rid of a god?" (*C* 186)

After the Gujarat campaign, the Maharaj Kumar has been kept away from the state affairs. During this phase of exile, there grows an intimacy between the Maharaj Kumar and the

Greeneyes, of course, not as husband and wife, but as companions. During the cholera, epidemic she works shoulder to shoulder with the Maharaj Kumar in helping and providing moral support to the populace. She has to pay a price for her deep involvement when she also suffers from cholera. The Maharaj Kumar nurses her with an utter care and her life is saved. The relationship between them receives a new dimension.

In spite of this new realization, the crisis of the Maharaj Kumar remains as it is. It just intensifies his perplexity. He ponders over the thought, "...Is my wife Greeneyes real? Is she nothing but a great actress, a phony all the way? Is she one person or many more? Does she love someone else and hurt me? Is she lying?" (*C* 297) The intimacy and companionship neither suppresses the Maharaj Kumar's 'ego', nor does it lessen his possessiveness. Thus, the moment comes in his life when he aspires to get rid of 'this obsessive disease'.

With this fear of obsession, the Maharaj Kumar disguises himself as the Blue God. He paints himself with deep indigo solution, wears the silk pitambar, the finely meshed gold belt and headband. Finally, he tucks a peacock feather in his hair, takes a flute with him and enters the room of the Greeneyes. The Greeneyes welcomes him, adores him. At one instance, she worships him by washing his feet. To his horror, the indigo colour washes away with water. But the Greeneyes doesn't complain about it, at least he feels like that. Then onwards, it becomes a routine for him. Every evening he is transformed into the Blue God. The notes of her bhajans and the rhythm of the raas leela bring ultimately some kind of solace to him. He remains under the impression that the Greeneyes is accepting him as her husband. But these pleasing moments are disillusioned when once, while love making, at an intense moment she calls him, "Krishna Kanhayya. Krishna Kanhayya" (*C* 496). For the Maharaj Kumar, this is a kind of revelation. With a deep sense of understanding, he is left with the ultimate reality that the Greeneyes's life is pervaded with her Blue God where there is no place for him. With this realization, a deep sense of melancholy pervades in his life that takes him to an altogether different kind of world. He is now a defeated being in every sense.

The novel ends with a disastrous defeat of the Rajputs in the battle of Khanua against Babur. The Maharana is successful in eloping from the battleground but later on is killed treacherously at the hands of the loyalists of Vikramaditya. As far as the Maharaj Kumar is concerned, the novel reveals multiple ends. As per one story, the six butchers from the side of Vikramaditya kill him. Another story maintains that the Maharaj Kumar escapes to Mandu and elopes with Leelavati[8] into the mountains. One more story suggests that he goes to Mathura, becomes a 'mendicant' and follows the little saint. But the narrator is more startled by the Maharaj Kumar's another mysterious story of disappearance. In his view, 'this story' seemed to suggest 'something more complicated' (*C* 601). Pursued by the six butchers, the Maharaj Kumar runs to the temple of the Flautist at Baswa and addresses the God:

> How long will you nurse this enmity? How long will you fight this personal war? And to what purpose? Do you not know that you and I are one? My flute and song are on your lips. We love the same woman. Why, you fool, no power on earth can separate or divide us. (*C* 602)

With these words, he raises the sword to kill himself, and dramatically, the Flautist embraces him. The six men are struck by terror and astonishment. There is left just the Maharaj Kumar's 'turban' and 'kesariyabana'.[9]

The end of the Maharaj Kumar's submission into the Blue God opens up a different kind of interpretation of his life journey. Though the crisis between the Maharaj Kumar and Greeneyes begins on a very human level, by the end of the novel it reaches the metaphysical level. Rejection by the Greeneyes is a challenge the Maharaj Kumar's machismo. But it would be incorrect to say that the Maharaj Kumar is obsessed with the human flesh. He has other sources to fulfil his urge of sex and which he confesses frankly. And at the same time, he is that much sophisticated that he dislikes "the sexual proclivities of others" (*C* 144). That means his attraction for the Greeneyes is only a matter of his 'manly ego' and the 'possessiveness'.

The ordinary story of cuckolding that begins with a doubt, suspicion and vengeance takes a different course in the novel, and in a wider context, it becomes the Maharaj Kumar's 'quest for truth' and through that the quest for 'self'. To comprehend the truth, the 'Absolute', the *Bhagavad Gita* proposes three different paths – path of knowledge (Jnana), path of action (Karma) and path of deep adoration (Bhakti). As far as the Greeneyes is concerned, her objective of life is well defined. She has an ardent desire to become one with her Blue God, for which she has chosen a path of deep adoration. Her path reveals the 'Madhurya Bhava.' She considers herself the beloved of the Almighty. Her bhajans, songs, as they come in the novel, reveal her ardent desire to become one with God. It is no wonder that the Maharaj Kumar considers them very erotic. Though deeply infused in the love and worship of the Blue God, she never ignores her homely duties. She looks after the father-in-law, cares for the people of Chittor, and proves herself a good companion to the Maharaj Kumar. But, in spite of the different roles, her prime concern is always the Blue God. In that sense on a metaphysical level, her journey is a journey to know, to understand 'the Absolute' for which she has chosen the path of 'Bhakti'.

In the same way, the Maharaj Kumar's quest encompasses a torturous journey. The only problem with him is his inability to determine the destination. His quest begins with the Greeneyes. The common human elements like doubt and suspicion mar his quest initially. With the realization that in the marital affairs, his rival is none other than the Blue God, his crisis becomes more acute. Once, he also adored the Blue God. In the moment of crisis, he always relied on his Flautist. But this deep adoration, all of a sudden turns into hatred. At this juncture, he fails to realize that 'hatred' is also one way of 'Bhakti' which is seen through the relationship between Shishupal and Krishna or Ravan and Ram. All the well wishers of the Maharaj Kumar consider his love for the Greeneyes as the fatal obsession.

In course of time, the husband-wife relationship transcends into a new form. Like the Greeneyes, the Maharaj Kumar also perceives that the attainment of the 'Absolute' is possible through 'self- forgetfulness' and 'self-abandonment'. Both of them become the fellow-travellers on the path of sublimation. That's why, after the defeat at Khanua, while finishing the memoirs, the Maharaj Kumar announces, "...there is only woman for me. It is not Leelawati and it is not Kausalya. It is my wife. I will follow her to Brindaban, to Mathura, to the gates of hell, even to heaven if the gods will have me" (*C* 600). If the Greeneyes follows the path of 'Bhakti', the Maharaj Kumar follows the path of 'Karma'. However, his is a lonesome journey. The Greeneyes is at least imbued in her adoration of the Blue God. There is nothing in the life of the Maharaj Kumar which can solace him. His crisis involves a twofold journey – one is at the social level, the other one is at the personal level. On one side, he has to jostle with the external enemies like Malwa and Gujarat. On the home front he has to fight against the stepbrother and the stepmother. And at the very personal level his confrontation is with the Greeneyes and her Blue God. The only consolation he finds is in the company of Kausalya, Sunehria,[10] and Leelawati who, however disappear from his life one by one. He becomes absolutely lonely. But, for him, by this time, this loneliness is no more pathetic.

Like his loneliness, the Maharaj Kumar is accompanied with humiliations. He has been humiliated at every moment right from his wife to the people of Mewar which leaves a deep sense of gloominess on his life. Vikramaditya spares no opportunity to humiliate him publicly. After the victory against Gujarat, the Maharaj Kumar receives unceremonious welcome at home. It is Vikramaditya, who provokes the people to declare the Maharaj Kumar as a coward and traitor and welcome him showing the black flags. Even the Maharana[11] doesn't offer the Maharaj Kumar the 'Veer Vijay Safa' after his victory against Gujarat. On the contrary, under the pressure of Queen Karmavati,[12] he asks him to relinquish his rights on the throne and to leave Chittor. When the Greeneyes is seen singing and dancing publicly in the Brindabani Mandir, Queen Karmavati insults the Maharaj Kumar saying, "Do you see to what depth your spinelessness has brought us?. . . . Get up, you pansy and drag her home" (*C* 170). His passes through a series of humiliations. His getting lonely and getting humiliated becomes a part of his quest which helps him to move on in the direction of 'self-forgetfulness' and 'self-abandonment'.

The Maharaj Kumar's 'self-realization' that comes in the final scene of the novel, where he addresses the Blue God:"...Do you know that you and I are one. . ." (*C* 602) is very near to the Vedantic principle of 'Advaita'. 'Advaita' proposes that the distressed soul finds salvation in the knowledge that there is no diversity, no evil, and no separateness. The mind of the individual may be conscious of evil and of suffering; but 'the great mind' knows nothing of these. Identification with 'the great mind' is the source of all bliss, the sense of separateness is the root of evil. To be emancipated from all the sense of a separate individuality is the real knowledge, the real bliss. This emancipation is expressed in the formula, "tat- tvam-asi" - "thou art it".[13]

This is how, in the novel, the Maharaj Kumar is confronted with a deep moral problem where he finds a separation between him and the Greeneyes on one level and he and the Almighty on the other level. During this metaphorical journey towards sublimation, at first, he transforms himself into the Blue God and then the Greeneyes transforms him into a Gopi which involves his process of the extinction of the 'self'. For him, through gradual changes comes a moment of realization of the inseparability of the Divinity and himself.

In this way, in the novel *Cuckold*, Nagarkar uses the legend and the folklore, experiments in the narrative techniques to handle the difficulties of restructuring history in a fictional mode, and emphatically poses the individual's moral, psychological and metaphysical anxieties from an altogether as different perspective.

To conclude, it can be said that the biblical myth and the epic world of the *Ramayana* in *Ravan and Eddie* and the legendry folk literature in *Cuckold* provide a space to Nagarkar to construct his narrative open for the multiplicity of interpretations.

References

1. H.R. Mackintosh, "Christian Sin", *Encyclopedia of Religion and Ethics*, ed. James Hastings, Vol. 11, New York: Morrison and Gibb Ltd., 1959, 538-544.
2. Kiran Nagarkar, *Seven Sixes Are Forty Three*, Tr. Shubha Slee, New Delhi: Vikas Publishing House Pvt. Ltd. 1981, 68.
3. Quotations from *Ravan and Eddie* are cited in the text with page numbers in parentheses using the abbreviation *RE*: Kiran Nagarkar, *Ravan and Eddie*, New Delhi: Penguin Books, 1995.
4. There is a distinction between the concept of 'salvation' and the concept of 'liberation'. If the Christian theology talks about 'salvation', the Hindu theology talks about 'Mukti' or 'lib eration. As Kapil Kapoor states, "In 'Liberation' you are not asked to re- establish your relationship that has been disrupted with God nor are you under punishment. No – it is a continuous process of evolution, your own evolution in which you free yourself from your own 'self'. You are not freeing yourself from tyranny which comes from outside you, but you are freeing yourself from your own inner self". Kapil Kapoor, "Sin, Suffering and Salvation", *Sin*, and *Salvation in Literature*, N. Delhi: Radha Publications, 2004, 9.
5. S.A. A Rizvi, *The Wonder That was India: Part II*, New Delhi: Rupa and Co., 1996 (Fifth impression), 367–68.
6. Quotations from *Cuckold* are cited in the text with page numbers in parentheses using the abbreviation C:Kiran Nagarkar, *Cuckold*, New Delhi: Harper Collins Publishers India, 1997.
7. Chandrashekhar Jahagirdar, "After Modernism: Marathi Poetry of the 80s and 90s", *Journal of Shivaji University: Humanities and Social Science* 35, (2000) 21–25 .
8. Leelawati is a daughter of a moneylender to the royal family. She belongs to the Jain community. She is much younger than the Maharaj Kumar. Even then the novel reveals the complex relationship between the Maharaj Kumar and Leelawati. At times she reminds the Maharaj Kumar

of his younger sister who dies untimely; at times she is the Maharaj Kumar's companion and the beloved.

9. Actually this ending of the Maharaj Kumar's life has been inflicted on Saint Meera by the folk tradition. Nagarkar very significantly subverts this folklore.
10. Sunehria is the washerman's wife that is seen in the opening part of the novel. In course of time, there grows an intimate relationship between the Maharaj Kumar and her.
11. The Maharana is Rana Sanga, the great king of Mewar and the father of the Maharaj Kumar.
12. Queen Karmavati is the stepmother of the Maharaj Kumar.
13. D. Mackichan, "Advaita", *Encyclopedia of Religion and Ethics*, ed. James Hastings, Vol. 1, New York: Morrison and Gibb Ltd., 1959, 137-139.

4

The Historicity of Texts and the Textuality of History: A Comparative Study of Karnad's *Danda* and Kalburgi's *Fall of Kalyana*

S. Lavanya

Karnad and Kalburgi's plays are based on the historical and legendary facts relating to Basavanna's life history. The playwrights have refracted upon the contemporary social issues by reflecting upon the life of Basavanna, a twelfth century religious and social reformer. Karnad has adapted the legendary life history of Basavanna and focuses upon his struggle against caste discrimination to address the communal violence of the present day. While Karnad's play *Tale-Danda* is a social realistic play, Kalburgi's *Fall of Kalyana* is a historical play which focuses on rebuilding the ideology of Basavanna's religious and social reforms which has transcended the rigid bonds of the past and has attained universal connotations in the present. History according to Frederic Jameson is "fundamentally non-narrative and non-representational; what can be added, however, is the proviso that history is inaccessible to us except in textual forms, or in other words that it can be approached only by way of prior (re)textualization" (82).

Kalburgi is a Kannada scholar, academician and former vice-chancellor of Kannada University, Hampi. He was awarded the National Sahitya Akademi Award in 2006 for his collection of research articles. His other honours are the Karnataka

State Sahitya Akademi Award, Janapad and Yakshagana Janapad Prashasti, and the Pampa Prashasti. Dr. M. M. Kalburgi has taken meticulous efforts in collecting literary evidence regarding Basava's life and ideology and has combined his vision as a playwright to put across the mission of Basava. Basavaraj Naikar is a Professor Emeritus at Karnataka University, Dharwad. His translation of the original Kannada play has paved the way for instilling the historical consciousness of our rich and variegated culture amidst our younger generation. The youth of today lack role models to emulate and are led astray by the illusion of the electronic media:this lacuna will be filled and the youth may have a strong hold on values if the forgotten real legendary heroes are brought back to life through literature. In an interview with Dr. Vishwanath Bite, Dr. Basavaraj Naikar has stated motives for selecting the historical genre.

> I choose the genre of historical novel or drama because I feel that we Indians have very little historical consciousness as compared with our vast and variegated history. I wish to write about the historical celebrities of my area i.e. North Karnataka and get national and international recognition for them.

Girish Karnad had his education in Dharwad and then in Mumbai where he obtained his Masters in Economics and secured the most prestigious Rhodes scholarship. He was awarded Padmashri in 1974 in recognition to his artistic achievements as an actor, producer, director and writer par excellence. The primary duty of a creative writer is to throw light upon the darker aspects of the society and to suggest ways and means to recuperate itself from the clutches of unwarranted practices and beliefs. Girish Karnad being a playwright with social consciousness draws his theme from history and mythology and makes it relevant to contemporary situation.

The period of 1980s was a phase of watershed in Indian history as the nation was torn between nationalism and communal discontent. Religious fanaticism, communal sentiments proved detrimental to the economic and spiritual growth of a nation. The communal violence which broke the twelfth-century city of Kalyan to shreds is relevant to the present society. The ideological conflict between orthodox Hindus who believe in hierarchical division of caste system and the Sharana movement bent at creating an egalitarian society which is confined to a small city at a particular time in history evolves with universal connotation in the play. Karnad in the preface to the play *Tale-Danda* states the consequence of historical continuity in the present day.

> I wrote *Tale-Danda* in 1989 when the 'Mandir' and the 'Mandal' movements were beginning to show again how relevant the question posed by these thinkers were for our age. The horror of the subsequent events and the religious fanaticism that had gripped our national life today have only proved how dangerous it is to ignore the solution they offered.

Myths are different forms of legendary stories traditional and religious in nature. "Myths are uncanny phenomena. They are at once regional and yet universal; static and yet dynamic; stable yet protean; archaic and yet contemporary; profligate yet hallowed; fantastic yet highly-structured; divine yet human in that they are as much about gods and goddesses as about human beings" (Dorairaj 9). Within the precepts of cultural anthropology myths are essential for stabilizing the norms of the society. The French Marxist critics believe that contemporary socio-political events have the potential to evolve into myths.

> Myths are different from legends which detail the adventures of a human cultural hero (such as Robin Hood or Annie Oahley) and tend to be less focused on the supernatural. Whereas a legend may exaggerate – perhaps even wildly- the exploits of its hero, it is likely to be grounded in historical fact. Myths also differ from fables, which have a moral, didactic purpose and usually feature animal character. (229)

In his article "Myth and History", Ricoeur spells out the difference between myth and history, "Myth is a narrative of origins, taking place in primordial time [...]. History is a narrative of recent events, extending progressively to include events that are farther in the past, but that are, nonetheless, situated in human time."(273)

Historicism is one of the strategies of postcolonial discourse wherein an attempt is made to revive their lost pride by recreating history in literature. Society and culture have evolved through various facets of history. Historicism is the explanation of the historical actuality of a culture. Post-structuralists such as Lacan and Foucalt emphasized that historicism is a critical theory which insists that the problems raised in the literary text should be solved within the limits and confines of the culture or society in which it is raised. History is a transcendental signifier through which multiple meanings could be derived. History has never lost its significance for it has become indistinguishable with its referents. If history is the signifier, culture and social context becomes the signified. Historicism is a school of thought which employs literary scholarship to express or react against the hierarchical power structures operating in the society.

> The post-structuralist orientation to history now emerging in literary studies may be characterized chiastically, as a reciprocal concern with the historicity of texts and the textuality of history. By the historicity of texts, I mean to suggest the cultural specificity, the social; embedment, of all modes of writing .... By the textuality of history, I mean to suggest, firstly, that we can have no access to a full and authentic past, a lived material existence, unmediated by the surviving textual traces of the society in question ... and secondly , that those textual traces are themselves subject to subsequent textual mediations when they are construed as the "documents" upon which historians ground their own texts called "histories".
>
> (Montrose 781)

History has the potential to shape the course of the society and changed the colour of the culture. Culture is a collective unconscious force that determines the dynamics of social hegemony. Texts are always related to the context in which they occur and literature makes historical percepts universal by applying it to the present scenario. Literature has the poignant vigor to resolve the age old cultural and social problems such as amalgamating the low and high culture; dissipating the difference between dominant and subjective factions of the society.

The New Historicist have destabilized the difference between historicity of texts and textuality of history for the narrative constructs of literature has contextualized the negotiation and discursive power equations that has maintained the hierarchical structure of our society, culture and religion. A literary author has the social responsibility of responding to the uncertainties in his society and has the moral responsibility of correcting the chaotic situation through his creative power. According to Greenbalt "the work of art is the product of negotiation between a creator or class of creators, equipped with complex, communally shared repertoire of conventions, and the institutions and practices of society" (12) .

> The New Historicism, while trying to understand the historical conditioning, contends that our knowledge of history cannot be objective and we can never recover the past without our present self modifying what used to be considered objective and stable. What is more radical about New Historicism is that it recognizes a 'variety of competing centers of cultural power'.
>
> (Seturaman 574)

Rice Phillip and Patricia Waugh define New Historicism as: "...informed by and arising out of the theoretical format of 1970s so that its concern to examine the textual traces of the past is premised on the notion that the text is available to us only in the form of textuality which is also embedded in that of the present" (259).

Continuity of history depends on the congenial link between the past traditions and the present existential reality. By continuity Girish Karnad means not repetition but the dynamic interaction of culture and history which would give rise to a better society. By re-reading history Karnad construed an opposition and a perception between the past and the present. In an interview with Allen Mendonca, Girish Karnad had stated: "The notion of originality is a romantic tradition. Edgar Allen Poe didn't need it. Neither did Shakespeare. What I do is to hold a mirror to the present incorporating elements not so much from the past, as that of our collective story telling tradition."(4)

> The play centers around a few major incidents:a] Sovideva's medling with the treasury, b] Basavanna's resignation from the post of Chief Treasury Officer, c] the death and funeral ceremonies of Jagadeva's father, d] the inter-caste marriage of Sheelavanta and Kalavati, e] Bijjala's abdication and death, f] Basavanna's union with God, g] Sovideva's coronation. Though the series of events look perfectly historical, it is not.
>
> (Ravindranath 141)

In the preface to the play *Fall of Kalyana,* Kalburgi states the structure and thematic concern of the play thus:

> Basaveswara's life passed through three stages:one, the agrahara-culture of Bagewadi; two, the temple-culture of Kudala-Sangama and three, the palace culture of Kalyana. All through those stages he grew from the static to the dynamic level and by transforming the former into the latter. He progresses from karma to dharma in Bagewadi; from the spiritual to the social in Kudala-Sangama and from spiritual to the social in Kalyana. Basaveswara, who faced problems arising in the first two environments, came to the third environment, where he was tortured by the triple forces. (*FK*)

Kalburgi and Karnad have articulated the greatness of our past legendary hero who fought for a noble cause from the niche of history. Basaveswara or Basavanna as he was popularly known tried his utmost to reform the cultural, religious, political and economic ideologies of the society. Ironically the social evils Basvanna strived to erase from the fabric of the twelfth-century society is still rampant, hence significant in this present scenario of dissection and division in the name of caste, creed, and religion. A revolutionary in spirit and with reformist zeal Basvanna broke the institutionalized cultural hegemony and instilled the values of universal brotherhood and gender equality. He consecrated the ideal of equality by making the citizen to realize the intrinsic value of human life. Basvanna's reformist movement completely dismantled the varna ashrma dharma which segregated humanity by creating hierarchies based on caste system. The fire of discontent that started in the agrahara engulfed the whole empire. The religious ideology and social reformist movement started by Basavanna with a foresight of creating a utopian society based on humanitarian zeal was completely shattered. The Sharana literature and vachanas propagating ethics and motto of Basavanna are still maintained intact and the followers of Basavanna have evolved into a close sect within Hinduism called Lingayats or Virashaivaites. Basavanna was instrumental in eradicating the imbedded delusions within each individual such as the opposition between high / low, privileged / marginalized, oppressor / victimized, man / woman, haves / have-nots which was instrumental in operating the rigid structure of society which ensured stiff segregation of man from man.

> Basava is endowed with a three-eyed mind; one eye (intellectual) gazing greedily at a new sky that leads to the establishment of Socio-Spiritual Academy; another eye (religious) that furthers the cause of vacana literature; and the third eye (social) that pushes forward the idea of a casteless society. A person of rich inward culture, he strives hard to reinstate the core values of humanism in the hearts of masses. (*FK xi*)

Basavanna, the poet, philosopher and minister of Kalyan, initiated religious reforms to propagate the ideas of universal brotherhood. The reformist cult was known as Shaivism or Virashaivism or Lingayats who considered Lord Shiva as the Supreme Self. The followers of the reformist cult were known as Sharanas. They opposed the caste system not in theory but in practice. The radical views of the Sharanas threatened the privileged position enjoyed by the high caste people. The inter-caste marriage planned by the Sharanas brings the communal hatred to the forefront and the ultimate destruction of the city of Kalyan.

In Girish Karnad's *Tale-Danda* the agrahara phase of Basava's life is attributed to the character of Jaganna, the chief disciple of Basavanna. Jagadeva returns to his house to see his father in the death bed. Unlike Basavanna, Jagadeva seems to be a split personality caught between two worlds. He conforms to the pressures of his brahmin society and cremates his father according to the rituals and ceremonies of brahmins and later feels acutely the absurdity of his situation. The problem of untouchability is evident when Jagadeva, a brahmin by birth brings his friend Mallibomma, who belongs to a lower caste to his door step. The women who have gathered in the household show their abhorrence by instructing Mallibomma to stand a little away from them. The manner in which Amba, Jagadeva's mother invites Mallibomma into their household envisages that humanism remains at stake. The belief that a human beings presence could pollute the environs shows the pathetic condition of the subalterns.

> Amba:My son won't come into the house unless you do, so come in, please. I will have the house purified later. Please, I beg of you— with folded hands - (*TD* I i 4)

Kalburgi delineates the life of Basava from his ancestors to revive the prestigious status of the forgotten legendary hero. Basava hails from an orthodox family steeped in tradition. His forefathers were awarded the Bagewadi agrahara as a grant from the Chalukya King. His family enjoyed a prestigious position in the society as his father was the mayor of the agrahara. Instead of enjoying the benefits of the socially ordained significant position, he at the age of 15 keenly felt that the caste distinctions were manmade bonds to keep humanity segregated. The play opens with him refusing to wear the sacred thread, a mark of his high caste. He says, "No, no I don't want this sacred thread, which makes me a Brahmin instead of a human being" (*FK* I i1). His mother advises him that ideal and reality are different. The priests say that these rituals are essential to retain their topmost position in the social hierarchy. He disregards the sacred thread with contempt, for caste system is the root cause for inequality in the society. The brahmins of the agrahara ostracize his family. He strongly opposes the decision as maladministration in the name of religion. He openly disregardes the rules of *Manusmriti* upon which the codes of Hindu society functions and leaves for the Shaiva monastery to gain knowledge in the scriptures. His parents who have enjoyed a revered position in the society are deeply affected by losing their status. His mother breathes her last in her brother's house. She is lucky enough to be cremated according to the brahminical rituals. He returns from the monastery only to see his father in his deathbed. His father passes away leaving him and his younger sister Nagalambika orphans at a tender age. The leaders of the agrahara arrive on hearing the news, and wait presuming that Basava would apologise for his rash behaviour and plead with them to cremate his father. Later they decide to cremate Basava's father on a humanitarian gesture. But Basava, a man of self–respect, refuses their help and cremates his father with the help of his sister and servants. He distributes all his wealth to his servants and walks with his sister towards the Shaiva monastery of Kudala Sangama.

In the play *Fall of Kalyana*, Kalburgi deals with Basava's life in the temple monastery where he formulated his religious ideology, whereas in Karnad's *Tale-Danda* the formulative phase of Basava's life lies in the shadow of the past and only his popular phase as the minister of Kalyan is highlighted. After spending a year in the monastery of Kudala Sangama, Basava feels that the priestly culture is as dominant as the brahminical culture was dominant in the agrahara and there is no scope for democratic principles. He feels, "The intelligence of Saiva's has been tarnished by the smoke of sacrificial fire" (*FK* I vi 14). Isanyaguru, a teacher at the monastery, takes a special liking for the straightforward and independent thinking Basava. Isanyaguru is instrumental in making his extraordinary student to evolve an exemplary religious ideology through constant discussion and criticism. Isanyaguru questions the necessity of the religious symbol known as ishtalinga for Basava's philosophy emphasizes the purification of the self rather that external worship. Bassava says: "Yes, sir. Spritual purity is of utmost importance for man. Meditation is very necessary for that. But nowadays the worship of idols and the spiritual meditation are separate. In order to prevent the rift one should consider one's soul itself as God and worship its symbol i. e. the istalinga" (*FK* II ii 26). Though Basava argues that ishtalinga is the symbol of one's soul, Isanyaguru associates it with the sacred thread which divides society into compartments. Basava clarifies his stand thus:

> No, no, sir. Though both are hung around the neck, they are not the same. A man becomes a Brahmin as soon as he wears the sacred thread. From that day, he starts classifying the society into Brahmin, ksatriya, vaisya and sudra. On the contrary, the istalinga removes this social division created by the Vedic people. Whereas the sacred thread divides the society, the Siva-string unifies it and considers its members as believers and the rest as non-believers. (II ii 26)

Isanyaguru tests Basava's credentials by raising the doubt that his ideology might pave the way for segregation in the society. Basava sheds light on his ideological percepts thus: "Not like that sir. The sacred thread classifies people on the basis of their birth; the istalinga does it on the basis of merit. In the former approach, birth is more important whereas in the latter, merit is more important" (II ii 27). Basva learns that the temple priests and the heads of the monastery plunder the poor in the name of rituals. He learns that the religious heads are into blackmarketing, who squander the ill-gotten wealth for self-aggrandizement. He determines to educate the masses to defy the temple in order to create equality in a society which remains crossly divided into the exploited versus the exploiter operating at the various levels of the society. Basava says: "We must defy the temples, which have become centers of misusing the God. Instead our legs should be pillars, our head, the golden pinnacle and our body, the temple. Every man should be a moving temple. Our personality should be transformed from static to dynamic" (*FK* II iv 33). He intensely understands the necessity for erasing the hierarchical oppositions in the society, so he resolves to create his religious ideologies into social reformatory movement.

Kalburgi throws light upon various social reforms undertaken by Basavanna in detail while Karnad highlights his efforts to annihilate the caste system. In *Fall of Kalyana* Basava is elevated to the post of Finance Minister but in *Tale-Danda* he resigns his post as the Tresurer of King's treasury and involves in social reformist movement. When Sovidevsa, the King's youngest son, meddles with the affairs of the treasury, Basavanna resigns his post as the Treasurer and he makes it clear that he took up the responsibility of safeguarding the treasury because the wealth belonged to the people and not to please the King. Basavanna refuses to address Sovideva as the Yuvaraj in spite of King Bijjala's insistence. Basavanna says: ".... Kingship is a calling. A source of living, yes, but also a duty and service to humanity. It is also an inheritance, not a family gift but a right to be earned, to be justified by diligent application" (*TD* I iii 20). Basvanna considers war to be a senseless self-indulgence that would create widows and orphans and would necessitate new laws to incur the expenditure. Basavanna says: "Inscriptions need eyes to decipher them. Panegyrics need tongues to sing them. Meaning is generated by this moving body and it is this human body that should be our primary concern" (*TD* I iii 18). M. K. Naik outlines the theme of the play *Tale-Danda* in the following words:

> The play deals with the final crisis in the life of Basavanna, the great social reformer of the 12th century Karnataka, and the founder of the Lingayat faith. When he was chief minister at the court of

> King Bijjala of Kalyan, Basavanna tried to propagate his revolutionary philosophy the main tenets in which were: the abolition of caste; equality of the sexes; rejection of idol worship; repudiation of Brahminism, and of Sanskrit in favour of the mother tongue, i.e., Kannada.

The play shows how the higher castes recent Basavanna's iconoclasm, and how the resentment reaches its highest peak when one of his brahmin disciples gives his daughter in marriage to an untouchable. The culprits are severely punished, and in the subsequent holocaust, King Bijjala is dethroned by his orthodox son, while Basavanna dies in mysterious circumstances. (1-2)

In *Tale-Danda* Basavanna tries his utmost and yearns to create a society where civilization will gain new meaning . He prays to God to see a new dawn of compassion among his people.

> Basavanna (to himself) Father, don't make me hear all day
>
> 'Whose man, whose man, whose man is this?
>
> Let me hear:
>
> 'This man is mine, that man is mine. '
>
> O Lord of the Meeting Rivers, make me feel
>
> I am a son of the house.' (*TD* II v 52)

The third and important phase of Basava's life starts at Kalyana, the capital city of Kuntala Empire which is elaborated in Kalburgi's *Fall of Kalyana.* King Bijjala, attracted by Basava's honesty and straightforward approach, offers him the post of Chief Accounts Officer. The King feels elated when Basava sets right the accounts of the treasury and elevates him to the post of finance minister. King Bijjala considers Basava as a ray of hope sent by God to set right the treasury which is an important pillar of the kingdom. Basava uses his new post to enlighten the masses on various human values and tries to elevate the downtrodden by casting away the unwarranted and unprecedented social practices. He implements various social reforms to curb the breach between the haves and the have-nots. Basava says: "The caste difference between the privileged and the underprivileged is born out of 'religion' whereas the difference between the poor and the rich is born out of 'labour'" (*FK* III, iv 50).

The social tapestry of Indian society is woven with different colourful threads called caste. The caste system is deeply rooted in the Indian ethos and it is rather impossible to erase this firmly embedded sensibility. The caste system has not only caused barriers among the higher caste and the oppressed, it has set in an unequal balance in the society which is detrimental to its growth. It is an irony to note that caste still takes the centerstage in implementing government policies and in social reforms, community-based reservations in education and in employment; while on the other hand we continually pledge on equality in a democracy. In an article entitled "The Playwright, A Discussion/ U. R. Ananta Murthy, Prasanna, Girish Karnad", in the journal *Indian Literature,* Karnad states:

> We talk of removing caste barriers and becoming one. But the moment we speak, our caste identity too comes out like- this is a Brahmin, that is a Lingayat, etc. Everyone is born into a language. Will it be possible to give up caste without giving up the language that comes along with. This applies to occupation as well. Socially caste and occupation are so much interwoven among us .... The word Kshorika (barber) is not merely a reference to one's occupation, but to caste as well. Sharana's concept of 'work without caste' generates a cultural dilemma. (133)

As the finance minister in *Fall of Kalyana* Basava takes the initiative to mitigate the poverty of the marginalized people. He distributes money from the treasury for fulfilling the basic needs of the marginalized section of the society and advocates them about the importance of work ethics. He makes the citizens understand that the treasury belongs to them for they have contributed to the wealth of the nation. He makes the citizens understand that they are the real wealth of the empire and the King's foremost duty is to care for the welfare of the citizens. He advocates the citizens to wear the ishtalinga as a symbol of social equality so that it would erase the distinctions as upper and lower caste. He educates the masses about the divinity of labour through the philosophy of 'kayaka' and 'dasoha'. He explains the philosophy of Kayaka thus: "Kayaka means not only physical labour but mental labour as well. It means one has to work not only for oneself but also for the society" (*FK* III v 54). He explains the nuances between charity and *dasoha* principles:

> Charity is different from dasoha. Charity involves the transferring the ownership of an object to others. But dasoha means ownership by neither one nor other. It presupposes the ownership of an object by God and use of it for another man. There is no chance for hoarding in dasoha. By not hoarding material things we can live happily and develop our treasure. (FK III v 55)

By following Basava's ideologies the citizens start to worship their work and to lead a simple life. The ideology of ishtalinga gives the untouchables self-respect and esteem in the society. The citizens live a peaceful and happy life as their standard of living improves and the King is happy as money is flowing into his coffers. When Basava starts to eradicate inhuman religious practices he gains the wrath of the brahmins but they cannot instigate the King against Basava for the King is not ready to impair the economic development of the country.

Basava stops the evil practice of 'velevali 'and 'masti'—the Vedic practice of servants sacrificing their life, as a symbol of loyalty to their master and wives dying in the funeral pyre of their husbands. He makes them comprehend that they have been beguiled into believing these inhuman practices as holy rituals. He says:

> These are not values, man. On the contrary, these are exploitations masquerading as values. These are exploitation of common people by the royal ones and of women by men. (*Basaveswara goes near the women.*) Matrons, "you cannot spoil your holy body consecrated to Lord Kundalasanga."Your husband's severing his head for exhibiting his loyalty to his master is an inhuman practice,

> indeed. Similarly, your dying on the funeral pyre is another inhuman practice. The concepts of Heaven and entry into Heaven are all false notions and illusions. (*He lifts the child.*) You have to live at least for this child's sake." (*FK* III ix 66)

Basava takes steps to mitigate the suffering of the untouchables. He stops a low caste boy passing through the streets crying 'samboli, samboli'; he is holding a stipoon in his hand and drags a thicket of thorns tied to his back. On hearing the announcement 'samboli' people run and hide in their houses, for they believe the sight of an untouchable would pollute their purity. Basava stops the child and removes the thorns. He is deeply moved by the inhuman practice and carries the child to his house. The lane of the untouchables is marked by a skeleton hung near a well. Basava orders them to remove the stigmas attached to their under-privileged status. He enters the house of Nagimayya, the headman of the untouchables, and accepts his hospitality. His recognition of their self-worth improves the status of the untouchables and they contribute towards the economic improvement of the empire. His attempts to enhance the status of the downtrodden create an uproar among the brahmins.

Basava create a socio-spiritual academy to advocate his ideologies. His followers known as Saranas, write vachanas to promote their philosophy. Basava is a man ahead of his times for he advocates women empowerment. King Bijjala's sister Nilambika is attracted by the respectable status of women in the Sarana society and is willing to marry Basava. Basava advocates inter-caste marriage as a poignant weapon in eradicating caste differences. To set an example to others he accepts Nilambika as his second wife. Nilambika's answer to her brother is evident of the necessity of women's emancipation in the present society.

> No, brother. Sometimes woman may have wealth and glory, but she has been cheated of social justice because of the male-dominated society. She has been suffering many a sorrow, which is not heard by men like you. Removing this discrimination happens to be the motto of the Sharana Movement. (*FK* IV v 83)

Basava happens to see a prostitute being taken as a prisoner for trying to throw away her newborn infant. He intercepts them and takes the unfortunate lady to the Sharana socio-spiritual academy. He holds the society responsible for pushing the unfortunate women into the abyss of social dismay. A young Sharana youth comes forward to marry the abused girl and to give her a new lease of life. The Sharana youth comes forward to marry widows and unfortunate women. Thus Basava sows the seeds for social change amidst the younger generation.

Karnad has elaborated upon the friendship and subtle understanding between King Bijjala and Basavanna. The character of King Bijjala in *Tale-Danda* evolves as a person who has a leaning towards the Sharana philosophy but is cunningly overthrown from power in order to culminate the religious reformist movement initiated by Basavanna from gaining momentum. In reality even King Bijjala cannot overcome the pain caused by the stigma of low caste. The psychological pain endured by him due to the caste distinction is evident in his thought-provoking answer to his wife.

> Bijjala: Your family – the Hoyslas, you may be Kshatriyas. But I am a Kalachurya. Katta churra. A barber. His Majesty King Bijjala is a barber by caste. For ten generations my fore- fathers ravaged the land as robber barons. For another five they ruled as the trusted feudatories of the Emperor himself. They married into every royal family in sight. Bribed generations of Brahmins with millions of cows. All this they could have the caste of Kshatriyas branded on their foreheads. And yet you ask the most innocent child in my empire:What is Bijjala , son of Kalachurya Permadi, by caste? And the instant reply will be:a barber! One's caste is like the skin on one's body. You can peel it off top to toe, but when the new skin forms, there you are again:barber – a shepherd- a scavenger!
>
> (Pause)
>
> In all my sixty- two years, the only people who have looked me in the eye without a reference to my lowly birth lurking deep in their eyes are the *sharanas:*Basavanna and his men. They treat me as what? - *(Almost without a sense of wonder)* as a human being.

> Basavanna wants to eradicate the caste structure, wipe it off the face of the earth. Annihilate the varna system. What a vision! And what prodigious courage! (*TD* I ii 15)

Though King Bijjala admires the vision and courage of Basavanna's idealistic motto of creating a utopian state he never forgets to point out the thread bare reality. He says to Basavanna:"If you really free them from the network of .... and let them loose in a casteless society, they will merely sputter about like a pile of fish on the sand and die!" (*TD* I iii 21). King Bijjala realises that the economy of Kalyan has flourished because the Sharanas consider their work as worship.

In *Tale-Danda* the plot reaches a climax when the Sharanas arrange an intercaste marriage between the upper and lower caste. Basava of *Tale-Danda* is reluctant to conduct the marriage anticipating religious violence. Madhuvarasa, a brahmin, has agreed to give his daughter in marriage to it son of Harlayya, a cobbler by caste and profession. Basavanna hesitates to approve the alliance for he foresees it to be a hasty decision. Until equality is a theoretical proposition it is not detrimental but when implemented it would cause havoc not only to their lives but also to their ideology.

> Basavanna :.... The orthodox will see this mingling of caste as a blow at the very root of varnashrama dharma. Bigotry has not faced such a challenge in two thousand years. I need hardly describe what venom will gush out, what hatred will erupt once the news spreads. (*TD* II v 38)

In Kalburgi's *Fall of Kalyana* Basavanna himself marries Nilambika, a kshatriya, to advocate intercaste marriage among his followers. In *Fall of Kalyana* the denoument reaches due to Basava's stance that dismantles the basis of caste-based self-proclaimed privilege by elevating Allamaprabhu, a low caste by birth, to the highest religious chair known as Sunya–chair. The religious priests known as Jangamas who are equivalent to Vedic brahmins are enraged at Basava's decision of appointing a Shudra as the chairman of a religiously significant chair. The Shaiva–Jangamas join Basava's detractors and pave the way for the downfall of the foresighted vision of a great visionary of all times. They plan to foreground the intercaste marriage planned between a brahmin bride and a Shudra bridegroom at the court as a case of violating the social system but their real ideal is to take revenge on Basava's blow at their religiously ordained honoured position.

Damodara Bhatta, the Queen's priest, and Manchanna Kramita, a brahmin adviser to the King, protest against King Bijjala's support of the Sharana movement led by Basavanna. The brahmins are worried because they would lose the privileged position they are so long enjoying in the society if Basavanna's new cult prospers. The Sharanas are growing in numbers as Basavanna has initiated numerous untouchables and tribals into their fold. Many high caste youngsters who are also attracted by the idealistic motto of Bassavanna refuse to abide by the age-old superstitious and ritual practices. The young Sharanas not only defile age old traditions but also break the caste boundaries that separat man from man. King Bijjala claims that he supports the Sharanas for they are instrumental in developing the economy of the country as they demonstrate the same reverence to their work that the brahmins have for their gods

King Bijjala succumbs to the pressure of the high caste priests and banishes Basava from the capital city. He passes death sentence on Haralayya and Madhuvayya for planning the intercaste wedding of their children as an offence against the varna system. Though the Sharanas, basic principle is compassion and non-violence, Jagadeva, a Sharana, takes revenge on King Bijjala by murdering him. Violence and hatred lead to unrest in the city of Kalyana which results in the denouement of culturally and philosophically rich phase of our history.

The people of Kalyan are ruined and they desert the city in order to save their lives. Jagadeva, the chief disciple of Basavanna, suffers from identity crisis and harks for popularity; he kills King

Bijjala to imprint his name in history and commits suicide like an absurd hero. The disillusioned and heartbroken Basavanna commits suicide, unable to endure his edifice of idealism crumbling to pieces. The Sharanas learn that Basavanna has merged with the elements. With this an exceptional epoch which made a brave attempt to rectify the society and revitalize their culture comes to a disquieting end.

Postcolonial discourse argues the opposition between 'other' versus 'I or we'. The 'other' is a specific social group which is not the privileged 'I or we', and each group is ordained a specific place in the social hegemony. Historical sense is part of the collective memory of humanity that could be retrieved to realize the importance of the excluded and oppressed and are as important as that of the privileged. The American critic, J. Hillis Miller, has stressed the importance of history in the literary text.

> Works of literature do not simply reflect or are not simply caused by their contexts. They have a productive effect in history. This can and should also be studied. To put this another way, the only thing that sometimes worries me about the turn to history now as an explanatory method is the implication that I can fully explain every text by pre- existing historical context. But the publication of these works was itself a political or historical event that in some way changed history. I think that if you don't allow for this, literature is not much worth bothering with. (152-153)

Both the plays taken for study focus upon the evils that have plagued our society from time immemorial. The title 'The Fall of Kalyana' is not indicative of the economical or political downfall of the empire but the moral fall of the citizens of Kalyan who fail to realize the ideals of the great saint and philosopher. Basava's ideology had stood the test of time and still proposes multi-dimensional meanings to the readers. Basavaraj Naikar, Dr. M. M. Kalburgi and Girish Karnad have placed Indian literature as the foremost among the firmament of world literature by upholding the significant and superior period of our history. The plays are to be read from the historical perspective to acknowledge the prescriptive measures it propounds for the present crisis of intolerance in the society. The cultural problems of the present are explicitly understood with connectivity to the historical past. The solution to the present crisis of inequality and inhumanity lies in the past historical events.

Though many philosophers have advocated their ideologies based on humanistic credentials yet in due course each ideology evolved into a closed sect within Hinduism. To bring men to live together on compassionate grounds and to respect each other's worth and not to judge them by their birth remains a challenge even in this present moment. The plays proves that history repeats itself for we have failed to learn the lessons taught by history.

Work Cited

Dorairaj, Joseph. A. *Myth and Literature.* Palayamkittai: Folklore Resources and Research Centre (FRRC), 2003. Print.

Greenblatt, Stephen. "Towards a Cultural Poetics." *The New Historicism*. Ed. H. Aram Veeser. New York: Routledge, 1989. Print.

Jameson, Frederic. *The Political Unconscious: Narrative as a Socially Symbolic Act.* Ithaca: Cornell University Press, 1981. Print.

Kalburgi, M.M. *Fall of Kalyana: A Historical and Religious Play.* Trans. Basavaraj Naikar. New Delhi: Sarup Book Publishers Pvt. Ltd, 2010. Print.

Karnad, Girish. "Circle of Reason: Allen Mendonca's interview with Girish Karnad." *Times of India.* 26 January 2003, India: 4. Print.

_______, "The Playwright, A Discussion/U.R. Ananta Murthy, Prasanna, Girish Karnad." *Indian Literature.* 38 (1995): Print.

_______, *Tale- Danda.* New Delhi: Orient Longman Ltd, 2004. Print.

Miller, Hillis. J. *Hawthorne and History: Defacing It.* USA: Blackwell,1991. Print.

Montrose, Louis. "Professing the Renaissance: The Poetics and Politics of Culture." *Literary Theory: An Anthology.* Ed. Julie Rivkin and Michael Ryan. USA: Blackwell Publishers. 2002. Print.

Murfin, Ross and Supriya M. Ray. *The Bedford Glossary of Critical and Literary Terms.* London: Macmillan, 1998. Print.

Naik, M.K. "Cindrella Still: Recent English Drama."*Littcrit* 27: 1-2(June-Dec 2001): Print.

Naikar, Basvaraj. An Interview with Dr. Vishwanath Bite. *The Criterion: An Internationasl Journal in English.* Vol. I Issue III 6 December 2010.

Phillip, Rice and Patricia Waugh, Ed., *Modern Literary Theory: A Reader.* London: Edward Arnold, 1992. Print.

Ravindranath, S. "Caste as Curse: A New Historicist Reading of Girish Karnad's *Tale-Danda* and Vijay Tendulkar's *Kanyadaan.*" *Critical Essays on Commonwealth Literature.* Ed. K. Balachandran. (New Delhi: Sarup and Sons, 2006). Print.

Ricoeur, Paul. "Myth and History." *The Encyclopedia of Religion.* Vol. 10 ed. Mircea Eliade. New York: Macmillan, 1987. Print.

Seturaman, V.S. Ed. , *Contemporary Criticism: An Anthology.* Madras: Macmillan India Ltd., 1989. Print.

Tripathi, Vanashree. *Three plays of Girish Karnad; A Study in Poetics and Culture.* New Delhi: Prestige Books, 2004. Print.

5

Image as Meaning: A Study of the Select Poems of Vikram Seth

L. Judith Sophia

"Image," one of the most common terms used in criticism, significantly contributes to the meaning of the text. The meaning of a particular text differs from one reader to the other depending on the mental pictures evolved by the readers based on their previous experiences. Vikram Seth (1952), one of the contemporary Indian English poets, a novelist, travel writer, children's writer, biographer and memoirist, employs different patterns of images in his poems in the collection, *Beastly Tales from Here and There* (1992). This paper attempts to identify the poet as a "bricoleur" who has borrowed from texts of different heritages to illuminate the readers and to study the different patterns of images employed which appeal to the sense perception of the readers. The poems chosen for analysis are, 'The Crocodile and the Monkey,' 'The Louse and the Mosquito' and 'The Hare and the Tortoise' from *The Collected Poems* (1995).

Derrida, a post-structuralist, borrows from the French Anthropologist, Claude Levi-Strauss the term "bricolage." It is not a new device or invention but a discourse of method which affirms that it utilizes those instruments which already exist. In his book, *The Savage Mind,* Strauss emphasizes the mytho-poetical nature of "bricolage" (17). To the post-structuralists, a text is a system of signs. Text in literary studies refers to the poem, plays and novels. Some of the theories offered by post-structuralists seem to be very difficult to digest and apply to the texts and they make the readers feel "how difficult it is to read a book" (Jackson 15). In the postmodern scenario, text and discourse are used as synonymous. Discourse occupies a larger semantic space than the text. In Derrida's words, "If one calls *bricolage* the necessity of borrowing one's concepts from the text of a heritage which is more or less coherent or ruined, it must be said that every discourse is *bricoleur*"(202). To Strauss the engineer differs from the *bricoleur* and "in this sense" says Derrida "the engineer is a myth" (202). With brilliant audacity Frye, in his *Anatomy of Criticism*, identifies myth with literature, and asserts myth is a "structural organizing principle of literary form" (341). "Myth" as Frye perceives, "is the imitation of actions near or the conceivable limits of desire" (136).

Myth as an "organizing principle of literary form" or an integrative force arises from the depth of mankind's collective psyche. Therefore, myths are collective and communal. Myth critics view that "mythology encompasses more than grade school stories about the Greek and Roman deities or clever fables invented for the amusement of children" (Guerin 159). In his attempt to define myth, Allan W. Watts says, "Myth is to be defined as a complex of stories—some no doubt fact, and some fantasy – which, for various reasons, human beings regard as demonstrations of the inner meaning of the universe and of human life" (qtd. in Guerin 160). People of all culture have their own myths reflected in their legend, folklore, and ideology and they are shaped by their cultural environment in which they grow (Guerin 160).

As myths are reflected in folklore and legends, a fable becomes naturally a part of myths. *The Penguin Dictionary of Literary Terms and Literary Theory* defines fable as "a short narrative in prose or verse which points a moral" and their characters are "Non-human creatures or inanimate things" (Cuddon 300). Fables also can be described as didactic literature for their purpose is to impart a lesson or value. Animals are their protagonists and anthropomorphic characteristics are given to them. Vikram Seth rewrites and reinterprets fables as enlightened discourses in his *Beastly Tales.* In the light of the usage of the term 'bricolage' it is appropriate to call Seth a 'bricoleur' for his utilization of the existing age old fables of the World. While explaining the genesis of the collection of "ten animal fables in rhymed couplets" Seth writes in "Author's Forewords": "Because it was very hot in my house one day and I could not concentrate on my work, I decided to write a summer story involving mangoes and a river. By the time I had finished writing 'The Crocodile and the Monkey'... another story and other animals had begun stirring in my mind. And so it went on until all ten of these beastly tales were born—or re-born." (xxxii) He also acknowledges the sources of these ten story-poems as "the first two come from India, the next two from China, the next two from Greece, and the next two from the Ukraine. The final two came directly to me from the Land of Gup" (xxxii). Critics like Wimsatt W. explains what the King's blood contains:

> That the royal blood contains
> Remedies for aches and pains—
> Ginger, honey, sugar, spice,
> Cardamom, and all things nice. (55 - 58)

The kinesthetic images are revealed through the arrival of a mosquito: 'One day a mosquito flew / Through the window' (17, 18); its 'parabolic leap, / Landed not too far from Creep [louse]' (27, 28); detecting the danger the mosquito has 'hidden in the canopy' (93) and in the end its leaving away as 'the mosquito flew' (96). The louse occupies the King's bed as its 'ancestral home' (2) for 'three decades' (4) and with his kin it enjoys an undisturbed and delightful life at the expense of the King's blood. This undisturbed delight is disturbed by the new entrant, the mosquito. This arrival brings all change including the tragic end of the louse clan.

In 'The Hare and the Tortoise', the 'laughter,' 'babble,' 'humming,' and 'giggling' of the hare and her friends, the 'muttering' of the tortoise and the 'idle boast' of the hare constitute the auditory images. The tactile image is formed as the tortoise 'Daily counted all his toes' (26), in the proud words of the hare: 'I would thrash you anywhere— / Marsh or mountain, hill or dale, / Field or forest, rain or hail!' (84- 86); as hare is 'wearing her silk nightie, kept on staring at a mirror' (103), 'satin shorts' (137) of the hare, and is got diverted by 'a field of Mushrooms' (156) whereas the tortoise slowly and steadily wins 'crossing line and the tape' (194), and in the end of the race receives 'the gold cup' (181). Ironically the deceptive world is ready to adorn the hare with a golden cup filled with 'Gorgeous rubies' (231), and 'front page in all the papers' (238), a book, a travel magazine have allotted space to highlight this defeat as a heroic one. This brings income to the hare and she has invested it in 'a manor house' (251). The smell of 'sauerkraut' (8), (chopped pickled cabbage), and the delicious mushroom treat which diverted the hare not only kindle the appetite of the readers but also contribute to olfactory images of the poem. The hare used to 'eat her eggs and sauerkraut' (8) and when it reminds the readers of the mushroom treat:

(This last mushroom, I suspect,
Has a cerebral effect.
Every time I eat one, I
Feel I'm floating in the sky.)
How delicious! What a treat! (159- 163)

The secretion of the digestive hormones is induced. These situations constitute gustatory images. The kinesthetic image, race is the central metaphor of the poem. The poet describes the movement of the tortoise as follows:

But the tortoise plodded on
Like a small automaton,

Muttering, as he held his pace:
'I have got to win this race.' (133- 136)

On the contrary, the tortoise begins 'Leaving all her friends astounded / At her rocket-fuelled pace' (151), soon it changes its direction on seeing 'a field of mushrooms' (156) and moves 'towards the wood' (167) to 'go exploring' (170). In the meanwhile 'the tortoise plodded on .... Very steady, very slow— / And he saw the finish line' (175, 178, 179) and in the end won the race. The tortoise teaches the lesson:

that sure and slow
Is the only way to go—
That you can't rise to top
With a skip, a jump, a hop—
That you've got to hatch your eggs,
That you've to count your legs,
That you've got to do your duty,
Not depend on verve and beauty. (207- 214)

Whereas the hare's race ends up in 'a feature with the news:/ 'All the World Lost for a Snooze' (241- 242) and a story 'of her three hour expedition / To the wood – called 'Mushroom Mission'' (248). In his essay, *A Retrospect'* Ezra Pound writes, "An 'Image' is that which presents an intellectual and emotional complex in an instant of time" (59). This "intellectual emotional complex" cannot be experienced or understood in "an instant of time." It takes a long way to trace back the similar pattern if not the same. Every poet has his /her own unique formation of images. In Northrop Frye's view, as expressed in his essay "The Archetypes of Literature," these images are bound "into an archetypal symbol of literature" (426). In his mission he has identified few identical image patterns. To him, "One essential principle of archetypal criticism is that the individual and the universal forms of an image are identical" (432). The archetypal critics have identified 'the questmyth' as the central myth of literature. This quest-myth exists in the chosen poems. In the poem, "The Crocodile and Monkey", monkey undertakes this quest. This quest begins from a world of innocence where the monkey is totally unaware of the intention of the crocodiles even then the crocodile suggests his wife's conspiracy through selective words:

> When she takes you by the paw
> Something at your heart will gnaw.
> When you gaze into her eyes
> You will enter Paradise. (85- 88)

The poor innocent monkey fails to understand their tricks and plans to go with the crocodile. In the mid way of their journey the crocodile reveals their vile intention to eat the monkey's heart and asks the monkey:

> Which would you prefer—to drown
> In the Ganga or to be
> Gutted by my wife and me?
> I will let you choose your end. (122- 125)

The monkey attempts to stop the crocodile as it 'slowly started sinking' (127) by asking it to wait. It tries to change the adverse situation with a powerful poetic discourse:

> Death by drowning, death by slaughter
> —Death by land or death by water—
> I'd face either with a smile
> For your sake, O crocodile! (129- 132)

And it decides to con the crocodiles and announces:

> If you had not rushed me so,
> I'd have found the time to go

To the hollow where I keep
Heart and liver when I sleep
....
Why did you not speak before?
I'd have fetched them from the shore.

(139-142, 147, 148)

In their attempt to con the monkey the crocodiles lose the sweet and pleasant friendship of the monkey and its gift, the ripe and rare mangoes. In this quest the realization comes in the middle and the monkey rises to the occasion and weaves a story and cons the crocodile. This paves way for its journey back home and answers to the crocodile's call:

I'm not such a double-dunce (171).

In the end, after gaining knowledge, the monkey escapes leaving the crocodile to learn how to overcome fate by wisdom. In the second poem, 'The Louse and the Mosquito', Seth presents Creep, the louse 'Lived in her ancestral house' (2). The lice live in group occupying the place of safety for a long time. It reveals,

They had dwelt here as of right
For three decades, and each night
She and her enormous brood
Drank the King's blood for their food. (3-6)

They silently and happily 'Nipped and sipped and drank the blood' (10) of the King and 'pursued their gentle lives /—Lives of undisturbed delight' (14, 15). They do not undertake any physical journey but their peace is disturbed when 'a mosquito flew/ Through the window' (17, 18) and demanded little space. Mosquito's plea:'Let me sleep here for one night / And I'll catch the morning flight' (35, 36) melts 'the tender hearted Creep' (39) who overcoming by compassion accommodates the mosquito.

The quest-myth prevails with the journey of the alien, the mosquito. This mosquito doesn't undertake the quest with any purpose but it dislikes the domination of the louse. It behaves like an anti-hero who brings destruction to the louse community. The 'fiery sting' of the mosquito leads the King to pass the command: 'Search the bed/ Find and strike the creature dead!'(89, 90). Causing annihilation, 'the mosquito flew / Looking out for further prey, / Humming mildly on the way' (96- 98).

In the poem, "The Hare and the Tortoise", both the characters undertake the quest to win the race. The 'hot and heady' (3) hare loses as it boasts its talents and sleeps in the middle of the journey. Its overconfidence and pride defeat it in the end. The 'slow and steady' (4) tortoise remains as a 'Major in accountancy' (41) and eventually, achieves the end. Though the writer takes license to twist the original end with a modern flavour the tortoise excels the hare by its earnest attempt and regular, slow and steady pace. 'Water' image has the symbolic meaning of 'the mystery of creation; birth-death –resurrection; purification and redemption; fertility and growth' (Guerin 161). The poem, 'The Crocodile and the Monkey' consists of this image having the symbolic meaning of 'birth-death-resurrection.' When the monkey realizes that he has been swindled it has to undergo a state of dilemma. There in the river it receives an intuitive idea of resurrection and regains life. The river image thus plays its symbolic role of the 'transitional phase of the life cycle' (Guerin 161).

The poem, "The Louse and the Mosquito" lacks the explicit water image whereas it has the image of 'blood.' The louse and clan enjoy drinking the blood of the King. This signifies their 'violent passion' for someone else's life that ends in 'disorder' (Guerin 161). Some of the colour images highlighted by the archetypal critics are used in these poems. The locale in the first poem, "The Crocodile and the Monkey" is 'Ganga's greenest isle' (1) and the crocodile appears in 'greeny brown' (3). In positive context the green colour symbolizes "growth, hope, and fertility" (Guerin 161) as indicated in the case of the locale. In the negative context, green is associated with "death and Decay" (Guerin 161) as the crocodile exposes its vile and deadly nature in the end. Drinking the King's blood the lice grow 'plump and smooth and white' (16). It is not used in its positive aspect but in the negative sense and it denotes "death" and "terror" (Guerin 161) as they sip and drink the King's blood which in the long run may cause the death of the king. On the contrary they are founded and killed. The blood here brings death to the lice. Number image is used when the tortoise counted its toes and his grand sons as: 'one, two, three' (32). This indicates the integrated and meticulous nature of the tortoise.

In the poem "The Crocodile and the Monkey", the crocodiles signify the role of "the trickster" (Guerin 164) as the female crocodile reveals:

> But I now desire to eat,
> As an anniversary treat,
> Something sweeter still than fruit,
> Sugar-cane or sugar-root:
> I must eat that monkey's heart. (47- 51)

Instead of showing gratitude for the sweet and rare mangoes, the crocodile asks the heart of the monkey to taste it. This shows the vile nature of the crocodiles. Tree in archetypal criticism symbolizes "life of the cosmos:its consistence, growth, proliferation, generative and regenerative processes" (Guerin 165). The monkey asks the crocodile to:

> Eat, my friend, and take your wife
> Nectar from the tree of life—
> Mangoes ripe and mangoes rare,
> Mangoes, mangoes everywhere. (73-76)

The metaphor 'tree of life' is used for the mango tree to indicate life. The fruits strengthen their friendship to some extend though the crocodiles misused it. Vice is defeated in the end and the monkey gains life and continues to live. 'The gold cup' in the poem, "The Hare and the Tortoise" stands for the ultimate aim of one's life. The race is an image that symbolizes the life journey. At the outset, the poem suggests the way to achieve the goal in life. If anyone determines to focus the goal after fixing it without heeding to any other diverting ideas that person will reach the end.

Though Seth is better known as the author of the novels, *A Suitable Boy* and *An Equal Music,* his verse-fables, *Beastly Tales* reveal that he is quite at ease with writing them for children. This delightful collection of story- poems proves to be a modern classic and reinterprets the age old Fables across the world and shows his astonishing versatility. Bruce King identifies Seth as "a very different young poet with a sense of humour, parody and a hedonistic enjoyment of life" (44). This is quite true and he sets apart as he retells the fables decorated with images not only to give pleasure and to teach moral but also make it relevant to the present context. Vivid imagery and humour make these poems extremely readable and constitute the meaning of the poems. This collection leads to various interpretations if poststructural theories are applied and it is a fine example of 'bricolage.'

Works Cited

Abrams, M.H, *A Glossary of Literary Terms.* Australia:Heinle. th 7 ed. 1999. Rpt. Singapore:Thomson Asia Pvt. Ltd. , 2003.

Cuddon, J.A, ed, *The Penguin Dictionary of Literary Terms and* th *Literary Theory.* 4 ed. London:Penguin Books, 1999.

Derrida, Jacques, "Structure, Sign and Play in the Discourse of the Human Sciences." *ModernLiterary Theory:A Reader.* Eds. th Philip Rice and Patricia Waugh. 4 ed. London:Arnold Publishers, 2002. 195 – 210.

Frye, Northrop, *Anatomy of Criticism:Four Essays.* Princeton:Princeton UP, 1971.

______. "The Archetypes of Literature." *20 th Century Literary Criticism.* Ed. David Lodge. London: Longman Group Ltd., 1972. 422-433.

Guerin, Wilfred. L, et al. eds. *A Handbook of Critical Approaches to Literature.* New York: Harper & Row Publishers, 1979.

Jackson, Leonard, *The Poverty of Structuralism: Literature and Structuralist Theory.* London: Longman, 1991.

King, Bruce, *Modern Indian Poetry in English.* Oxford: Oxford UP, 1987. Revised ed. 2001. Levi-Strauss, Claude. *The Savage Mind.* London: George Weidenfeld & Nicolson, 1966.

Pound, Ezra, "A Retrospect." *20 th Century Literary Criticism.* Ed. David Lodge. London: Longman Group Ltd., 1972. 58- 68.

Seth, Vikram, *Beastly Tales from Here and There* (1992). *The Collected Poems.* New Delhi: Penguin Books India Ltd., 1995. xxxii, 279-289, 304-312.

Wimsatt, William K, J.R. and Cleanth Brooks, *Literary Criticism: A Short History.* Rpt. New Delhi: Surjeet Publications, 2007.

6

The Plays of Girish Karnad: A Socio-Linguistic Study

Krishna Singh

Language in Karnad is a social tool and it is simultaneously shaped by socio-cultural factors. His plays adhere to Indianized version of standard English defying the notion of superiority of King's English, freely indulges and incorporates the popular Indian slangs, dialectic words, words from various Indian languages, metaphors, symbols, irony, imagery, idioms and phrases, specific sentence structures which are pregnant with Indianness.

Karnad is a master of rich vocabulary. Though, for him, English was a language of adulthood not mother tongue, he has perfectly used English to discuss certain important socio-cultural and political issues of the contemporary India through his plays. He never hesitates nor feels inferiority complex to use English in the Indianized twist. English, in his hand, has become a tool to make people conscious of the evils which have envenomed our whole society. His translation or transcreation of his earlier plays as well as the plays i.e. *The Dreams of Tipu Sultan, Two Monologues: Flowers, Broken Images* and *Wedding Album* of the later phase of his dramatic career show a marked distinction and accomplishment in linguistic expression. We notice the evolution of themes, techniques and language in his plays. He chooses apt and suitable words from a rich treasury of vocabulary. His words are suggestive and reveal both character and situation. He writes dialogues in lucid, pointed and precise language which possess decency and decorum. His plays are in prose, the use of poetic rendering is not excepted. He has translated original Kannada verses into English.

Karnad's characters use language which suits their status and temperament. Frequent use of Indian vocabulary, idioms and phrases, symbols, images, metaphors and irony facilitate to create an Indian atmosphere and lend his style the charm of familiarity. Grace in his style is hardly sacrificed for social cause or idea. His style is, however, straightforward and idiomatic. There is a typical Indianness about his style in his plays. His style is not loose but periodic—a complete whole or a part of a bigger whole. It has specific form that cannot be easily tempered. Aristotle has laid down two essentials of good writing: "clearness and propriety" (46). Clarity or intelligibility and propriety or suitability are necessary to convey the writer's meaning to the audience; and these can be attained by the use of current words, use of unfamiliar words—archaic words, foreign words, dialect words, newly-coined words, metaphors and all kinds of words are used in a judicious combination to make the work a dignified composition. Karnad has dexterously handled all these rhetorical techniques. He makes use of traditional as well as personal symbols which are employed to highlight his concern for the psychological problems of the protagonists and their revolutionary outlook towards old values.

Karnad's plays from *Yayati* to *Wedding Album* present a variety of themes, characters, techniques and situations which require a specific language to suit the context. For instance, *Yayati* draws its plot from the myth of *Mahabharata*, characters, situations, atmosphere, and socio-cultural practices. Different status of characters cannot be presented in a natural way without the congenial vocabulary, structure of sentences, idioms and phrases, symbols and metaphorical representation of certain aspects of life, compound words, poetic expression to yield charm and beauty to the dialogues suiting the personality and status of the speaker. Above all the air of ancient mythical culture would flow due to the corresponding language. Even the names of the characters of the play immediately takes us to nostalgic cultural past of India—Yayati, Pooru, Devayani, Chitralekha, Sharmishtha.

In the Prologue of the play, Sutradhara, like the Greek Chorus, introduces the content and characters of the play in a very lucid and pointed language to let the audience know the backdrop of the play. King Yayati, Prince Pooru and his wife Chitralekha, the Princess of Anga, Queen Devayani, Sharmishtha, the slave to Queen, and Swarnlata speak a language that suits their temperament and character. For instance, Swarnlata reacts against Sharmishtha who has bewitched King Yayati, a talks to Devayani: "That spiteful whore—I would have torn her hair out if you hadn't stopped me. Taught that fiend a proper lesson. A proper lesson. The rakshasi. You heard us, madam… She didn't even spare His Majesty. I…I can't bear it" (7). Even Devayani's condemnation is very sharp and penetrating, "Bitch, I'll kill you. I'll feed you to the…" (13). It's ironical that due to moral transgression Yayati is cursed to old age and he is planning to exchange it with his own son Pooru and indulge in filthy sexual gratification knowing the way of immunity: "—the curse will not have its effect on you if a young man agrees to take it upon himself and offers his youth to you in exchange" (44).

The protest of Chitralekha is well founded and it imbibes its force and meaning from a very stunning and aggressive language. Yayati, Pooru, Chitralekha, Devayani and Sharmishtha all are symbolical representation of lust, obedience, woman's protest, and jealousy. The metaphors used to denote certain peculiar traits of Sharmishtha are: "treacherous hyena" (27), "Satanic" (8), "spiteful whore" (1), "Bitch" (13), "reptile" (30), and "fiend" (7). The gentleness of Pooru "like a waft of cool breeze"; Rakshasi, guru, Arya, Aryavarta, arti, namaskara, Devi etc. yield indigenous pulse to the story.

Tughlaq draws its story from Indian history—the reign of Mohammad-bin-Tughlaq which was remarkable for two reasons—numbers of experiments Tughlaq carried out, and his character. Karnad remains close to the original and gives philosophical dimension to the play and psychological depth to the character of Tughlaq—a tortured soul. Apart from structural design, art of characterization, mental and emotional reactions, Natak company conventions, which the playwright has employed skilfully in the play, language with its various properties has been used to suit the historical context, controversial figure, dialogues, conspiracy, anger, frustration and polarities among characters. Use of Arabic, Persian, Urdu, dialectic words, idioms and phrases, symbols, irony, metaphors, cryptic, sketchy as well as long sonorous poetic sentences have been used to create congenial atmosphere and proper meaning to make the presentation highly awarding. The announcer has been used as a Greek Chorus that goes on providing basic information hence his language is clear, straightforward, highly informative and arresting. The very first line of the play: "God, what's this country coming to!" (1) conveys the anguish of an Old Man of Delhi Sultanate who is generic. Tughlaq has been introduced in a traditional fashion, language full of adjectives, conceits and pomp: "Attention! Attention! The warrior in the path of God, the Defender of the Word of the Prophet, the friend of the Khalif, the Just, His Merciful Majesty, Sultan Muhammad Tughlaq" (3).

At the onset, Tughlaq unlocks his plan of shifting capital from Delhi to Daultabad, his speech is full of humility, the sentence structure is periodic, lines are run-on and continuity is maintained artistically:

> MUHAMMAD: My empire is large now and embraces the South and I need a capital which is at its heart. Delhi is too near the border and as you well know its peace is never free from the fear of invades. But for me the most important factor is that Daultabad is a city of the Hindus and as the capital it will symbolize the bond between Muslims and Hindus which I wish to develop and strengthen in my kingdom. I invite you all to accompany me to Daultabad. This is only an invitation and not an order. Only those who have faith in me may come with me. With their help I shall build an empire which will be the envy of the world. (3-4)

In the later scenes when Tughlaq is disillusioned and frustrated his language expresses his tortured soul:

> MUHAMMAD: God, God in Heaven, please help me. Please don't let go of my hand. My skin drips with blood and I don't know how much of it is mine and how much of others. I started in Your path, Lord, why am I wandering naked in this desert now? I started in search of you. Why am I become a pig rolling in this gory mud? Raise me, clean me. Cover me with Your Infinite Mercy. I can only Clutch at the hem of your cloak with my bloody Fingures and plead. I can only beg—have pity on me. I have no one but You now. Only You. Only You...You...You...You...(67)

Karnad has succeeded in creating a proper Indian atmosphere in the play, i.e., fourteenth century India when Tughlaq reigned, by the use of words and idioms and phrases from different sources: Sultan, Jiziya, Kaji-i-Mumalik, dhobi, dar-ul-Islam, Darbar-i-Khas, Allah, Sukrat, Koran, Mussulman, hakim, Kafir, Khalif, Maulvis, Islam and the Muezzin's call for prayer has been twice given in Arabic: "Alla-Ho-Akbar! Alla-Ho-Akbar...La Elaha Illilah" (41 & 86). Idioms and phrases used in *Tughlaq*: light up our path, went wild, hold your tongue, the end of my tether, to breathe life into, play the game, torn into pieces, backbone of rebels, an incompetent fool, get rid of, an honest scoundrel, crush into dust, get to ooze out spittle, mug's game, etc. "roads lined with skeletons" (70)—are imageries that create an unpleasant and dismal experience.

OLD MAN's speech:"I survived. But my family was more fortunate. They all died on the way" (52) and FIRST MAN's reaction:"We starve and they want us to pray. They want to save our souls" (70) are finest instances of irony and satire. Symbols in the play enlarge the expressive range of the language due to emotional and associative significance attached to it. The whole play is a symbol of the political situation of India of the sixties that "...reflects as no other play perhaps does the political mood of disillusionment which followed the Nehru era of idealism in the country" (Murthy "Introduction" vii-viii). This mood is revealed even in the very first line of the play: "God, what's this country coming to!" (1). Aziz and Aazam symbolize opportunistic and unprincipled people who exploit the liberal ideals and welfare schemes of the government meant for the poor.

Chess symbol has a unique significance as it runs through the play. It suggests the intrigue in Tughlaq's nature. As a skilled chess player he uses his political opponents as pawn on the chessboard of politics. The python in Scene Eight symbolizes Tughlaq's barbarity and inhumanity. It is a symbolic of the complete degeneration of his personality from a human being to a wild beast, a huge snake. Daultabad is a symbol of Hindu-Muslim unity which Tughlaq wants to foster. The vulture and other birds of prey that thrust their beaks into the flesh of Muhammad so that he knows no peace either by day or night are also symbolic. They symbolize the frustration of an idealist and visionary, and his spiritual agony. The prayer symbol which has been used as a leitmotif (theme associated with a person or a thought) is highly significant. The Muslim chieftains along with Sheikh Sham-ud-din, a pacifist priest, conspire to murder Tughlaq at prayer time. The use of prayer for murder is reminiscent of what Tughlaq adopted to kill his father. The prayer is symbolic of the fact that his life is corrupted at its very source. Rattan Singh also tries to exploit prayer to murder Tughlaq. Tughlaq is fanatic about prayer, and when disillusioned about the futility of prayer prohibits it in his kingdom. The word 'prayer' has been used in an ironical way in the play. It is introduced after an interval of five years. Tughlaq falls into a sound sleep and gets up when the Muezzin's call to prayer fades away; so he fails to offer prayer. The prayer symbol is the very basis of the play.

Hayavadana is based on Thomas Mann's mock-heroic novel *The Transposed Heads*, which is rooted in Somedeva's *Kathasaritasagara*, an ancient collection of stories in Sanskrit. It is full of myths, allusions, references, archetypal beliefs, identifiable characters, narrative design and plot rooted in Indian soil. Karnad, in the play, deals with the identity crisis—the mad dance of incompleteness—illustrated through Devadatta, Kapila and Padmini triangle and sub-plot in which Hayavadana figures. Bhagavata, Kapila, Padimini, Hayavadana, Ganesha, Kali, Rudra, Indra, Ridhi, Sidhi, Yakshagana, Gandharva, King Vikram, demon Vetal, Vatsayayan, Shakuntala, Uravashi, Yakshini, Indumati, Mt. Chitrakoot, Ujjain, Kashi, Pavan Veethi, Kathakali, pooja, pativara, punyasthala, arti, dhoti,"Jhanda Ooncha Rahe Hamara" (64), "Sare Jahan se Acchha Hindostan Hamara" (64), "two pieces of heart" (28), "dog's eye" (31), "apple of very eye" (92), Kapila and Devadatta "Like cocks in a pit" (61) etc contribute to the richness of language and develop a distinct sort of world, different from us—a world of incomplete individuals, indifferent gods, dolls that speak and children who cannot, a world indifferent to the desires and frustrations, joys and sorrows of human beings. The image of Ganesh, Kali, Rudra, river and scarecrow, horse rider, Hayavadana extend something deeper associated with the theme and characters of the play. Doll I, II, III symbolize the mental dilemma and reactions of Padmini. Like the Sutradhara of *Yayati* and the Announcer of *Tughlaq*, the Story of *Naga-Mandala*, Bhagavata in *Hayavadana* goes on supplying background information and comments on the development of the story. The use of verse and use of prose—that is balanced, uniform, precise and pointed—suit the context. Bhagávata introduces the scene and characters of the play in a very lucid and straightforward manner:

> This is the city of Dharampura, ruled by King Dharamsheela... Two youths who dwell in this city are our heroes. One is Devadatta. Comely in appearance, fair in colour, unrivalled in intelligence.... Having felled the mightiest pundits of the kingdom in debates on logic and love, having blinded the greatest poets of the world with his poetry and wit, Devadatta is as it were the apple of every eye in Dharampura.
>
> The other youth is Kapila. He is the only son of iron-smith Lohita.... He is dark and plain to look at, yet in deeds which requires drive and daring, in dancing, in strength and in physical skills he has no equal.
>
> [*sings*] Two friends there were —one mind, one heart—(1-2).

Two friends ironically develop into deadly enemies due to entangled relationship after transposition and kill each other. Whenever Karnad had to emphasize anything, he creates space with dashes between the words: "KAPILA: I mean—who—is—it—this—time?" (12). The fear of the Actor has been expressed in a very natural way by the use of broken, cryptic and incomplete structure of sentences: "ACTOR: Sir...oh my God!—God!—/ I—I—I—Oh God!" (2). After transposition Devadatta, Kapila and Padmini make a circle and sing a song; though simple in diction and clear in expression it carries deeper psychological dilemma they all are facing:

> ALL THREE [*together*].
>
> What a good mix! No more tricks! Is this one that or that one this? Ho! Ho! (35)

In nature and landscape description Karnad is purely Wordsworthian; he goes beyond physical charm and fascination, and suggests the inner conflict that runs parallel. His language is simple and highly poetic with the touch of emotion. The image of Ganesha symbolizes perfection and victory, Kali—power; and river and scarecrows in the choric song the mental crisis of Padmini; Hayavadana stands for incompleteness, Devadatta Apollonian tendency and Kaplia Dionysian tendency; Padmini symbolizes erotic urge, horse energy, and Doll I, II, III symbolize Padmini's psychic reactions and reverie.

Naga-Mandala which is a richly textured dramatic transmutation of two folk-tales of Karnataka deals with gender-bias, subalternization of woman and prospect of the emergence of women in orthodox Indian society in which patriarchy dominates all the domains of life, i.e., religion, culture, social conventions, beliefs, man-woman relationship. Plot, character and thought have been developed due to dignified composition—consummate excellence in language. Kusbi oil, Ayyo, but'ting, ogress, demon, Naga, Cobra, Yaksha woman, Flames, Indianized similes and metaphors, i.e., "juicy as a tender cucumber" (24), "wife locked up like a caged bird" (30), "Ears like hibiscus. Skin like young mango leaves. Lips like rolls of silk" (32), "change like a chameleon" (51), "spreads hood like an umbrella" (58), and transferred epithet—" tender bud like you"; and the image of Cobra (58), haunted well (48), Flames floating in the air (23), ruined temple (Prologue) and symbols extend innovativeness and novelty in expression. The ruined temple (dilapidated temple also figures in *Bali: The Sacrifice*) symbolizes seclusion and desperation, Flames represent the socio-psychological condition of woman, Naga—a romantic lover or poetic imagination, Rani stands for woman's status, role and emergence, Appanna male-chauvinism, Kappanna filial obligation, Kurudavva motherly love and worldly wisdom, Village Elders patriarchy, Dog, Mongoose tools of subjection of woman and Rani's tresses—wedded bliss.

The evolution in Rani is noticeable and Karnad dexterously correlates language with the character. The protest and latent frustration is let loose emphatically to convey it to the audience: "I was a stupid, ignorant girl when you brought me here. But now I am a woman, a wife, and I am going to be a mother. I am not a parrot. Not a cat or a sparrow. Why don't you take it on trust that I have a mind and explain this charade to me? Why do you play these games? Why do you change like a chameleon from day to night?" (51). Appanna's anger over Rani's infidelity is expressed by sharp and piercing abuses: "harlot" (52), "slut" (52), and "whore" (53). The imagery of the Cobra is highly thrilling and awesome duringthe the Ordeal: "the Cobra slides up her shoulder and spreads its hood like an umbrella over her head. The crowd gasps. The Cobra sways its hood gently for a while, then becomes docile and moves over her shoulder like a garland" (58). Naga's jealousy and sense of loss haunts it with reminiscences that morbidity is poetically drafted by the playwright. M.K. Naik has rightly commented: "the play moves at a brisk pace, and the dialogue, which is in clear, simple every day English without any conscious straining after 'Indian-ness', suits the rustic folk-tale it presents as a surface structure, without causing harm to the deep structure of the symbolism beneath" (46).

Tale-Danda is a historical play that deals with the problem of caste which has poisoned the Indian life and its institutions. The medieval history of Karantaka, its socio-political milieu, characters rooted in the medieval past of South India, conflict between traditional Sanatana dharma and *Lingayat* faith, ideals of new faith—static versus progressive, royal priests, deserve a kind of language that can be a natural vehicle of conveying the vision and thoughts of the playwright and suit the character and their personalities. Religious fanaticism and its consequences occupy the central position in the play; the character of Basavanna posed a threat to religious fanaticism and the result is awesome. The words and expression of various stocks enrich the text and correspond to the issues, deeds, actions and reactions of the characters: King Bijjala, Sambashiva Shastri, Savitri, Jagadeva, Mallibomma, Sovideva, Damodara Bhatta, Manchanna, Kallaya, Kakkaya, Gangambika, Haralayya, Sheelavanta, Madhuvarasa, Kalavati, Kalyan, "jungle of Uluvi" (90), Ayyo, "*Thoo! Thoo! Thoo!*" (81), "laughing stock" (83), "heap of shit" (83), "ocean of saffron" (74), *Sharanas,* Shiva, Jain, "Om namah Shivaya" (31), untouchables, Nandi, Bhakti, Varna, guru, bhakatas, Darshan, tribals, low-caste, Vedic dharama, *linga,* aryavarta, *Lingayat,* Lord of meeting rivers, Kappadi, "Yuvaraja Kalanjara-Puradhishwara Suvarna-Vrishabha-dhwaja Someshawara Rajendra Bho parak! Bho parak" (57-58). Even the full length expression in Sanskrit takes us to the twelfth-century Karnataka dominated by Hindu rituals and marks an instance of Indian imagination. "

Human Body" (29) has been presented as a symbol of holy temple which facilitates our spiritual advancement and well-being of the whole society. "Fire" (91) stands for anger—the anger of Sovideva and the entire Satanatana Dharmi against Basavanna and the forces of change. Killing of Bijjala in the sanctum symbolizes the degeneration of human values similar to Prayer in *Tughlaq*; Mariappa sitting on the shoulders of King Bijjala symbolizes harmony between low and high castes; Basavanna represents revolution for change, progressive ideas and establishment of egalitarian society; Damodara Bhatt, Manchanna and Sambashiva Shastri stand for traditional values of Hindu religion; Jagadeva and Sovideva symbolize players in power politics, *linga*—power and generation; and Kappadi—a meeting place of rivers symbolizes peace and spiritual introspection. The similes and metaphors used in the play heighten Indianness: "a woman is just a ripe mango on a roadside tree" (42), "Brahmin like a jackal" (56), "snake" (62)—a metaphor of Sovideva who traps his own father King Bijjala, "city is dead—like a cemetery" (82); the inter-caste marriage of Sheelavanta and Kalavati—"cursed wedding" (48), "absurd wedding" (49), "unnatural alliance" (55) etc. The fear after violent reaction from brahmins led by Sovideva is exquisitely presented: "GUNDANNA: *Ayyo…Ayyao…*Kala! Malli! I can't bear it. I can't…Mother!" (81). Use of capitals, space, italics and dashes between the words have been the technique Karnad has used to emphasize the meaning or make the expression forceful throughout his plays.

The Fire and the Rain with its solid thematic richness has proved a great success. It draws the story from the myth of Yavakri who figures in the *Mahabharata.* Karnad gives modern meaning to the myth which stresses the dangers of knowledge without wisdom and power without integrity. Fire sacrifice, origin of drama, and the history of theatre in India, penance, oblation, kritya, Brahma, Lord of All Creations, Vedas, Fifth Veda, Bharata, Hymns, Indra, God of Rain and Sky, demon Vritra, Vishwarupa, Paravasu, Aravasu, Yavakri, Vishakha, Nitillai, Raibhya, Andhak, Braham Rakshasa, adhvaryu, Brahmin soul, famine, drought, sudra, outcaste, gurus, mantras, kamandalu, nether world, champak tree, "jack fruit grove" (121), "wheel of Time" (173), "Hell-hole" (176), dhoti, "dogs sniffing around my daughter-in-law's bottom" (138), council of Elders (tribal), "tamarind hill" (143), tribal customs, Vedic practices, Yavakri's rigorous penance for ten years etc. fill life in dry-bones of the age-old myth and vindicate Karnad's interest to revitalize Indian imagination.

The language used in the play has various levels. "Sick of silence" refers to Vishakha's sense of alienation similar to Rani of *Naga-Mandala*; Yavakri's penance is described in such a way a complete picture is drawn and we are transported to a world of romance, magic and supra-mundane: "Ten years of rigorous penance. And still Lord Indra would not oblige. Finally, Yavakri stood in the middle of a circle of fire and started offering his limbs to the fire—first his fingers, then his eyes, then his entrails, his tongue, and at last, his heart—that's when the god appeared to him. Restored his limbs, and granted him the boon" (115). Simple and stately diction is noticeable in the play. Use of similes and metaphors make the expression more lively and meaningful:"dry like tinder" (103), "dying like a sacrificial animal" (172), "like a bandicoot" (131), "drying up like a dead tree" (142), "a soul locked in nothingness like a foetus stitched up inside its mother's sac" (146), "let's be together like brother and sister" (153), "bodies drenched in blood like rats that pour out during the plague" (154), "like an eunuch" (155), "dance like a celestial being" (161-62), "wave of blood breaking out of the sacrificial enclosure like a flock of fear-crazed jungle fowl" (170); "bitch of yours "(138) refers to Vishakha and "trees loaded with fruits" (121) and "savage" (126) metaphorically represent Vishakha and Nittilai tribal society condemned by brahmins. The words 'bitch' and 'whore' symbolize condemnation of the fair sex by male-chauvinists. The 'fire' symbolizes lust, anger, vengeance, envy, treachery, violence and death. The 'rain' symbolizes self-sacrifice, compassion, Divine Grace, forgiveness, revival and life. The image of Brahma Rakshasa (128), Raibhya in meditation (128), big banayan tree (110) and Nittilai's killing (172) are marvellously employed to create a cathartic effect.

Bali: The Sacrifice deals with the instinct of violence and morality of substitution. Inspired by Sanskrit and Kannada epics Karnad delves deep into the problem and treats in a dramatic manner to expose the ways of violence and hypocrisy involved in it. At the centre it's Bali, i.e., the sacrifice of animals for material gains. The Queen and the Mother represent two opposite standpoints whereas the King is in between these two. The Mahout symbolizes the subalternity of the lower class. The instinct of violence, character development and dialogue has been given artistic expression by the use of verse as well as prose that suit the above. Brilliant use of select words, phrases, similes and metaphors add beauty and power to the play: Bali, Savior, Jain, pallu, dhoti, Mahout, "black and blue" (76), "bazzar woman" (78), namaskara, "World is divided into two orbs...so also the human soul" (74), "ugly as a bandicoot" (75), "ruby lips" (77), "shunned and starved like outcastes" (98), "naked like Saviors" (120), "rainy nights" (125), "Death yields to life like monsoons piled on monsoons so the life follows" (125). The abusing terms like 'harlot' and 'whore' have been used to denote the subalternity of the fair sex. The imagery supports the meaning and create proper background to the context:"inner sanctum of a ruined temple" (73) which also figures in *Naga-Mandala* and *Hayavadana* stands for a haunted place, seclusion and lifelessness, "four armed deity" (74), "replica of cock" (118) etc. The Mahout symbolizes "low-born" (80) and its subalternity, protest and masculinity. The Mother Queen has been used as a symbol of traditional practices prevalent in orthodox Hindu society, especially concerned with animal sacrifice; the Queen is quite antithetical to her and symbolizes Jain beliefs, the cock symbolizes hypocrisy involved in rituals.

Certain expressions deserve close scrutiny to endorse Karnad's skill of craftsmanship in language: Night has got a poetic expression—"Nice. The mist's cleared. Nice breeze. It's a beautiful night. Full moon. You can see very leaf in the tree. It's such a bright night; you won't know when it dawns. It'll flow from one into the other, seamlessly" (76); the erotic experience nowhere got such power of words:"Good. Oh God, you are good! uh...uh...uh.... You're like no one I know.... Oh! you are good—good..." (85); the old belief is treated in the following words: "My maid says that if a boy pees on a bush and then if a girl smells the flowers from that bush, that's how babies are made" (91), the Mahout is ugly because he was born on "full moon. There was an eclipse. As you know, the worst thing you can do to yourself is to be born during an eclipse. The sun or the moon—the god whose eclipse it is—is already in the grips of the demons" (80). The protest of the Queen is remarkable, the language used is quite potent to convey the cinder latent in her mind:"I'll not agree to the sacrifice. I'll never" (114). The acknowledgement of Mahout's love, the Queen's frankness and courage are expressed in a spontaneous manner:"I do not regret anything that has happened. I will not disown him or anything he gave me.... Because it just happened. Without my willing it. It just happened. That's all.... And what happened was beautiful" (118-119). The use of verse is highly contextual and throws light on the action of the play; language used is simple and stately.

The Dreams of Tipu Sultan provided an opportunity to Karnad to deal with Tipu Sultan, "one of the most politically perceptive and tragic figures in modern Indian history" ("Preface") and explore the inner world of Tipu Sultan which was recorded by him in his diary. Tipu's valour, political acumen ship, struggle against British colonialism, antagonistic forces within the country, innovation in trade and agriculture, familial love and affection, conspiracy, failures etc. widen the canvas of the play. It is a world of various cultures and practices, people with numerous traits of their personality, political ambitions, wars, psychic reactions, dreams, and the fall of the protagonist all have been treated by the playwright in a language which unhesitatingly embraces the words, phrases, idioms, similes, metaphors, irony, symbols, imagery from Arabic, Persian, Urdu, Hindi, Sanskrit, Kannada, Marathi etc. He develops the proper context and succeeds in communicating the ideas implanted in his mind: Nizam, *Arthshastra,* Diwan-i-Aam, Diwan-i-Khas, kebab, Imam, Caliph, caravanserai, Rajah, Quilledar, Sarkar, Goddess Sharda, "*Arre suno—Tum nahin—Han! Tum!*" (10), "*Jee Huzoor*" (10), "*aao dekho. Inko pehchante ho*" (12), "*Han! Han! Yahee hai hamare padshah! Yehi hai—Allah ab kya hoga?*" (12), "*Yeh murdah kya yeh tumhare Sultan ka hai?* "(10), "*Yahan aao...dikhai nahi de rahoa.... Andhera*" (10), "*jaldi jaldi*" (13), "*Thehro! Yeh hain*" (13), "*Jee han*" (14), haram, exclamations of horror in Urdu and Kannada:"*Arre—Roko—Ayyo! Ayyo!Yeh kya kiya?* "(15), "Sarkar-e- Khudadad" (36), "I'm never not serious" (59), Inshallah, Sufi Zikr, zenana, Kaharajas, etc. and the host of dramatis personae soiled in Indian multicultural milieu take us back to our history and culture.

Use of similes and metaphors is also very apt and they heighten the dramatic effect:"apple's texture...so delicate like a woman's cheeks" (21), "Persian sword" (49), "The English generals squabbling like women in the market" (63), "White Plague" (64). The image of "temple—dilapidated" (18), "White elephant" (20), "English withdrawing" (63), and the dream image artistically fused with the plot. "Roar of tigers" (23) symbolizes the ferocity of Tipu Sultan, "fair-skinned and light-eyed—young man" (228) represents the nature of Marathas in disguise; "white elephant" (20) symbolizes peace and power. The Postscript is full of irony, i.e., how we treat our legendry heroes:"When India became independent in 1947, the families of maharajas who had bowed and scraped before the British masters were granted sumptuous privy purses by the Government of India while the descendents of Tipu Sultan were left to rot in the slums of Calcutta" (65).

Two Monologues: *Flowers* and *Broken Images* mark a significant change in subject and form. The *Flowers* is a narrative that treats religious devotion and erotic love and finally by the miracle of the *Shivlinga*, the power of the Priest's worship is recognized and he is a chosen priest. *Broken Images* discusses the politics of language in Indian literary culture, particularly in relation to literatures of several regions of India, i.e., Indian writings in English versus Bhasha literatures. The genre in literary writings is another issue that has been highlighted. *Linga, pooja, aarti, dhoti,* flowers common in India—*malligai, sevanti, chandu, hooru, sampigai, kanakambara etc;* and *Prasad, pallu,* neem, *Prajata, tritiya, namaskara, gurus,* have been incorporated in the play to accentuate the folklore atmosphere and the obsession with *linga* and *Prasad*; photographic transcription of the erotic excitement reads like a pornographic video clip, have been skilfully handled:

> I watched the mole, poised on the inward plunge of her right breast, peering precariously into the darkness of her cleft. I was longing to kiss it, but didn't dare move for fear of disturbing her. Finally when she had fallen into drugged sleep, I laid her back gently on the carpet, still moaning in defiance and resisting sleep like a child. I bent down and kissed the mole. (255)

The Priest is a symbol of religious devotion, Chandravati sensuality, and *linga* stands for power and divine blessings. "Squabbling like a married couple" (277) is an apt simile. Karnad, in the *Broken Images* has adopted terms used in modern technology; expressions, creative image. Self-exploratory reactions used in modern psychology are quite supportive to advance the conflict and focus on the theme of the play. Lapel mike, plasma screen, Elephantine lights, Headphones, Cameras, sound studio, broadcasting studio, *Arthapoorna, artha, Prayaschitta, namaskara*, guru, Literary Agent, hypocrisy of the speaker on the screen, use of paradox, "And this time I had one advantage. She was dead and I was not" (283) and self–disclosure are blended together to justify technological innovation and the dilemma of the protagonist—Manjula Nayak. One instance of self-exploration deserves mention:

> *Namaskara.* I am Manjula Nayak. I must mention that officially I am Mrs. Manjula Murty, but my creative self continues to be Manjula Nayak.... The first question—you have probably guessed it already. After having written in Kannada all your life, why did you choose—suddenly—to write in English? Do you see yourself

> as a Kannada writer or an English writer? What audiences do you write for...Intellectuals whom I respected, writers who were gurus to me, friends who I thought would pat me on back and share my delight—they are all suddenly breathing fire. How dare I write in English and betray Kannada. (263)

The choice of the words and the beauty of the expression are noticeable: "But my response to the charge that I write in English for money would be:Why not? Isn't that a good enough reason? Would you like to see what royalties I earned when I wrote in Kannada?" (264). The self-image symbolizes the inner self of the protagonist, i.e. Manjula Nayak who broadly represents the crisis the writers of Bhasha literatures are confronting; *Broken Images*, the title itself stands for split-personality, Malini—young talents exploited by kiths and kins for market profitability.

Wedding Album is a dramatic version of marriage in urban middle class family in India which depicts the culture and practices involved in it. The use of self-exploratory, argumentative and reflective style; use of words, phrases, similes, metaphors, symbols, irony and specific expressions augment the atmosphere requisite for the play. The words and phrases from different stocks of Indian languages are dexterously linked with the plot, characters and their mental and emotional make-up:*dupatta, hafta, namaskar, kameez, salwar, pandal, gunas, Amma, bendi, muhurta, Appa, Kanjeevaram Sari, Ma, dhoti, arzee, triphala, vagar, tamasha, Ayyo, avatara, Amma*, Sati, Savitri, Shastri; "Oh, god! No. Shiva-Shiva" (48), "God broke this forehead" (21), "cool your top" (22), "make a mountain out of a molehill" (82), "fire altar and seven steps round it" (15), the blend of humour, satire is characteristic of Indian culture and creates the strong feel of our society:"This is India, you know. Not Australia. We have a solution for everything" (49), "they reserve their harassment for Saturday mornings" (28), "hasn't your weekly dispatch arrived" (33), "That's all that remains to me to do now. Sit down. Place a betel leaf on my head, and do penance under the jackfruit tree" (22). The following expression, very obviously expresses the psychic disturbance:"Radhabai, tea, please. Three cups. (*To Vidula*) It's disaster. Call mother. No. actually don't call her. Not yet. Where is she?" (46).

The play deals with the marriage—both traditional as well as modern, twenty-first century marriage. Hence vocabulary and expressions used in modern society are also given due space: "fuck off" (90), "fucking right to harass me" (90), Cooking Quotient, video tapes, SMSes, mobile, phones, video games, dating, tele - serial, ad, laptop, video chatting, camera. Similes and metaphors used are appropriate:"a smile like a toothpaste ad" (11), "Indian women...obedient Sati Savitri" (17), "marriage is a gamble" (27. Mother symbolizes traditional housewife with progressive ideas, Ashwin—modern young man who believes in "simple registration" (16) for marriage, and "spiritual crisis" (78), Vivan stands for teenage phantasies and sexual urge, Internet Café symbolizes twenty-first century culture to find out life partners, the family of Nadkarni—urban middle class family with multicultural and cosmopolitan ideology, Vidula symbolizes modern youth, Hema opposite to Vidula, Gopal touching the feet of Rohit represents culture of marriage and compulsions of bride's family in marriage.

Works Cited

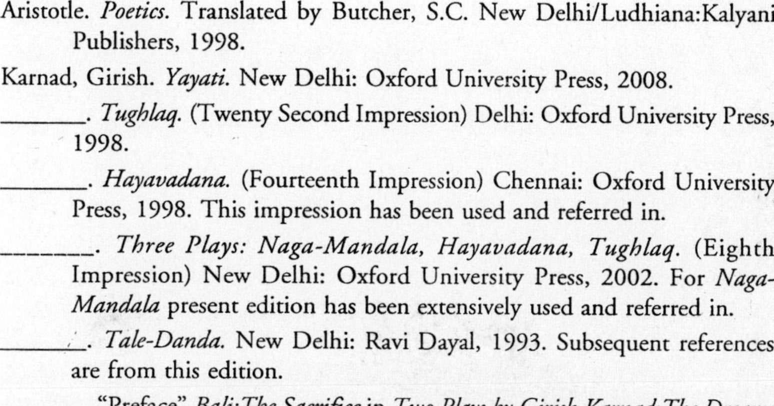

Aristotle. *Poetics.* Translated by Butcher, S.C. New Delhi/Ludhiana:Kalyani Publishers, 1998.

Karnad, Girish. *Yayati.* New Delhi: Oxford University Press, 2008.

_______. *Tughlaq.* (Twenty Second Impression) Delhi: Oxford University Press, 1998.

_______. *Hayavadana.* (Fourteenth Impression) Chennai: Oxford University Press, 1998. This impression has been used and referred in.

_______. *Three Plays: Naga-Mandala, Hayavadana, Tughlaq.* (Eighth Impression) New Delhi: Oxford University Press, 2002. For *Naga-Mandala* present edition has been extensively used and referred in.

_______. *Tale-Danda.* New Delhi: Ravi Dayal, 1993. Subsequent references are from this edition.

_______, "Preface" *Bali:The Sacrifice* in *Two Plays by Girish Karnad:The Dreams of Tipu Sultan, Bali:The Sacrifice.* (Fourth Impression) New

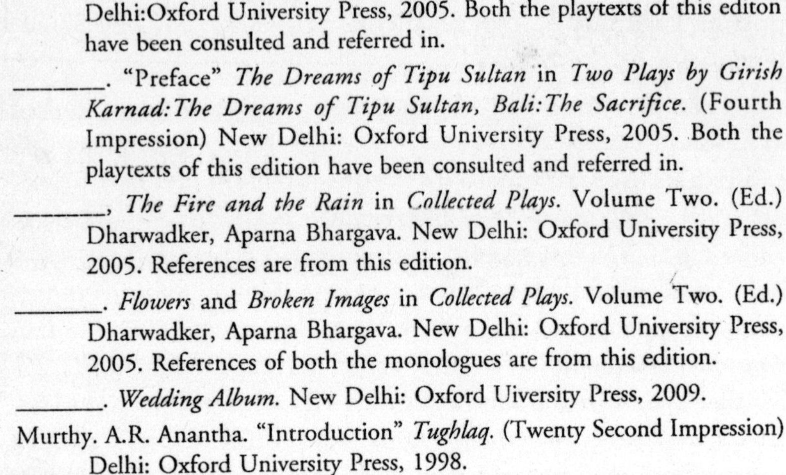

Delhi:Oxford University Press, 2005. Both the playtexts of this editon have been consulted and referred in.

_______. "Preface" *The Dreams of Tipu Sultan* in *Two Plays by Girish Karnad:The Dreams of Tipu Sultan, Bali:The Sacrifice.* (Fourth Impression) New Delhi: Oxford University Press, 2005. Both the playtexts of this edition have been consulted and referred in.

_______, *The Fire and the Rain* in *Collected Plays.* Volume Two. (Ed.) Dharwadker, Aparna Bhargava. New Delhi: Oxford University Press, 2005. References are from this edition.

_______. *Flowers* and *Broken Images* in *Collected Plays.* Volume Two. (Ed.) Dharwadker, Aparna Bhargava. New Delhi: Oxford University Press, 2005. References of both the monologues are from this edition.

_______. *Wedding Album.* New Delhi: Oxford Uiversity Press, 2009.

Murthy. A.R. Anantha. "Introduction" *Tughlaq.* (Twenty Second Impression) Delhi: Oxford University Press, 1998.

Naik, M.K. "Cinderella Still: Recent Indian English Drama" *Littcrit.* Volume 27, Number 1&2, June-Dec, 2001.

7

Kalidasa's Overpowering Celestial *Shakuntala* versus Gokhale's Detrimental Namesake *Shakuntala*

Sangeeta Das

Drama is one of the various rich branches of our literature which has been gathering immense attraction in the recent years. Sanskrit carries the credit of strengthening the foundation of our literature. Sanskrit was the language in which the great educationists of the ancient Indian literatures conversed and wrote. The renowned *Vedas* were also written in this language. The famous dramatist Kalidasa, whose famous play *Shakuntala* was written in Sanskrit, is a masterpiece.

Though no one can stand before the august playwright, the comparison between the two Shakuntalas – one of Kalidasa and the other of Namita Gokhale—gives an interesting turn to this article. I enjoyed a lot while writing this and hope the readers would also approve of it.

The dramatist not only emphasizes the omnipresence of love in our life but also reforms and levitates the impact of love in our life. Such human-feelings and their importance in human life have been totally ignored in the source of the play which therefore is rather humanized by Kalidasa by decorating it with such enhanced concepts. The source has no importance of its own unless it is associated with a play so renowned and written by such a remarkable dramatist, Kalidasa. Namita Gokhale has very smartly on the other hand materialized the character of Shakuntala by taking away from her the uniqueness and celestial spirit and transforming her into a common person belonging to this mean world.

Our Indian literature is extensively rich with many branches, drama being one, which has been drama was the most popular form of literary system since the ancient times. All the important treatises and works conveying messages to the public were written in drama form. It was called 'Nataka' in the Vedic as well as post-Vedic or epic period. Most extracts from the *Ramayana* and the *Mahabharata* were represented through drama and dance. The great pioneers of Indian drama, responsible for taking it to the pinnacle of renown are Bhasa, Kalidasa, Ajnaghosia, Bhabhuto, Sudrak etc. Of these, Kalidasa was the most remarkable who illustrated all the precepts related to the theories of dramaturgy perspicuously in his dramas. Consequently, he stands shining at the top while the others fade out before him. Neither his contemporaries nor his successors could supersede him in his expression of meaning, style, structure and spiritual wholeness. He is like the pole star that stands uneclipsed through ages.

Though this may look absurd and eccentric to bring in anyone beside Kalidasa, I have dared to make a feeble attempt to bring up Namita Gokhale's 'Shakuntala' which is a rephrase of the ethereal Shakuntala into a mortal Shakuntala with all her vices and dereliction. Although the present Shakuntala is no comparison to the celestial prototype, the diversity in the personalities and preferences in the two women with the same name, made the study both esoteric and enigmatic.

Shakuntala in its complete and accomplished form is the sole creation of Kalidasa the renowned dramatist, whose renown not only spread in this country but also abroad. This play was widely accepted and eulogized even in those days among men of calibre and acumen. None of his contemporaries could stand with him in the ranking of this drama. Reckoning this, drama fades out the existence of all his contemporaries just spotlighting Kalidasa. But behind this wonderful articulation of the story lies the secret of its source, which has been traced to the Adiparva of the *Mahabharata*, which is our ancient encyclopaedia of history, mythology, philosophy, ethics and politics. Nevertheless, the crude presentation of the story has been picked up roughly and deftly dressed, trimmed, designed and moralized by the expert Kalidasa in such a way that an insignificant incident in one of the folds of the great epic *Mahabharata* stands scintillating and exuding the pre-eminence of the art of the great dramatist.

Shakuntala seems to be a most calculated and worldly-wise woman who does not desist from clinching her compliance of physical submission to Dushyanta by confirming the throne for the child born out of the union. Dushyanta appears to be a lecherous and unscrupulous person whose sole intention is to bed down Shakuntala and enjoy her beauty for which he even promises to send for her to his kingdom where she will acquire the place of his queen and their issue subsequently will inherit the throne. Here the physical attraction and sexual inclination of Dushyanta can be likened to that of Nearchus who took the mortal Shakuntala with him and enjoyed her physical beauty without any futuristic prospect except for lust. Both these male characters stand in sharp contrast to that of Srijan, Shakuntala's husband who married her for an heir but loved her honestly from the beginning. The twist in the two stories is that Dushyanta's love gets waylaid by the curse and hence the ignorance and disfavour towards Shakuntala. The ardour of love is revived with the retrieval of the ring. Gokhale's Shakuntala has no such dramatic twist and turns in the story. Her falling in love and honesty are severely punished by fate in the end.

Further, in Kalidasa's 'Shakuntala', their marriage was not as a result of a contract based on selfish gains but pure love and devotion for each other. This is obvious by the lapse of time, which sees both the lovers pinning and paling for each other. Unlike the source, the lovers give each other ample time to judge the intensity of love between them. This time was given to them by the long absence of Kanva Rishi from the ashram for the purpose of satisfying the stars, which were to play havoc in Shakuntala's life. Whereas dubiously, in the original story, Kanva Rishi goes to the forest to gather fruits and within this short span, both fall for each other and quickly abed each other. Dushyanta perfunctorily promising Shakuntala, rushes out of the ashram lest Kanva Muni sees him there and curses him for molesting his treasure. Everything seems unrealistic and illogical in the original text. Kalidasa through his expertise notches all the flaws and steers through commendably, in transforming the whole story remarkably.

The touch of Kalidasa's high intention in filtering the source of his masterpiece through rigorous shuffling and reshuffling has almost rejuvenated the whole story and ricocheted it to the public consideration and appreciation, which, it in its original form wouldn't have been achieved ever. The characters were insignificant naturally-selfish fools which received a complete physical, mental and emotional transformation in the hands of the great dramatist. Shakuntala, in the original text has been shown as a selfish and coquettish woman, whereas, the great dramatist has escalated her position in his drama by highlighting her innocence and beauty strikingly out-placed in the ascetic precincts which further lead to her ignorance of worldly hazards and consequent waylay by Dushyanta's magnetic personality. Gokhale's *Shakuntala* has no such master-craftsmanship. Her story revolves round four main characters: Shakuntala, Srijan, Kamalini and Nearchus. All the characters being mere mortals had every characteristic of a mortal while Kalidasa had celestial and divine souls for his character-cast.

Dushyanta has been presented as a philanderer and an unscrupulous person who stoops low to coax a humble forest girl into submitting herself before him just as Nearchus, the Yadur, exploited the insecurity in Shakuntala's life coupled with an inner revolt against her husband bringing in Kamalini from nowhere between them. Here Kalidasa with his expertise softens the incisiveness in the character of Dushyanta, who, as in the original text, was not projected acceptably. Reference to Kalidasa's 'Shakuntala' has been made by Gokhale in her 'Shakuntala' making the difference more pronounced.

The mortal Shakuntala was impressed with the love story of the celestial Shakuntala and yearned for her Dushyanta to come and take her away from the monotonous and drudgerous life in the unchanging hills. Such an unnatural dream makes Gokhale's Shakuntala very much a part of this materialistic world and a human being in the true sense. She lives in a world of fantasy and clutching onto it, tries to fly away from the hazards of the life. Gokhale's Shakuntala is a village girl and a novice with regard to the reality of life looking through rose-tinted glasses. Little does she know about the pernicious life ahead. She has no proper friends or guide who would direct her to the right path. Even her mother who could have been an appropriate guide and a friend to her, treates her roughly. Her imaginative man-woman relationship is never shown the reality and hence her dreams of a smooth and lovable life with her dream man, is dashed into smithereens. In reality, a man-woman relationship is not only physical and romantic; it has many twists and turns which she comes to realize with time but not until she has ruined her life irreparably. Even Shakuntala and Dushyanta have to undergo pangs of separation and insult in their life on this earth.

Besides romance, another aspect of Kalidasa's Shakuntala' that caught the mortal Shakuntala's fancy was the explicit description of her beauty. She has a persistent desire to be called as beautiful as the celestial Shakuntala and hence when her mother mentions her resemblance to herself while her brother's to divinity, she is filled with disgust and utter disappointment. Gokhale's Shakuntala is a prey to a society where male-chauvinism is predominant where as Kalidasa's Shakuntala is loved at her foster father's ashram. But she too cannot stay free from the evil impact of the male predominance when she is turned out of the court with disgrace by Dushyanta. Gokhale's Shakuntala pines for all such things that a mortal would always desire out of life.

In one respect, both the Shakuntalas identify each other – one is intoxicated with love for Dushyanta, eager to be with him so much that she carelessly neglects the importance of his gift and loses it by her absentmindedness. The other is eager to associate herself with a man and run away from the boring life which she is leading, to a changed life irrespective of love. Gokhale's Shakuntala has no idea about love and there is no mention of any pangs of love that she feels for her husband except for a feeling of jealousy for the second woman brought in their life by her husband. Kalidasa's Shakuntala is deeply in love with Dushyanta and experiences the sweet and sour feeling for him throughout. Due to the absence of such a feeling, Gokhale's Shakuntala does not have serious feelings for Srijan and has no qualms in indulging in the debasing act of eloping with Nearchus. Both the Shakuntalas disregard the feelings of their other half; one by losing the ring and the other by losing the honour though Kalidasa's Shakuntala loves her Dushyanta with a pure heart and soul and is lost in his dreams when she lost the ring, whereas Gokhale's Shakuntala elopes with Nearchus in her full senses and their association is nowhere based on love except on sexual desire and animal instinct.

Both Shakuntalas come from a rustic background but the stark difference between a mortal and an immortal being can be seen in their thoughts and approach towards life. One extremely beautiful, pure and loving with helping friends in an ascetic environment while the other is ordinary, poor, differentiated from her brother, living in extreme want and deprivation, pining for worldly pleasures and having no moral values.

Both long for the company of their husbands at a certain point of time. Shakuntala, the wife of mahasamant Srijan, craves for his love and togetherness denied to her after the rituals just as Shakuntala, the wife of king Dushyanta is denied his love and togetherness after he is called back to his kingly affairs of the state, and later due to Shakuntala losing the fateful ring given to her by Dushyanta as a token of love and remembrance. Giving herself the privilege of being called Shakuntala as the celestial namesake, she expects her life to take a romantic course. The story of the celestial Shakuntala brings in her mind the yearning for a lover turned husband who would not only love her immensely but also take her away from the boring life that she is leading. The excitement and budding desire mixed with lust makes her menstruate for the first time and turn into a woman in the true sense. Nevertheless, the celestial being is nowhere identically related to Gokhale's Shakuntala; she is totally given to duty and decorum and her love for Dushyanta is more spiritual and platonic than sexual and lustful like her mortal counterpart. Gokhale's Shakuntala is on the other hand, totally given to lustful and sexual love and has nothing in common to Kalidasa's Shakuntala. Moreover, Kalidasa's Shakuntala is a sober, elegant and docile woman whereas the mortal counterpart is absolutely different with an incisive hunger for freedom, lust and information. She has no qualms about leaving her nuptial home and relationship behind.

Her identification with Kalidasa's Shakuntala further prove to be a hoax when she sees the play staged on her jealousy with her paramour. Is surprised and a bit taken aback because she has to recall herself as Shakuntala, for her association with the Yadur Nearchus has changed her into a Yaduri. Even Nearchus does not react on hearing the name Shakuntala as for him Shakuntala has transformed into a yaduri after her elopement with him. The revelation, though shocking, is both alarming and saddening for Shakuntala as she has lost every trace of resemblance to the celestial being by her derogatory actions.

Nevertheless, in both the cases, they fall prey to the ambition of man. Dushyanta has to leave in haste for his kingdom for looking into its affairs while Nearchus has his unending expedition to unknown lands for which the pregnant Shakuntala is proving a hurdle. Another similarity in both the cases is their situational union. The celestial Shakuntala gets into a hasty gandharva marriage with Dushyanta in the absence of Kanva Rishi, her guardian, and the namesake Shakuntala gets into a clandestine relationship with Nearchus without the knowledge of her husband. Though both the unions are made without a proper condition, the namesake Shakuntala does a hateful and discrediting act, by flouncing the restrains of marriage and eloping with a stranger just to satiate her lustful desire. In this condemnable pursuit, she kills herself and her unborn baby. It can be said that the namesake Shakuntala is the distorted form of the celestial Shakuntala, who is far enhanced in her position in Indian history for her sanctity and forbearance.

Subsequently, the namesake Shakuntala's sin dawns on her and she realizes the blunder done by her but it is too late for her to retract. Realizing the greatness of the name of Shakuntala, she laments over the defamation caused to the sanctity of the name by herself. Her eyes open to the awareness of her failing the name 'Shakuntala' who has maintained the sanctity of her love and marriage even after being disgraced and ousted by King Dushyanta from his court denying her the lawful position as his wife. She on the other hand has betrayed everything and everyone, in return belying the greatness of her name; she likens herself to a Yaduri, the unmentionable one.

Thus we see that both the persons with the name of Shakuntala are poles apart. There is more dissimilarity between them than similarities. One has the mind ruling over her body while the other has the body ruling over her mind. One accepts the suffering as a penance for carelessness and disregard while the other overshadows the realization of sanctity, stifles the voice of the conscience and takes to a mad pursuit of sexual satisfaction irrespective of disastrous consequences.

Works Cited

Gokhale Namita, *Shakuntala* (*the play of memory*) Penguin Viking, 2005.

Khosla Shakti Batra, *Kalidasa's Abhijyana Shakuntala* (*A critical study*) et. al. N. Delhi 2005.

8

Floral Motifs and Vibratile Emotionality in Girish Karnad's *Flowers*

O.P. Budholia

The text of *Flowers* analyses the triangulated version of human relationship. Enmeshed in erotic sentiment (*rati*) it brings into being the effectiveness of folk motifs and the orality of literature. The existing two female characters in the text—the wife of the priest and Ranganayaki—create the sensuous perception and arouse visual and auditory stimulus-response for awakening the latent emotions (*sthayibhavas*). It ascertains the fact that the contents included in the text of *Flowers* are conditional by the social obligations and moral responsibility. The devices of folklore and the application to the oral signs of literature as an inclusive mode in showing the complications of relational values set forth the metaphoric connotations in the text. The sense of horrification and fetidness as the *sthayin* (latent) of *jugupsa* (disgust) prevails in the structural properties.

Any text of literature is a true reflection of an insight into culture and social matrix. The literariness of the literature as the universal appeal in the text innovates and re-innovates the literary signifiers which control, and re-define the changing values of social structures and the understanding of national traditions as culture. The cultural configurations and the social structures determine the conscious level, and thus enrich the unconscious mental powers as the empiric mode of human knowledge. The genre of drama in its suggestive pattern encompasses the codifying system of the associational clusters between the actors and the spectators. Girish Karnad as a dramatist experiments with some definitive movements in the structural. He has made an application to the two antagonistic situations: the worship of the Linga and the development of carnal desire in the priest for his relationship with Ranganayaki, the courtesan. As Karnad chooses an oral tale from the folklore, he brings into being its efficaciousness in revealing the interior motifs of drama and the theory of dramaturgy.

Aparna Dharwadkar in her *Introduction to the Collected Plays of Girish Karnad* (Vol II) comes out with the facts related to the structural resources of this monologue, *Flowers. Flowers* in contrast, returns to the world to folklore, and in the first work in this genre of focus on the male rather female desire, thus registering a small but important shift in Karnad's dramaturgy. The legend of Veeranna on which the play is based belongs to the Chitradurga region and became widely known when the Kannada writer, T. R. Subbanna (known as Ta Ra Su), included in his novel, *Hamsgeethe* (Swan Şong). (Dharwadkar, xxxi)

The only difference between Subbanna's version and Karnad's monologue is this: In Subbanna's novel the wife of the priest and the mistress exist with their passive role and remain the marginal characters to the text and context. In Karnad's monologue, *Flowers,* the character of the priest's wife and the courtesan, Ranganayaki, stand actively and extend the concrete structural plan of the dramatist. Unlike *Hayavadana, Flowers* osculates us with the triangulated version of the human relationships. At its outset, the structural design of *Flowers* offers to be seen as the carnal desire in the priest who makes a curving moment in the love of two women—his wife and the courtesan. The narrative as the oral tale, re-invents the memory lanes and a force that disjoins the conscious and the unconscious mental forces, the subtle cultural signs and the empiric mode of knowledge. The cognizance as the behavioural trait in the priest is surrounded by such visual images that set his routine to live.

In the devotional offerings to the worship of Shiva-linga, the oft recurring images in the text, such as the temple, the tank, the rough grey boulders, the flowering shrubs and the trees, the chirping of the birds and the changing of the seasons are symbolic of the phenomenological approach to syntax and the cyclicity of time. The association of the priest with these natural objects seemingly appear in his romantic activities. He confesses undisguisedly about his association with these natural objects and his unstinting worship to Shiva-linga.

> I am the priest here. I have lived here all my life and discouraged all friendly attentions from the world outside. And in the isolation of this place, I spend most of my time with the Linga—talking to it, singing to it even discussing recent political developments and most of all, decorating it with flowers. The Linga is not ornately carved like some in the neighbourhood. It is essentially a plain phallic stump with a smooth crown and a rough-hewn vulva for the base.
>
> (Karnad 244)

The description of the Linga with its different visual forms such as a "plain phallic stump" and his "step-wife" brings into being the symbolic features of the temporal and the transtemporal features of the puja being performed daily in the temple. The referential intake of the four characters (the priest, the chieftain, the wife of the priest and Ranganayaki) perpetually occurs frequently in this monologue. The priest remains enamoured and spellbound by the beauty of Ranganayaki. The main incident in the temple happens when Ranganayaki comes usually to the temple during the Shivaratri celebrations. In her usual meetings with the priest, she holds a promise from him that he will decorate her body from the remnants of the flowers in the same way as he decorates the *Linga*. It so happens that on the occasion of Shivaratri, the priest wait for a long time for the chieftain to begin with the rituals of the puja. But the chieftain does not come to the temple. The priest is with his wife in the temple and remains for a few hours in isolation and loneliness while awaiting the arrival of the chieftain; and the priest after sometime finds his wife sleeping in the inner sanctum of the temple.

The repressed feeling as the carnal desire seeks first to be experienced with the courtesan and than those repressed feelings re-visit the psychic turmoil of the priest when he sees his sleeping wife in "the recumbent figure" (Karnad 253). In her sleep she arouses the deeply rooted repression of the priest. Her sleep like "a wet rag" with mouth half-open expresses many things that become semiotically symbolic of mental restrictions of *conjugal relationships.* The awakening and the proximal presence of the priest leave some indelible impressions of wifely relationships with her husband. This scenic relationship makes the priest put a flower in her hand and for his attraction she tucks it in the knot of her hair. Apparently the theatrical motifs become visual when she begins to see the enquiring look in the eyes of her husband. She, through her enquiring eyes, raises so many complicated questions that arouse an emotional outlet of the repressed desires and feelings. The priest, out of the burden of the repressed desires, confesses candidly the uncontrollable situation that prevails in the inner sanctum of the temple.

> My wife and I were there, just the two of us, alone, as we could never be at home. . . . And for once her infinite self-control had slipped and she had let her Pallu drop from her bosom to expose her blouse and let it hang unretrieved. Any other time, just giving quarter of the thought of sex while in the temple would have horrified her, but at this moment she was inviting the shame of it.
>
> (Karnad 253)

The narrator through the orality of literature works out the interiority of human intents. The process of letting her pallu stretch justifies the erotic sentiment (*Rati*) in the recess of his wife's mind. Moreover, the priest as the narrator has conceded the fact about the restrictions being imposed at their home for their relational proxemics. The verb "expose" used for her blouse makes her a catalyst agent who arouses the latent and repressed feelings of the priest. The priest on his part too exhibits the limits and possibilities for the consummation of their carnal desire inside the sacred precincts of the temple. Amidst these developments the Linga as the Supreme Powerful Force looks at them "and snarled silently at it" (254). The priest listens to his inner voices and finds that the continuity with these irrational thoughts will certainly defile the purity of the sanctum. The active participation of his wife creates a sense which opens the possibilities for the triangulated love to the connoisseurs. The divisiveness in relationship is worked out when he compares the social and moral status of the two women: his wife and the courtesan. He accepts the fact that Ranganayaki would "never be allowed to step in here" (254). His wife too judges the inside of her husband's mind and she makes him aware of the situational and contextual realities:

> The gesture proved fatal. The desire faded. The glow went out of her eyes. Bleakness seeped back into her voice as she muttered: 'Don't go in the dark. Snakes, poisonous insects. Why don't you stay home?' The whining tone insinuated that she already knew my answer and that infuriated me.
>
> (Karnad 254)

The semantic sway of the noun-verb phrase "bleakness seeped" becomes reflective of the suppression of the sudden stimulants that re-visit and exhibit the rebuses of vocables. She as a passion-ridden woman forbids her husband to go into the dark where he can meet the poisonous snakes and other injurious insects. As a folkloristic tale, this monologue reveals the deep structure of linguistic and cultural properties. The orality of literature is generally meant for revealing the passionate and erotic relationships:

> In terms of genres, the folktales live out of interior language. Mythologies are part of the outer world. They have to do with wars. They construct cosmologies and deal with social issues. In the folktale everything is interiorized. You do not see big social issues except through the detail intimate relationships.
>
> (Daniels 72)

The literary essence that creates the subtle signs for establishing a link between literature and society, is concerned with the production of these two aspects of human relatives, but they also construct the mental structure in the form of images and symbols. These mental structures bring into light the images and symbols that lie inherent as the empirical consciousness and as the creative imagination of the writer himself. Thus, these creative-mental structures symbolise the collective consciousness of the society or they may also be termed as universal elements of literature. Any literary text and more specifically the dramatic text extends over the tri-polar system of reflexology, the writer, the text and the connoisseur.

The textual structures of *Flowers* become a categorical assurance for exhibiting social, psychological and existential principles of human life and the ontological and homomorphic nature of the text:

> The categorical structure, which governs the collective consciousness and which are transposed into the imaginary universe created by the artist, are either conscious or unconscious, in the Freudian sense of the word, which presupposes a repression; they are non-conscious process which in certain respects, are a kin to those which govern the functioning of the muscular or nervous structures and determine the particular character of our movements and our gestures.
>
> (Albrecht 585)

The wife of the priest as a lonely figure in the premises of the temple determines her character—a character who, with her particular movements and gestural articulations—stimulates the passionate emotion that controls the endocrine glands of the priest. Thus the oral form of the text of the *Flowers* leaves an impression that can be better responded through reader-response theory of literature. The tripolar system of the text can be diagrammed thus:

Tri-polar System of Text

The entire properties of the text show preponderance of the memories that expand the mental structures of the writer. The writer follows the inherent social mechanism and the empiric mode which include primarily in its territories the economic, demographic, passionate and psychological concerns in order to build a deep structure of values, ideas, linguistic and ethnographic signs in his literary text. The audience as the connoisseur and the sensitive readers come through the mental level of the writer and make equal shares of the textual apprehensions. If there is a written form of the text, the cultural, relational and the ethnographic signs are to be decoded for the reconstruction of the real signs in the text. There are so many incidents in the text of *Flowers* and each incidence makes a separate text within the text.

Another incident on Shivaratri happens and that incident creates an inner conflict and an explosive disturbance in the latents of the priest. Ranganayaki becomes the catalyst agent for this incident. She comes to the temple for performing the puja and sees the priest in the temple. She lets the pallu of her sari stretch before the priest. The priest sees the pallu of the two saris: the first is of his wife and the second is of the courtesan. The courtesan during the worship of the Linga bends and her bending lets her sari loose, giving an opportunity to the priest to see the mole between her breasts. He is so enamoured and emasculated that he loses control of his senses; and the fire of passion in his loins. The confession of the priest about his love to the courtesan unveils the mystery of relationships:

> I wanted her. I had never lusted for a woman before and so felt emasculated by the sudden weakness. Yet I could not control the

> fire raging in my loins. During the rest of the week, I started the day impatient for a glimpse of hers.
>
> (Karnad 245)

The oft-repeated meetings of the priest make him completely sink in the love of the courtesan. As he begins now to visit usually the cavernous house of Ranganayaki after the daily puja of the Linga for the floral decoration on her body, the momentary absence of the courtesan baffles and teases him. One day, he reaches her house late in the night and feels shocked when he does not find an opportunity to meet her. Every day, he used to collect the garlands that were offered to the Shiva-Linga and he used to come to the house of Ranganayaki for the floral decoration. He thus becomes sinuous and now appears desperate to see the physical beauty of Ranganayaki so much so that he even finds the natural smell in her body. The physical beauty of the courtesan stupefies him with erotic sentiments (emotions of *rati*): "When I finished decorating her, I would lay her down and kiss the mole. With a sudden movement she came alive" (Karnad 251). The priest tries to explore the functionary role of floral motifs that lie engraved inside his unconscious mental forces as the text which is to be brought to its deconstruction. He thus experiences the fragrance of different flowers in two distinctive ways: the first remain in the specified decoration of the Linga and then the decoration of the body of Ranganayaki. Sometimes the analysis made in silence by the priest for the various experimentation becomes *reducto ad absurdum* in his monologic speech-act. In the principles of Indian poetics, the art of drama:

> comprehends in itself, all the branches of learning, all arts, all crafts, all skills, all aspects of human nature and worldly behaviour represented through the gesticulacious.
>
> (Walimbe 2)

The theories of aesthetic influence on bringing the emotional properties to be shared equally by the actors and by the audience are worked out here. Thus the emotive-content expressed in the acting of an actor creates another text according to the situational referents. A thing of beauty with its aesthetics joy is meant for grasping the abiding appeal of literature. These are the latent sentiments or interchangeability of *bhavas* according to the situational realities and the referral context which make the priest as a protagonist comprehend the pleasing instincts in two distinct ways:

> I looked for wider variety of flowers now, chose them with great care and experimented with floral motifs on the Linga which would be distinct from those I would device later on Ranga. The garlands were the same, inevitably, but God was not to be the preliminary model for what I would do with her body. Each day I coaxed the flowers to say something special to God and then something different to Ranga.
>
> (Karnad 251)

The floral motifs bring into being the intramural and the intracellular metamorphosis in the priest for realizing the *sthayin* of his emotion (latent sentiment). If the floral decoration of the Linga makes him mechanical in approach, the decoration on the body of the courtesan arouses in him the vibratile emotions. The garland used for the decoration of the Linga and Ranga are of the same natural attribution. The one makes him mechanical and repetitive while the other (the sensuous body of the courtesan) creates in him a sense by which he stares "breathlessly at her bare bosom" (249). This process combines different *bhavas* (the rudimentary mental states) together and he in the presence of his wife and children breaks the code of social obligations and moral values. Thus, this monologue is replenished with various gesticulations and is enriched with the means of entertainment. The drama as the literary genre unites in its content the physical and the spiritual features in an equal proportion.

The total experience of delight makes the spectator undergo "a kind of unique homogenous experience—in the realization of rasa" (Walimbe 3). The art of drama as *drashyakavya* (visual poetry) includes in its contents the range of various emotions, physical sensations, the experience of pain and pleasure, the excitement and repose and the steady feeling-tones of the conscious mental structures.

It is again on *tritiya* (the third day after full moon), there comes another incidence that helps in the development of structural plan of this drama. The priest and his wife have been waiting for the chieftain for the usual puja at the temple, but he does not come till late night. The priest sends his wife home and makes the floral decoration of the Linga and usually collects the flowers for the decoration of the courtesan. When he reaches the house of Ranganayaki, he finds faint light spilling out from inside the house. He meets her and asks about her. The meeting of the priest with the courtesan arouses in the latter the feeling of pleasure-seeking instincts. The erotic sentiment is so heavily loaded with repression as he thinks of sharing the love of Ranganayaki in her house. When he cups his breast in his palm, the scenic image in the text arises to a fresh phase: "You must support them; otherwise they began to hurt from their weight" (255). Girish Karnad, while showing the passionate relationship between the priest and Ranganayaki, reveals the carnal desire of the priest and an eagerness for its fulfilment at the same time. The priest concedes to his erotic sentiment before the audience:

> I watched the mole, poised on the inward plunge on her left breast, peering preciously into the darkness of her cleft. I was longing to kiss, but didn't dare to move for the fear of disturbing her. Finally when she had fallen into the drugged sleep I laid her back gently on the carpet, still moaning in defiance and resisting sleep like a child. I went down and kissed the mole.
>
> (Karnad 255)

In Indian poetics, the origin of *shringar* (love) is derived from its root *shringa* meaning the peak of love. But it doesn't show the consummation of love between the low-born characters. If the love between the two such characters is allowed for consummation there comes the sentiment of *rasa dosha* in the form of *shringara bhasha* (an illusion of eros). Karnad here fails to develop the sentiment of *shringara rasa* in accordance to the principles of Indian poetics. He makes an application to the fulfilment of passionate desire of the protagonist, and not of the emotional intensity for the realisation of the sentiment of love (*rati*). With the sense of defiance the protagonist fails to realize the highest joy of erotic sentiment (*rati*) in his love for the courtesan. When he thinks about the stupor in Ranga ("fallen into drugged sleep") he becomes symbolic of passion-ridden man who fails to fulfil his carnal desire.

The passion enmeshes in him so deeply that he ignores his social and moral obligations. Amidst these developments in his relationship with Ranga, he is disturbed by the sudden sound of the canon, for it shows the warning of the arrival of the chieftain in order to offer his puja in the temple. Hallucinated and disenchanted as he is, he collects all the flowers he decorated on the body of the courtesan and moves immediately to the sacred sanctum of the temple. As a passion-ridden man, the priest takes out his repressed feelings before the audience when he describes the spellbound effects of Ranganayaki's body on his psyche: "I saw Ranganayaki, naked on all fours, starting out stupefied, shivering" (256). He reaches the temple and decorates the Linga once again with leavings of the flowers. Thus the floral decoration becomes symbolic of the association between the spiritual and the physical principles of human life. As he begins to decorate the Linga, an unconscious sense of revulsion ensues his mind:

> I felt buffeted by the revulsions I could sense welling up inside her. We had already performed a Puja with these flowers. They were now the leavings, polluted discards. What further use they had been in Ranganayaki's house she didn't need to try too hard to imagine. To place them on the Linga again was the desecration.
>
> (Karnad 256)

The "buffeted revulsions" shows his disgust towards the mechanical process of focal decoration and the floral point in repressed desires that remain unfulfilled even in having the passionate relationship with the courtesan. Thus the adjective-noun phrase "buffeted revulsions" becomes symbolic of the binary between the goal-attainment and reward-expectation. The priest brings into light his counter irritation by the sounds of the canon, for he regards the leavings to be decorated on the Linga, as "polluted discards." His arrival in the premises of the temple makes him feel the sudden presence of the chieftain. He sarcastically thinks how the hairs grow on the Linga, because the chieftain finds a long hair in the flowers being offered to him after the Puja. ("I didn't know the God had long hair") the dramatist presents theatrically the sentiment of disgust and fear-psychosis in the priest after this incident. The priest was not in the position to face the world amidst such humiliations. In his reply to the king, the self assertiveness can be seen in the semantics used by the priest: "If we believe that God has long hair. He will have long hair" (257). He accepts the challenge of the chieftain; he kneels before the Linga and begins to pray before it:

> I had known the Linga since my birth. My association with it was longest and closest in my life. As a child I feed on it, and then in remorse wept on it. Even as an adult, I have poured out my woes to it, bragged about how my success with flowers had turned this place into the ruler's favourite shrine. Now I plead with it to save my face.
>
> (Karnad 258)

The placatory syntax shown in the verbal pattern such as "used", "feed", "poured out my woes" and "bragged" becomes symbolic and suggestive of two aspects: the priest's honesty and sincerity on worshipping the Linga and the sense of self-appreciation in showing his expertise in floral decoration. His association with the courtesan (Ranganayaki) induces in him the inner awareness of disgracing his spiritual act; he thus shivers at the thought of "facing the world in that state" (258). Engrossed in his thought, he experiences the heavy load of conflicting conditions which bring forth the psychological mechanism of drives, needs, wishes, purposes, tendencies and impulses. The fear to be exposed publicly for the act he has developed under the compulsive restrictions and psychogenic pressures for fulfilling his carnal desire makes him shudder; and in such circumstances he finds no other way except "to surrender to Him" (258). He begs now for a period of 12 days for facing trials with the challenge of the chieftain for proving the process of hair sprout on the Linga, he keeps himself in complete isolation in the vestibule of the temple. The priest thus retains the continuity of his prayer for twelve days in order to save himself from "public humiliation" (258); and after the expiry of the period the chieftain arrives in the sanctum of the temple. The presence of the chieftain in the temple makes the priest aware of the challenges:

> There was a pause and then the Chieftain gasped. I opened my eyes. The lights had not been lit and the sanctum was in darkness but not in such darkness that one could not see the long and thick hair that came cascading from the Linga, hiding it completely. He stared. I stared. He looked at me for some explanation. I had none. I was stunned as he was.
>
> (Karnad 258)

The act of starring and stunning becomes causative (*arthprakrti*) for the original thought that breeds the disbeliefs in both the chieftain and the priest. The cascade of the hair on the Linga re-invents the cauldron of the repressed desires. However the act of distrust related to the sprout of the hair on the Linga continues obstinately among the people who are with the chieftain ("they could be glued" 258). The chieftain orders to test the cascade of hair; and in accordance with the order, one of his brahmin courtiers twists a tuft of hair. He brings immediately that tuft for examining its root, but the brahmin sees the drops of blood in the roots of the tuft. Thus this scene produces the sentiments of disgust which causes stink, blood, flesh, fat, etc. to appear. The disgust (*jugupsa*) as one of the eight or nine *sthayins* (latents) presents the sign of spitting or vomiting or closing down one's eye, unconscious distress, sickness, fatigue and death from its accessories. As a matter of fact, the signs that come out from the *sthayin* of *bibhatsa rasa,* the sentiments of disgust, are to be discernible in the text-content:

> There was blood on his fingers. The Brahamin ran back to the Linga feet for the spot from where he had plucked the hair and collapsed, crying hysterically, it's bleeding. It's bleeding. I have wounded God.
>
> (Karnad 259)

The sense of horripilation and fetidness prevail among the devotees who are in the precincts of the temple. The chieftain falls down at the feet of the priest and begs his pardon. The crowds surge and seek the blessings of the priest. The priest momentarily falls in sound sleep and when he wakes up; he is told by his wife that she (courtesan) has left the town. The courtesan leaves the town with belief that the priest should remain in peace with the devotion of Lord Shiva. Thus there comes an end to falsehood and concealment from human relationship. Here, the dramatist succeeds in showing an integral relationship between the temporal concerns and the spiritual experiences of human life. The folkloristic tradition stresses repeatedly on the psychic aberrations and cultural configurations. Prof. A.K. Ramanujan reveals the visible spectrum that comes out from the oral tradition of literature:

> If we could listen we could hear the voice of what is fashionably called the subaltern—the woman, the peasant, the non-literate, those who are marginal to the courts of the kings and offices of the bureaucrats and the centre of power.
>
> (Nagendra 166)

In the text of *Flowers*, the inherent doubts are crashed from the mind of the chieftain and the solipsistic quest of the priest is achieved, but the courtesan still remains "a slave and guardian" (259) and misses all her fortune in having the priest "for her husband" (259). The thought process in literature is conditioned by following the social obligations and having the things bearable in life. The coded signs of syntax as visual pictographs carry forward the suggestive pattern in the structural plan of *Flowers.* The dramatist works out the theatrical motifs when he reveals the socio-psychological properties of the text. The priest finally brings into being the theatrical gestures when he exhibits the interior regions of his mind: "I am guilty of gross dereliction, of sacrilege. Guilty of cruelty to the two women I loved" (260). The postmodern trends of literature are worked out cautiously in displaying the conflicting conditions of the protagonist and in developing the subtle signs of physical relationship and spiritual awakening. "I shall seek in the narrow confines of that hollow the answers that God has denied me." (260)

Works Cited

Dharwadkar, Aparna. Bhargava *Introduction to Collected Plays.* New Delhi: Oxford University Press, 2005.

Daniels, Molly. Ramanujan and Keith Harrison (eds), *A.K. Ramanujan: Collected Poems and Prose.* New Delhi: Oxford University Press, 2005.

Karnad, Girish. *Collected Plays* (Vol II) New Delhi: Oxford University Press, 2005.

9

Locating Identity within Mizo Folk Narratives

Margaret L. Pachuau

This chapter attempts to portray the significance of identity as located intrinsically within the parameters of the history of Mizo folkloristics. In order to render justice to the topic, it shall examine the notion that most of the folklore within the Mizo arena has been located within the backdrop of nature, the animal world order, the world of spirits and the supernatural. Walter Ong has denoted that "orality is not an ideal for a community and never was." This aspect has significant bearing in terms of the Mizo society.

The society was an illiterate society, that was firmly etched within the confines of an oral sensibility, until literacy was attained with the advent of the Welsh missionaries in 1894. Orality then gave way to writing and thus there has never been looking back towards the period of orality, especially with Mizoram attaining the status of being the second highest in terms of literacy in India. However, orality by itself has not been regarded to be 'despicable' by the Mizo community and it has been realized by and by that both orality and the growth of literacy out of orality were increasingly necessary for the evolution of a Mizo literary consciousness. The interaction between the orality to which all human beings are born into and the art of writing has indeed been rendered inherently significant. Writing by itself, has become a mode of raising a semblance of consciousness for the Mizo community.

Sangkima, a noted Mizo historian has denoted that the sources of Mizo history and culture are predominantly oral in perspective. The oral sources include folklore, folksongs ,rituals and superstitions. Writing, as mentioned before was introduced to the Mizo community only in the latter half of the nineteenth century. The concept of the past as it is inrerelated to identity, thus needs to be reconstructed with the help of the oral narratives. Thus even in terms of the post colonial context, orality has continued to play a very significant role. Orality within the Mizo tradition is inherently central. Cultural historians denote that Mizos originated from the Chhinlung area.

It is traditionally believed that Mizos came out of a very big cave called Chhinlung, which was believed to be located around China. The folk songs and folklore of the Mizo are believed to revolve round this period. The transition from the oral to the written parameters have been significant in that it has produced a community that is highly literate, and as depicted earlier, Mizoram ranks second in the whole of India in terms of literacy and at the same time, here are literary bodies such as the Mizo Academy of Letters that publish and encourage writers to write and translate from Mizo to English and vice versa and this by itself remains a remarkable achievement in terms of the development of the written word.

The pre-colonial, pre-Christian lore are still referred to as 'literature' in every sense of the term which is remarkable because many of the writers who write in Mizo are still not regarded to be worthy of literary consideration. The pre colonial era, especially was filled with the abundance of Mizo folklore and the tales revolved around the creation of man and the creation of the universe and it also denoted aspects on how various forms of natural and human life came into being. Such narratives which were especially related to the concept of identity are remarkably different from the narratives in the post-colonial, Christian era where religion has occupied the central role and in the process there has been a relocation of beliefs and ethos that had once been associated with Mizo identity. It also seeks to advocate that the tribal dynamics have experienced a vast paradigm shift within the domains of a pre and post colonial perspective. This itself is unique in terms of the formation of identity because the Mizo culture itself is still predominantly tribal in its roots but at the same time it has continued to hold on to an inherently Westernized concept of 'identity'. Thus, hybridity comes into perspective in this regard.

A study of folklore in its oral parameters also reflects the inherent difference in sensibility that existed in terms of the pre and post colonial elements. In this regard a noteworthy observation has been that due to the advent of Christianity and the post colonial dynamics, especially after 1894, there has been an inherent loss of the status of myths within the Mizo community. Colonisation has brought with it a changing facet to the perspective of identity and the defining parameters of identity in the decades that follow after the advent of Christianity especially have been honed towards a redefinition of the Mizo identity. Mizo society is now (at the present time of writing) gradually involving into a society where there has been an increasing focus upon the nuances of religion. Subsequently, in the process there has been the consistent negation of the myths, folk and cultural lore.

The projection of identity itself is complex in any culture and the same is true of the Mizo race. As denoted earlier, the Mizos themselves have been regarded to be a race of Mongoloid origin and they are said to have come into existence from a large rock emerging out of the Chin-Lushai province known as Chhinlung. However, there is hardly any historical or anthropological claim to legitimacy on that perspective but it remains a central belief nevertheless. However it is out of this oral tradition that identities have been carved and it has been out of this belief too that many lore have been centred upon. In the pre colonial era which was prior to 1894, myths were significantly a part of the religious system and the status of a person or community depended very much upon the interrelationship between the resonant myth and the individual or culture. In as far as post colonial Mizo society and identity are concerned, Christianity has played a major role in terms of the formulation of the identity of the postcolonial Mizo. The contrast in terms of identity in the pre and post colonial parameters have been vast because, the colonized Mizo domains were previously under a culture that was inherently non-Christian and so subsequently it had a different sensibility altogether, whether religious or secular.

Identity in the pre-colonial Mizo society was inherently non Christian and it was one that existed in affinity with the flora and the fauna around them. While the concept of colonization has been significant, there must be an inherent comprehension of the fact that the narratives that existed within the pre colonial domains were intrinsic in shaping and formulating arenas that were pertinent to the concept of identity. As already indicated earlier, the aspect of the oral narrative within the Mizo cultural as well as literary context has been pivotal. For instance in terms of a significantly oral perspective there has been a marked focus upon the centrality of the animal world order in terms of Mizo oral narratives. Pre colonial sensibility has depicted a world that was replete with the co existence of animals in the larger arena of reality. It is inherently impossible to conceive a world that was bereft of the animal world order in terms of the Mizo domains. Animals were regarded to be on equal terms, if not on superior terms with that of human beings. In order to critically elucidate upon the same, it must be first comprehended that Mizos have been a predominantly tribal community and as such, a number of aspects pertaining to Mizo folklore have been drawn from animal imagery. This can be further exemplified through select Mizo narratives.

Narratives of the oral tradition such as 'Thailungi', for instance, focuses upon, a little girl by the name of Thailungi. She had a stepmother who wanted to sell her to the traders from the Pawih (a community who resided in the Lushai hills) community. All this was to be done in order that her step mother could procure some scrap iron. The tale also reflected upon the ill treatment that was meted out by the stepmother to Thailungi. After a long while Thailungi's brother discovered that his sister was missing and decided to go in search of her. After various instances when his stepmother's plans of disrupting his plans were thwarted, the boy was finally able to break free and so he set out in search of his sister. On the way he met several people and he kept asking them about the whereabouts of his sister. Ultimately the incident that eventually led him to his sister was because, he met an old man who was leading a gayal. The query he put forth was:

> "Kapu, can you tell me where my sister Thailungi is?"
>
> And the man replied,
>
> "Just follow the gayal that I am leading, and do exactly as he does. If he crouches, you should do likewise. If he stands up, you must stand up too, and if he nibbles grass then you too must do the same."

The boy then obediently did as he was told and eventually in this manner, they reached the village of the man who was leading the gayal. The lesson that has been evidently conveyed here is the significance of the gayal, which was portrayed as different from the rest of humanity that has been represented in the narrative. These are significant instances where man and animal have been put together in the world and where they have assisted each other in seeming comprehension of each other's dilemma. On the other hand, there are instances in narratives such as "The Monkey and the Tortoise", where the world in which the animals exist remain seemingly bereft of human company. It is a world where animals have been increasingly creating a bond with each other. In fact, they lived in a world that was seemingly harmonious. The narrative begins with the both the monkey as well as the tortoise wanting to pluck figs. The tortoise was not very eager because he was apprehensive about plucking the figs as he was unable to climb atop the tree. The monkey on the other hand was very agile. After a while the monkey suggested to the tortoise:

> "Just bite the end of my tail, and I shall help you climb up."
>
> Saying this the monkey led the tortoise up in like manner. After a time the tortoise even fell off while laughing because he found the entire aspect very amusing. One day, the tortoise invited the monkey to go fishing with him,but the monkey was very reluctant. However, he decided to go along and as they reached the lake the tortoise began to catch plenty of fish but the monkey stood by helplessly, and suddenly the tortoise said,
>
> "Just catch hold of my shell and I will carry you into the water and in that manner we will catch plenty of fish."

Eventually in the narrative the monkey died because he could not breathe in the water. The narrative denotes that his body became stiff and frozen and even then the tortoise could not make out what the matter was. Finally he thought that the monkey's frozen grimace was a smile of pleasure and even tried to give him his share of the fish. As there as no response from the monkey, the tortoise offered, "All right, you can take all the fish, otherwise you might get annoyed later."

And thus the narrative ends on that note. This tale is one that is bereft of the presence of human beings and it also records that there was a time when it was believed that animals could actually speak, just as human beings did. Mizo oral literature thus abounds with such tales. There are various tales where man and animal co existed in seeming mutual harmony. This need not be seen as peculiar ,rather it may be perceived as a totally natural environment to both man and animal.

In the narrative concerning Chepahakhata, who was a very ugly young man, it was realized that he was in a dilemma because no one wanted to marry him, due to his ugliness. Ultimately he did find a bride but she turned out to be a witch in disguise. One day in the town that they were living in, the people slaughtered an animal in his honour and as a result he even forgot all about the time. His wife then asked her daughter to call him but he took his time in going home, and ultimately he had such a merry time that he forgot all about returning home. In the meantime, his wife was enraged and she turned the entire town into a foliage of wild plantains (as she was a witch) and took her daughter up to the heavens to dwell with Pu Vana, the god of the heavens. However, upon noticing his plight, his daughter, began to feel very sorry for him, and so after pleading his case with her mother, she threw down a bottomless vessel which could hold an unending supply of food, in order that her father would not go hungry. Much later in the narrative, Chepahakhata had an altercation with the chief and in the process they tied him atop a banyan tree where the hill mynah and drongos were gathered together. Once again here the essence of the animal world became significant.

The debate was actually with regard to the fact that they were contesting about who were the more clever of the human race and they were debating over whether it would be the Mizos or the vais (non Mizos from the plains). The debate was overheard by Chepahakhata and very soon when it was actually time to put his skills to good use, he did so with the help of the argument that he had overheard from the birds. Due largely to this, he actually outwitted the contestants each time because of his wisdom, and eventually the villagers no longer felt the need to strap him astride the tree anymore.

Amongst the myriad aspects that are related to Mizo oral literature, there are also instances of different protagonists who portray differing personalities that are reflective of the then Mizo community. For instance, there are anecdotes that are related to Samdala, who has been regarded to be the laziest man that ever lived amongst the Mizos. It was believed that one day when he went out hunting he saw some ripe figs atop a tree. However true to his nature, he was too lazy to pluck them and so he lay underneath the tree with his mouth wide open and waited for the fruit to drop into his mouth, and ultimately in this manner, he was able to consume the fruit. Yet even after that he was still too lazy to chew the fruit. In this narrative, there exists a number of animals and the tiger was one of them. In fact Samdala did not even make an attempt to run away from the tiger, (so mutually conducive was the arena of existence between the animal and human world order). Instead he simply requested the tiger to carry him atop a hill, just so that he could be eaten by the latter. After this he placed a red fig leaf atop his back and surprisingly enough the tiger was really frightened, especially when Samdala denoted, "It is something that consumes men and beasts alike."

And eventually the tiger was forced to beat a hasty retreat. Samdala was very often seen in the company of the other animals of the forest such as the barking deer, the wild pig, and the elk. Ultimately the narrative denotes that all these animals were yet to decipher that Samdala was actually only a mere human being and they requested the tortoise to clarify the matter. After a great deal of reluctance the tortoise denoted, "He is the incorrigibly lazy Samdala."

Thus, once again the narrative denotes that there was a great amount of contact between the world of the animals as well as that of men and that they seemed to dwell together in many respects, as a harmonious whole. Within the realm of the animal world order, the narrative concerning Chemtatrawta (one who sharpens his dao) finds a very privileged place in terms of textual narration. This tale especially denotes aspects that are related to the animal world order and this existence has been inherently in terms of the animals who have been existing in tandem with man. Chemtatrawta was actually a young man who had set off on a hunt . In the midst of it he stops to sharpen his dao along the length of the river. The animal imagery becomes rampant from the very outset when it denotes that 'a prawn bit him on his testicles'. This spurred off a chain reaction in him and in his anger he cut off the large bamboo from where the *khaum* (a type of climber) hung. The *khaum* in turn landed atop the spine of the jungle fowl below and these in turn scattered the nest of the large ants, who in turn bit the testicles of the wild pig, who in turn scattered the wild plantains where the bats nestled. The bat was furious and it flew up the elephant's trunk. The elephant then destroyed the house of an old woman nearby and she in turn defacated by the mouth of the village well. Thus the villagers in anger began to rally in great rage.

Ultimately the source of the anger was traced to Chemtatrawta and the prawn that bit him. However it must be noted that the prawn was very clever and he took full advantage of the situation and was determined not to be punished. He managed to convince them to put him in the water and very soon he escaped from their clutches. However, these oral tales continue to have a predominant impact upon the postcolonial Mizo sayings that denote that after the prawn glided away to freedom, he swam inside a cave and because the people continued the chase, he was poked about with the leaves of the hnahthial plant. He was prodded and poked about so much that eventually the edges of his mouth became scruffy and grungy. And legend has it that this is the reason why the prawn's mouth retains such a shape till today. Thus, most folktales have retained an element of reality in terms of portrayal and most of them bear a semblance of truth to this day.

In terms of a tale like "The Egg and the Twig", the tale has dwelt predominantly upon the concept of *tlawmngaihna*. (Tlawmngaihna is an integral aspect of Mizo cultural domains that portrays aspects like charity,benevolence towards one another). In this tale, the egg and the twig were actually taking turns to help out each other and this was at the jhoom. This tale reflects a very agrarian set up especially because the Mizo community at large belonged predominantly to such an existence. Eventually when it was time for the mid-day meal they both realized that they had nothing to eat but rice and they were bereft of a side dish that was to go along with the rice. At this the twig asked the egg "Friend, what will we eat alongwith the rice?"

Later on it turned out that the egg went out and 'crushed herself atop a rock and fried herself'. And then both she and the twig ate the rice alongwith the fried egg. The concept of tlawmngaihna is relayed consistently throughout the narrative where both friends had no qualms about sacrificing whatever they had for the sake of the other. The tale goes on to expound upon the setting wherein the next day they realized that there was no fire to warm themselves in the jhoom. And the twig then 'set fire upon herself' and eventually she came back to the jhoom with a fire brand. This short tale depicts the Mizo concept of 'tlawmngaihna' in a very coherent manner.

Significantly, in a tale entitled "The Monkey and his Flute", the narrative depicts a tale where there are animals galore and this tale is again bereft of the presence of any human beings. The tale, once again very intrinsically remains an integral part of the oral tradition and it denotes the adventures of a monkey who had a flute. The flute was envied by the quail who used to hear the melodious music played by the monkey. After a series of attempts made by the quail while trying to fool the monkey all in order to procure the flute,(These included attempts like) "your mother has asked you to fetch water", or "your mother has asked you to fetch wood", and finally he managed to trick him by telling him "your mother has asked you to take a nap."Eventually, the monkey realized that he had not taken a nap and he decided to take one. Immediately the quail pounced upon this chance and seized the flute but he made such a noise that the monkey awoke. Eventually, the quail asked the monkey if he could play upon the flute but the monkey was wise to his ways and he was reluctant to agree. Finally the quail told him

> ...you may hold on to my tail while I play upon the flute.

The monkey agreed to do so, and he gave his consent. Suddenly the quail scampered away with the flute and though the monkey pulled with all his might, only the quail's tail came off. Later on, the quail did go back to the monkey and asked for his tail, but the monkey replied that he would give back the tail:

> "Only in exchange for eight gayals."
>
> The quail then decided against the matter and replied,
>
> "In that case I chose to remain without a tail."

And thus Mizo legend of course has it that this is the reason why the quail remains without a tail to this very day! In the narrative of *Rimenhawihii*, there is a depiction of a beautiful damsel who has very fine, long, hair and we are told that some strands of her hair fell into the water ,as she was bathing. Unfortunately, a local chief, upon seeing her locks of hair, decided that he wanted to acquire the damsel and have her for a wife. However, Rimenhawihii was married and her husband, Zawlthlia, had ensured that no strangers could actually come close to her or to their house. Thus for a long while, the chief's servants could not enter the house. Eventually they managed to lure her with the help of an orange and even as she was captured she hastily informed the dogs and the fowl in their courtyard on how she was taken captive. Upon returning home her husband queried,

> "O dog, where is my wife?"and "O hen, where is my wife?"
>
> Both of them replied "You must follow the strand of thread."

The husband did so and eventually was able to find his wife. Thus, even in this narrative animals play a predominantly significant role and they illustrate that while tracing elements related to identity, animals and man have always existed in tandem.

In an astounding display of strength and wit, the folk narrative, "The War Between the Creatures of the Air and the Creatures of the Land", discloses the series of adventures between various animals. A majority of the anecdotes that are involved panders to the aspects that are related to the elements of heroism and chivalry which are strongly embedded within the Mizo sensibility. The narrative began with the adventures of a tortoise who was keeping guard over the egg of a serpent. After a time a barking deer passed by and invited the tortoise to a high jump competition over the egg of the serpent. The tortoise in turn realized that as he was very slow it would be foolishness on his part to oblige to such a task and so he declined, especially because he was afraid that he would land on the egg of the serpent and it would break. The barking deer assured him that he would protect him if such a thing occurred.

In yet another tale, "Chungleng leh Hnuaileng Indo" or "The War between the Creatures of the Air and the Creatures of the Land", there is a depiction of a great war between the animals. War is common to tribal societies and tribal culture reveled in this aspect. This tale depicts only animals (as protagonists) as denoted in the title and there is no indication of the presence of human beings within the same. It all began with the tortoise who was asked to keep guard over the egg of a serpent. Soon he was challenged to a high jump competition to jump over the egg and he could not refuse the chance. As he was very slow he could not jump over the egg and he ended up by landing atop the egg and breaking the egg in the process. At this he ran amuck and sought refuge amongst his fellow animals but all the other animals including the barking deer, the bear ,wild goat, the elk and the wild pig refused him asylum, for fear of the serpent. Finally, an eagle granted him refuge. After a series of altercations wherein the eagle refused to give up custody of the tortoise the serpent flew into a rage and declared war between the creatures of the land and the creatures of the air. The battle then went on in full swing and soon all the various creatures were up in arms against one another in full force. And the war waged on.

The tale has an ending that is relevant to nature of the bat. During the war, he had joined the ranks of the creatures of the land for he claimed that he did not even have wings. And thus he had left the creatures of the air, whose ranks he had originally belonged to. After a time however, the animals gathered together and signed a pact and very soon they all became friends once again. As the bat had displayed cowardly behaviour during the war, he could not find an ally amongst either land or air creatures and in great embarrassment he fled and hid and did not dare to go out in the light of day. And the story denotes that this is why the bat wanders only in the darkness of the night, to this day. This belief is narrated till this day and it denotes that oral narratives are still inherently central to identity.

Chawngchili's story is more profound in a way, because it denotes the courtship between a young maiden and a serpent. The relationship was kept a secret from the maiden's father and he discovered it only when he realized that his son(the maiden's younger sibling) was losing weight despite the fact that his father packed a decent mid-day meal for him. When questioned, the young boy revealed the love relationship between the serpent and his sister wherein he added that the snake would consume his share of the food. Enraged by this turn events the man lay in wait for the serpent and he killed him. Later he also killed his daughter who by then was already pregnant with the serpant's child. Upon slitting open her stomach the man discovered to his horror that there were many small snakes inside his daughter's womb. He managed to kill all of these, save one. This lone survivor proved to be a source of great menace for the village, as it gobbled up everything in sight. Ultimately the villagers managed to slaughter a portion of it and the tale ends by denoting that all the villagers who consumed the flesh of the serpent were put to death while an old woman, became the sole survivor in the village because she was the only one who did not partake of the flesh of the serpent. Thus, Mizo folk tales bring out the myriad instances of man-animal relationships in the pre colonial times and it also conveys that there are many beliefs that are still kept alive to an extent even in the post colonial domain.

Myths within the ambit of a pre colonial Mizo culture have had a significant role in terms of the aspect of creation as well as life and death. Mizo narratives have denoted these features in an inherently significant domain. In the history of Mizo myth and folkloristics there has been coherent representation of these various parameters. For instance, the concept of creation has been portrayed in a manner that is very different from the creation of the post colonial era. Pre-colonial era has inherently depicted the existence of a world that was bereft of human beings and even the universe. This is in sharp contrast to the post colonial era where the Christian God becomes sovereign and is solely responsible for the creation of the universe as well as the first man and woman. Even the creation of the heaven and the earth ,the waters of the sea as well as all objects that were of the air and water and land, took place only with the emergence of the Christian God. This has been reflected in the *Bible* in the book of Genesis which is the first book in the Old Testament. The decades that followed the advent of the missionaries on Mizo soil saw a sharper and a more focused perspective emerging in terms of myths and creation beliefs. The colonial Mizo began to gradually identify with the image of the Christian precepts of thinking and fashioned himself within such parameters.

The pre colonial Mizo context was one that was rich in terms of carving out its own niche with regards to identity. It saw the existence of a being, (or a god) that was referred to as *khuazingnu* and the aspects of creation, including the creation of the earth and the addition of greenery around the earth were attributed to this being. Myth in this era also depicts that as the earth was very dry this all majestic being called *khuazingnu* would occasionally open the windows of heaven in order to water the earth. This explained the concept of rainfall and much later on, the same god was credited with the creation of animals and humanity, especially in order to consume the vast produce of the earth. It was also significant to note that within this world order there was the existence of both men and animals who could communicate with one another and this especially depicted the centrality of the animal world order within the ambit of the human race. The earth was basically reflected as a land of abundance. However, even within the pre colonial era, with the passage of time there grew conflicts amongst the inhabitants of the earth and eventually this gave way to the creation of the chief.

The concept of 'identity formation' within the pre colonial era was significantly inter linked with that of nature and animals as well as human beings. This was in sharp contrast to the post colonial Christian domains where the Christian parameters prevailed in terms of the identity formation, and it reflected upon an era where God deemed that man was supreme in terms of all creation. All the other aspects of creation were subservient to man even though man was created last of all. Woman was made to keep man company because it was realized that even as man had vegetation and the animals around him but there was an inherent sense of dissatisfaction around him. This world thus did away with the mythical world of creation in the pre colonial era, and it was no longer a world where man and animals could communicate with one another, at least verbally. It was only man that had access to the higher order of language and animals were hunted down for food or used as beasts of burden. The book of Leviticus in the *Bible* denotes passages where God legitimizes sanction upon the kind of animals that could be consumed for food and those that clearly could not be. Thus, in the formulation of identity the *Bible* became in coherent ways the legitimate parameter within the post Christian ethos.

Significantly, because man and woman were to be consorts to each other, woman was created from man's rib by God. Thus, the pre colonial era, was demystified and there was a gradual rewriting of the identity politics even in terms of the folkloristic perspective. Adam and Eve thus became the first man and woman within the dynamics of the post colonial order and this is the aspect of creation that Mizos currently advocate to. There has been an emerging sense of hybridity however in various other ways in the identity perspective. Though Mizos advocate to the Christian parameters of creation, the myths have been kept alive in many ways and are told and retold within the dynamics of the folklore perspective.

Within the ambit of the pre colonial Mizo, it must be reflected that the creature called *khuazingnu* played a significant role. However when she created the universe there was no mud at all to moisten the earth. The world was filled with rocks and thus because of this, there was no greenery or vegetation around the universe. This is again in contrast to the post colonial perspectives of creation where God reigned supreme and accounted for everything within the universe. There was nothing that was left unaccounted for and man was not in want or need. There was also the existence of a huge sea which was known as *tuihriam* and the waters of this sea was very cold, and it was believed that if one dipped one's hand in the sea the coldness of its waters would ensure that it was chopped away. On the other shore of the sea there was a small amount of mud and it was said that in order to procure that mud the various animals would make an attempt every now and then but because of the coldness of the waters of the sea, they could not even manage to swim halfway across the sea. Thus they could not get the mud at all. However after a while a porcupine managed to swim all the way across the sea and in this manner he secured a bit of the mud, and eventually he got back ashore. The other animals began to wonder as to how they could multiply the small bit of mud. While they were still debating the earthworm suggested,

> "If you are ready to listen to me I know how we can multiply the mud".
>
> As they promised to do so, the earthworm said:
>
> "I shall consume the mud and shall throw out the same in the form of excreta and it will then multiply". The other creatures cried:

> "We do not believe you, perhaps it is only because you want to eat mud."
>
> The earthworm replied:
>
> "If it does not happen as I say then you may break me up in three parts."

And because he was so daring the others decided to believe him. Thus the earthworm did as he had suggested and soon the mud grew to a large amount. All this mud was transferred across the various portions of the universe this myth is regarded to be how mud came to be spread across the earth. Once again this myth establishes the significance of the role that animals played in the creation of the universe, in sharp contrast to the post colonial ethos where man is regarded to be inherently supreme ,in accordance with the Biblical perspective. The role of animals is now very much secondary in the post colonial ethos and sadly enough there is little or no regard for the animals. The respect that was accorded to them at the orality stage where they were treated on par with man is decidedly an element of the past.

In sharp contrast to the Biblical parallels, in as far as the creation of the mountains and the rivers were concerned, it was discovered that even though the mud had been spread to increase a sufficient amount of vegetation on the earth, there were no other structures such as mountains and rivers. However, there was a place called Vanlaiphai that was situated in the midst of the heavens that contained a tall tree that was known as *thingvantawng* or tree that reached up to the heavens. The inhabitants around the area wanted to destroy the tree but they were scared that the mud ,precious as it was, would be destroyed too.

One day they sent a small bird called Lailen to test whether the earth was dry or not, and the bird flew around and pecked the earth and because it was so light in weight, it failed to make a dent in the earth. The bird then flew back and reported that the earth was dry enough to stand around it, and that the tree could be destroyed. Now the inhabitants of the earth gathered together to destroy the tree and they began to hack away at the tree but they soon realized that the earth was not at all dry. The increasing dent that was made by their combined weight resulted in the breaking up of the earth into various dimensions and this in turn created the rivers, the lakes and the mountains.

Even with regards to the inception of the first earthquake that occurred in the universe, Mizo myth denotes that there was a tortoise who carried the earth upon its back and it was regarded that if the tortoise moved the earth would fall. Thus, if such a thing happened all the inhabitants of the earth would be killed. In order to prevent such a calamity the guardian of the ends of the earth had requested the tortoise to not move away. However, there was a certain creature from the animal world order, who lied to the tortoise and declared:

> "The inhabitants of the earth are all dead."
>
> While saying this, he placed a heap of burning embers of charcoal upon the back of the tortoise. The tortoise was immediately forced to scamper away due to the heat. Thus the earth began to quake tremendously and immediately the inhabitants of the earth cried out:
>
> "Have mercy, we are not yet dead, we are still alive".

Eventually, when the truth was realized that the inhabitants of the earth were not all dead, the guardian of the ends of the earth requested the tortoise once more to stay still and to not wander away. The myth is one of the very few that are still kept alive today, because when an earthquake occurs ,it is very common to still hear old folks crying out to mother nature,to bring the quaking earth to a halt by pleading that they are still very much alive and to not destroy the earth.

Pre colonial dynamics were also clear with regards to the creation of an after world. Death and life were very much a part of humanity and Mizo myths did not have the existence of huge giants as well as ogres and ogresses who lived up to eternity.

were two places where the dead could go to after they had given up their human form on earth. These were places that were known as; *mitthi khua* and *pialral.* It was believed that whoever died would go to either one of these places. However the latter was actually only a place that warriors of great fame and their families could go to. There was a very significant difference between *mitthi khua* and *pialral. Pialral* is regarded to be a very pleasant place where every need is taken care of without the burden of physical toil and it is said that people vie to have a place there. However *mitthi khua* is a place where ordinary mortals reside after death and it was regarded to be inferior and more lowly even as compared to earth. The dead who were designated a place in the same, had to labour and toil in abundance but the food and drink that they could consume there were significantly inferior to even what they could consume upon the earth. Thus, such people lived in dire poverty and due to this, they were very weak and emaciated.

Within the parameters of this belief, there was a lake that was known as *Rih dil.* This lake was regarded to be one of the more significant places where the dead would visit. In fact this lake was so crucial, that it was regarded that all the dead had to necessarily pass through. In this event there was a plant called *mitthi pal* that was planted in honour of the dead. There was also a place that was known as known as *hruai kawn* that was erected in honour of the spirit of the dead. Again in order to commemorate the area and its interaction with the dead there were places that were known as *mitthi kawtkai* or passageway for the dead and even as the dead were on their way to the *rih dil*, there was the creation of a place that was known as *lung rah buk.* This was especially significant because this rock would create a lot of noise whenever someone stepped upon it.

After the dead stepped upon the same rock, they would leave for the abode of the spiritual world. Myth also denoted that the spirit of the dead would be very reluctant to leave the earth where they had dwelt for all time, on a permanent basis world. In order to aid them to bid adieu to the nostalgia of their past lives there was a mount that was known as *hringlang tlang*. Once a person set foot upon this mount, they could decipher and perceive the world of the human beings that they had left behind. Upon observing this it was but natural for them to feel very sentimental about the same and they would weep in regret. However, there were two remedies to this :one was in the guise of a very beautiful flower that was known as *hawilopar* and as soon as the dead who were to leave the earth were getting overtly sentimental, fortune would chance that they come across the flower and upon perception of the same, they would be enchanted by this flower. They would necessarily pluck the flower and adorn themselves with the same and in doing so they would never want to even give the earth a second glance. This ensured a permanent obliteration of the earth from their memories.

The other remedy was with regard to a clear spring water that was located on top of a mountain and this water was very tempting and refreshing to perceive. No one that walked about the place could actually resist the water, and once they drank that water they would immediately forget their past and everything else about the earth. In fact, the obliteration would be so immense that they would long and yearn all the more for the abode of the dead and they would hasten towards the same. This water is known in Mizo as, *lungloh tui*. This belief along with the other aspects are inherently different from the Christian beliefs because, there is the belief in an after life in terms of the latter, but only in the light of salvation and a heaven and hell parameter. All else was obliterated. There are references only to salvation and redemption. Thus, there are no believers amongst the Mizo society in terms of these myths at the present stage of time.

Hybridity has been emerging even within domains that are both sacral as well as secular. The myths have been kept alive for academic discourse and domains, but the practices have been negated and rendered redundant. There has not been vociferous protests with regards to the same. Predominantly because at least for the present time, Mizos have been a people where colonization has implanted and etched itself very firmly within the psyche of the people. Most, if not all, of the myths, that have been denoted in the paper, are still told and retold, in the original Mizo and perhaps at times in translation, but these exist for the sake of existence alone, as myths that suffice at best as tales to amuse and entertain or to create a sense of the mystical and exotic every now and then. Identity thus has been rewritten, and recreated for a small dimension of people in the far flung corner of an Indian tribal ethos; for in Mizoram, what began as myth, centuries ago, has actually come full circle by still existing as myth, for its own sake, in terms of situating the identity paradigm.

The aspect of identity has thus been inherently myriad and linked with the notion of complexity in many dimensions within the Mizo cultural context. It must also be noted that a rewriting of this dimension can only be interpreted in terms of the aspect of hybridity because there has been a significant amount of imparting the influences of both the cultures of the colonized and the colonizers within the domains of the Mizo community. This has been evident from the very outset where the missionaries had sought to emancipate the community by means of education and other administrative reforms. Thus, identity has come to a coherent circle, by situating the post colonial Mizo well within the folds of the religious parameters and yet still embracing aspects that are incorporated within the folds of the age, therefore acknowledging also, the notions of hybridity in terms of the Mizo identity paradigm.

Works Cited

Bhabha, Homi K. *The Location of Culture.* Routledge: New York, 2010.

During, Simon. *Cultural Studies, A Critical Introduction.* New York: Routledge, 2005.

Dahrawka, P. S. Mizo *Thawnthu,* Aizawl: Thankhumi, 1981.

Khiangte, LTL. *Thuhlaril* Aizawl: Felfim, 1997.

Lalthangliana. B. *India, Burma & Bangladesh-a Mizo Chanchin*. Aizawl:RTM Press, 2000.

__________ *Mizo Literature* Aizawl: RTM Press, 1993.

Nuchhungi. *Serkawn Graded Readers: Mizo Thawnthu*. Aizawl: Mualchin, 2003.

Ong, Walter J. *Orality and Literacy: The Technologising of the Word*. New York: Routledge, 2008.

Pachuau, Margaret L. *Handpicked Tales from Mizoram* Writers Workshop, Kolkata 2008.

Thanmawia, R. L. *Mizo Hnahthlak Thawnthu*: Aizawl: Gilzom Offset, 2009.

The Lushais. Tribal Research Institute. New Delhi: Alllied Publishers, 1978.

Thanmawia, R. L. *Mizo Hnahthlak Thawnthu Vol. II* Aizawl: Gilzom Offset, 2009.

Shakespear, J. *The Lushei Kuki Clans*. New Delhi: Allied Publishers, 2008.

Sangkima. *Essays on the History of the Mizos*. Guwahati : Spectrum Publications, 2004.

Vanlalchhuanawma. *Christianity and Subaltern Culture*. ISPCK: Delhi, 2007.

Vanlallawma, C. *Hman lai hian mawm* 4th ed. Aizawl: Zamzo Publishing House, 2000.

10

D.P. Sinha's *The King of Mathura*: A Megalomaniac's Story

A.J. Sebastian sdb

The King of Mathura portrays how King Kans, growing up under cruel circumstances, becomes himself an evil monarch full of malice, cruelty and jealousy. As a child, having fallen in love with a flute rather than a sword, his father thwarts his growth through evil machinations, making him a demonic character. In his turn, he becomes a megalomaniac, who destroys and kills everyone who crosses him in his inhuman ways. Kans himself narrates his story of extraordinary ambition which leads him to become a demi-god. Finally, his own demonic ambition leads to his destruction. The playwright traces Kans's growth and annihilation in several flashback scenes, proving him to be a megalomaniac.

D.P. Sinha, the distinguished Hindi playwright, in his short play *The King of Mathura* probes into the evil machinations of King Kans of Mathura. The play could be assessed in the absurd theatre tradition with its atmosphere of nervous tension, coupled with comical situations. The absurdists believe that reality is meaningless and senseless. The Absurd theatre presents the absurdity of modern human condition and the humanity's loss of religious, philosophical, or cultural roots. The individual is essentially isolated and alone. It presents the existential outlook of man depicting him lonely, confused and often anguished in a bewildering universe (Murfin 2). Kans's victimization in the hands of his cruel father leads him to become cruel, jealous and intriguing. The sensitive boy who fell in love with a flute rather than a sword, becomes a demonic character, destroying and killing everyone who crossed him in his megalomaniac dreams. The playwright has clearly demarcated two acting spaces for the play: the first, the open space of the palace terrace where there is a high stone pillar, a royal chair, a huge gong and a hammer; the second, the space in the jungle beside a big tree.

The play opens as King Kans enters, tired and exhausted, having spent sleepless nights with tension of his own making with his obsession with his own self. He wonders how his poor commoners sleep soundly despite their misery and utter poverty. He muses: "I the 'Brightest of the Bright', 'Bravest of the Brave', 'Mighty King of Kings', the Highest, Lord Kans, the God – roams about restlessly alone in the dark of the night, like a ghost..." (Sinha 132). He is so self-obsessed with his own superiority complex that has led to narcissist tendencies. He sits on the throne, closes his eyes and lets off a scream. He imagines as though some strange hands attempt to strangle him. He slips out of the throne and falls to the ground, crying for help. A palace Guard rushes to assist him as he wakes up from his delirious state. Regaining his composure, he drives away the Guard, who bows and exits. Recollecting the dream vision, he is all scared of the terrible hands and the gory faces of thousands of men, women and children. He begins to laugh ironically, taking possession of himself as the King, driving away all fears and dangers: "Afraid? Lord Kans! The Almighty God was frightened! The God was frightened. He was terrified" (132).

As he undergoes such a conflicting psychological trauma, he can overhear the sound of flute playing. The notes of the flute keeps haunting him as he recollects thoughts of the rebel youth leader Krishna hiding somewhere in the palace. He gets panicky and orders his guards to search the palace to capture Krishna. He is unable to sleep as he keep hearing the music of the flute, driving him crazy and utter:"What a torture. No peace... asleep or awake!

Death in life and living death! Sleeping and waking have become one" (133).

In his frustration, Kans comes forward and begins to narrate the story of his life. His was the story of an ordinary young boy, with extraordinary ambition, which led him to become a god. His demonic ways led him to his own destruction. The sequence shifts to a flashback in childhood, when his father King Ugrasen asked him to choose his favourite weapon among sword, bow and arrow, spear, thunder-bolt and mace. Surprisingly, the boy Kans opts for a lute. The King is so infuriated that he calls his son a woman in the garb of a man. The flashback ends as King Kans recollects the scornful insult of his father when he opted for a lute in childhood. The insult becomes part and parcel of every fibre of his being.

Flashback II begins with Prince Kans in the company of his beloved, Swaati, a village girl. The sequence in the open field presents the duo in exchange of affectionate words. She wishes him, her god, solace and happiness all the time. She acknowledges that she finds him most handsome when wrapped in thought. He wonders and queries if he has lost his masculinity as his cruelty is synonym for manliness. He speaks of callousness, violence and murder as hallmarks of a man. He doesn't accept her praises referring to the ridicule heaped on him by his father which has forced him to subscribe to his new found conviction: "A man is one who kills and takes joy in shedding blood. Unfeeling, cruel, barbarous, blind and deaf – such is a man" (135). He is puzzled by his cruel nature and his feelings of pity for the sufferings of others lets him shed tears. Swaati doesn't consider it weakness on his part, instead he is ahead of his times. He lets out his cherished childhood dream of building a world devoid of barbarity, bringing equality, sympathy and love by which music of lute would become man's companion in solitude. But he realizes his times have become cruel as he has to snatch away all smiles from the faces of people.

Kans recalls the gruesome sights of cruelty meted out to animals by his father. As a child he had been groomed in cruelty like the way his father shot at animals for entertainment. Goats used to be tied and the king would shoot arrows at their eyes from a short distance to prove his expertise in archery. The young Kans was told to do the same. He mused: "Am I not myself an animal, about to kill a nearly dead creature? What is this madness?. . . I confessed to the king that it was not possible for me" (136). His father only taunted him telling him to wear bracelets on his hands and play on the lute as such masculine games were not meant for him. He shares his frustration with Swaati as he beholds such sights of corpses of men, women and children and heaps of goats with vultures hovering over them. He accepts it as his destiny. The flashback ends with Kans at the present time as king. He confesses to Swaati that he can't return back from cruelty in which he has grown as he is rendered a deflated and lifeless man, reaching the pinnacle of his life, lonely and frustrated.

In flashback III, Kans tells of his father Pradyot, giving audience to Baahuk, the special emissary of the King of Magadh. The king bursts into laughter as Baahuk pays obeisance to him. He places his sword on the emissary's chest calling him a captive. Suddenly Kans challenges his father's mocking remarks saying, "King, my father! I had sworn to myself that on your lips that twisted so often in mockery, there shall be entreaty for forgiveness one day" (139). He then goes on to challenge the king to ask his pardon. In shock King Ugrasen becomes dumb. He shows his helplessness as he has lost his power of speech. Kans orders the guards to imprison his father and declare in the Yadav empire that he has committed suicide. He is keen that his father should be kept alive to regain his speech to make him apologise for having ridiculed him. As the guards take King Ugrasen away, Kans is moved with emotions and in a state of confusion he cries out: "King, my father! What have you done? I had been waiting ever so long for the moment when you will ask my pardon" (139). The flashback ends with Kan's reminiscing his childhood days when his father had taken him to the middle of the forest as he engaged in hunting.

In flashback IV the king asks the young Kans if he could go back to the palace all alone in the thick of the night. The boy Kans is left alone there to fend for himself while his father rides away. The young Kans shivers in fear of dreadful beasts as he limps back home. Suddenly his father appears from behind a tree letting the boy run and cling to him. When the Prince begins to cry, his father brushes him aside for his lack of bravery. The boy Kans, shivering with fear, wets his clothes in utter shock and cries out: "Forgive me, Royal Father…I will never feel afraid. Never shall I wet my clothes… I am a brave Yadav of the Bhoj clan" (141).

The flashback ends with the various official discussing King Kan's plan of building a powerful Yadav republic like his father-in-law, the mighty king Jaraasandh of Magadh. The officials Pralamb (Minister of Mathura), Pradyot (Military Chief of Mathura) and Baahuk (Army Commander of Magadh), heap praises on King Kans who would establish his kingdom from the Himalayas to Kanyakumari, though surrounded by rebels. Suddenly a Guard rushes in to inform that Pradyot, the Military Chief, is busy searching for rebel Krishna in the royal palace as per Kan's instruction. Meanwhile praises are heaped on the King by the passing officials. The sequence moves to the arrival of Queen Asti. She brings the good news that she has brought Magadh soldiers as part of her dowry. She tells Kans to disregard everyone to spend time in her company and make love. Kans is still in great fear of the astrologer's predictions of destruction of Kans by the eighth son of Vasudev and Devakee. Asti brushes aside all fears of such impending danger. But Kans writhes in pain uttering: "How can one sleep! How can one relax when everyone is wishing for his death" (144). A furious Kans demands that Devakee be brought there and killed.

When Devakee, his sister, arrives and praises his greatness, all his bitterness is forgotten. She reminds him of their childhood days when he jumped into a river to retrieve her doll, risking his life. Now, she wonders why he has imprisoned her along with her husband king Vasudev. He has very paradoxical opinions when he says that he loves his darling sister and yet tortures her in prison. He has his argument: "Yes, demon-like and also god-like. This is the dilemma of a human being – split into a god and a devil – half and half" (146). As she begins to cry, he consoles her with utmost affection and begins to shed tears. She reminds him how he himself had selected her husband Vasudev. Kans acknowledges that Vasudev was his good friend from childhood, but now things have changed as he has become his enemy due to political ambitions and conspiracies. Though his sister pleads him for mercy, he drives her away.

The sequence moves forward when Asti, his Queen, arrives to dispel his fears. She ends up taunting his vain glorious attitudes inherited from his father. As she exits scorning him, Kans calls his officials Pradyot, Baahuk and Pralamb, ordering them to keep strict surveillance of his enemies and all tribes of the Yaadavs. In his suspicion of his own people, he wants to know what goes on in every household in his kingdom. He finds himself so lonesome as there is no one whom he can trust and confide in. He confides his predicament in Pradyot, his military chief, who reassures him of his allegiance till death. Pradyot also surrenders his life in his service, more out of fear and trepidation than affection.

In the next sequence Swaati enters as she had been summoned by the King. Kans confides in her how lonely he is imprisoned in his own palace. He expresses his passion for her and wants her to be beside him as he suspects everyone attempting to murder him. He tells her to marry Pradyot and to observe his every move and inform him. There and then, he summons Pradyot and makes him tie the marriage knot, as he is overwhelmed with the loss of his much loved woman.

Flashback V is one surrounding Kan's secret love affair with Swaati as a young man. Though scared of nurturing love for her, a village beauty, he reassures her that he wouldn't abandon her love even to the point of death. She is convinced of the invisible bond of love as he has promised. The flashback ends as Kans wonders if his love for Swaati is one of invisible bond of attraction and attachment. Suddenly he hears the chorus pleading, "Do not delay further, O! Deliverer!" (155). He wonders who the deliverer is and vaingloriously imagines himself as the great Mahaarajhadhiraaj Kans, King of Kings, the deliverer. Pralamb, his minister enters and tells him that the deliverer is fictitious. An argument ensues between them. Kans decides to smash the fiction and nip it in the bud.

> Kans: I shall smash this fiction.
>
> Pralamb: You cannot destroy it.
>
> Kans: What can I not do?
>
> Pralamb: As long as a single person lives, the fiction will continue to live in his mind.
>
> Kans: In that case, not a single person shall remain alive.
>
> Pralamb: Over whom will the King of kings rule then? ... At the root of all this are the religious beliefs and the discourses and teachings of the godmen...that in their time of difficulties God will take human form and appear on this earth to free them from misery.
>
> Kans: So these are my real enemies?
>
> Pralamb: Godmen, religious teachings... (155).

Pralamb informs the king that seven sons of Devakee had been killed as per his orders. Yaadav women had experienced killing of their male children like the Biblical account of the way wicked Herod killed all Jewish male children who were two years or under in Bethlehem at the birth of Jesus. It is a tragic report of how a wicked ruler tried to destroy Jesus, the Messiah and how God prevented it from happening (Matthew 2:13-23).

Pralamb brings news of a theatre group touring Mathura with their play on the incarnation of Narasingha entitled

"Narasingh Avataar" which the king longs to see. As the play unfolds the narrator speaks of the tyrannical rule of irreligious king Hiranyakashipu when he oppressed and plundered his people. As they prayed to the Almighty, Lord Vishnu revealed himself and promised that he would take birth on this earth and bring deliverance. When people rejoiced at the prophetic incarnation, the king Hiranyakashipu became most violent, but people continued to pray. A lotus grew in the mud and an ascetic Prahlaad, was born in a demon's house. Though the king raged in his fury, he was unable to harm the ascetic. In the end when the king raised his sword to kill the child, Narasingh burst out from a pillar and held the king by his stomach from where blood began to flow. At this juncture, King Kans screams and orders that no plays would be performed in his kingdom. He forbids all forms of worship in the land. As the actors are taken captive, Baahuk arrives bringing bad news of the Yaadav revolt. The soldiers had set the temple on fire as the people had taken shelter in it.

In Act II Pralamb brings news to the king that temples have been deserted with the ban on prayers and singing, driving God out of the kingdom itself. Kans promises to give them a new God in his own person and declares: "People can put Kans on the throne of their hearts as God, in both his forms, those of the benign and the angry destroyer…Let it be declared that from today in the kingdom of Mathura God Shri Kans alone will be worshipped…He who defies shall be put to death" (161). Pralamb prostrates before him and promises to execute the orders. Pradyot comes in to inform that the images of God Shri Kans have been installed all over and masses are worshipping him. Kans appoints Pralamb the High Priest of his religion. Baahuk enters with a poor and scared fisherman who reveals to the king that while fishing in the river he was swept away by the undercurrent. Uttering the Shri Kan's name in prayer he is saved from drowning. An elated king rewards him with his ring.

Swaati suddenly appears carrying a new-born baby, in the company of the officials. When Kans decides to kill the child, she tells him it is a girl. Without heeding her plea, he dashes the child to death. Suddenly an explosion is heard which the king thinks is that of the goddess, his destroyer, being annihilated. Meanwhile news arrives that a child had been born to Nand, the chief of Gokul village, whom the people considered the incarnated one.

In the following sequence Kans is found in the company of Swaati. She admires him as the most glorious and brave King of Kings. He confesses his helplessness though mighty in power, groaning in loneliness. He finds comfort only in her presence. He asks her to go to Gokul and kill the incarnation of Lord Vishnu. She decides to execute his orders to kill Krishna. Pralamb comes in to inform the king that the newborn baby sucked the life out of Swaati's poisoned breasts. To appease the people, the King orders that the body of Swaati, considered the killer of Yaadav children, be hung in public. Then he goes on to make peace with his father-in-law, the ruler of Magadh. Entrusting his kingdom to his officials, Kans goes to Magadh to fight for the king. The army chief of Magadh informs Kans that he is surrounded by enemies and his own people wish him dead. His officials Pralamb and Pradyot too join the rebels against Kans. Viritrighn, the Army Commander of Magadh, gives information received from his spies that the rebellion has been full grown with the young people at the vanguard. Kans is told of the latest developments:

> Viritrighn: Lord, you have prohibited music on the kingdom of Mathura; now every rebel carries a flute with him, as a sign of protest.
>
> Kans: Flute?
>
> Viritrighn: A symbol of their rebellion against the ban on music.
>
> Kans: A musical instrument.
>
> Viritrighn: Who is the leader?

> Kans: Krishna: (recollecting) Krishna! The son of the Yadav – chief Nand of village Gokul?
>
> Viritrighn: Yes, the son of Nand. But the Yaadavs consider him to be the eighth son of Devakee (170).

Kans asserts that Devakee never gave birth to the 80 sonns and calls it superstition. But Viritrighn claims that such superstition has become reality as the notes of the flute are more powerful in Mathura than the call of the conch-shell for war. He reiterates that the flute is the symbol of their rebellion under the leadership of Krishna. He has been very charismatic in collecting people for *raas leela* with the objective of music and love-making.

In flashback VI Swaati enters limping, complaining of a thorn in her foot. When Kans takes at her foot in his hands to examine it, she laughs away saying that she would tell everyone that the King had touched her feet. As Kans remains lost in his reverie, the flashback ends with Asti limping into his presence, asking him to take out the thorn on her foot. When Kans shows reluctance to look for the thorn, she insists that he search her leg. When he releases her foot, she laughs away and shows her ruby necklace presented by her father, the king of Magadh. With the pretence of showing the necklace, she comes close to him to draw his attention to her full, round breasts. She appeals passionately with her beauty to arouse his carnal desires, but he brushes her aside as nonsensical. When questioned why he can't make love to her, he claims his Godly position. As he pushes her out she taunts him saying: "I know why the God is so worried. The leader of the Yaadav youths, Krishna is organising resistance against god Shri Kans's despotism.... He is dark-complexioned but his figure is so winning that all girls go mad after him. I also want to see him once.... Resistance against God Shri Kans! God who is impotent!" (174). In utter disgust Kans attempts to strike her, but refrains from such a hasty act of violence. Instead, he begins to admire her beauty and then all of a sudden grabs her and strangles her to death. He throws her down and kisses her on her forehead. He begins to say that he had rendered her a service, freeing her soul: "I have only murdered that counter-ego which my ego could not brook, be it of wife or friend, sister or father. That has to be destroyed" (174).

When Pralam is brought before him, Kans queries if the flute-wielding Yaadav youths are organising themselves to destroy his power. Pralamb declares his open enmity with the king as the illegitimate son of King Ugrasen their common father. Being the eldest son of the king, he claims that he should have been made the chief of the Yaadav confederacy. When Kans threatens to kill him for his conspiracy, Pralamb declares that he has achieved him mission in hatching the plot to destroy him with the popular rising under the leadership pf Krishna. He happily goes to his death as the hang-men lead him to his execution.

Meanwhile, Kans is haunted by Krishna's flute playing in the palace. He sends the guards to search every nook and corner for Krishna. Pradyot tells the king that the sound of music could be a making of his imagination. Suddenly Kans threatens him with dire consequences for being a traitor. Pradyot keeps his cool and tells the king that he is prepared to face death and regrets for having served a tyrant all his life like a slave. He takes his own life by stabbing with a dagger. Kans keeps listening to the flute-playing which communicates fear to every fibre of his being. Still he puts on a brave face and declares himself the brightest God Shri Kans who is invincible. But the recurring flute-playing drives him crazy and as he breaks down he pleads, "No-no Krishna! No! No!" (178).

Kans is the epitome of a person suffering from Megalomania which is a psycho-pathological condition characterized by *delusional* fantasies of wealth, power, or *omnipotence*. He is characterized by an inflated sense of self-esteem and overestimation of his powers and beliefs ("Megalomania." http:/ /en. wikipedia. org). Freud's concept of *repression* by ignoring one's unresolved conflicts or traumatic past being forced out of conscious awareness into the realm of unconscious, could be applied to Kans' life. Freud's idea of *ego*, *super-ego* and the *id*, corresponding to *consciousness*, *conscience* and *unconscious* (Barry 97), delves deep into Kans life whereby he kills his conscience which eventually suppresses his consciousness and returns him to the stage of the unconscious. It is this that makes him a monster until the end of the play. Being forced to repress his childhood dreams, the echoing music of the flute which runs like the leitmotif finally crushes him to his own destruction.

Works Cited

Barry, Peter. Beginning *Theory: An Introduction to Literary and Cultural Theory*. Manchester and New York: Manchester University Press, 2002. Rpt.

Bible, The Holy. Revised Standard Version. London: Catholic Trust Society. 1966.

"Megalomania." http://en. wikipedia. org/wiki/Megalomania

Murfin, Ross & Supryia M. Ray. *The Bedford Glossary of Critical and Literary Terms*. New York: Bedford Books, 1998.

Sinha, D.P. "The King of Mathura." *Indian Literature, Sahitya Akademi's Bi-MonthlyJournal*, No. 226, March-April 2005, Vol. XLIX, No. 2, 131-178.

11

In Search of Universal Peace in Ratan Thiyam's *My Earth, My Love*

A.J. Sebastian sdb

My Earth, My Love revolves around myth and history, depicted in time past and present, as the dramatist dwells on Manipur's horrendous past. The seven mythical celestial nymphs weave a cloth at the loom to be offered to God, the Almighty, as their love offering to ward off warfare and destruction. The seven sisters represent human longing for peace and brotherhood. As they have premonitions of a bleak future, Puwari, the personification of history, recounts the prophesies on Nostradamus about Hitler's atrocities and the bombing of Hiroshima. The eldest nymph gathers information from her six sisters about pain and destruction in different parts of the world.

Through *My Earth, My Love*, hinged on the wheel of time, Manipuri dramatist Ratan Thiyam, makes an appeal for peace and harmony in the world. Mixing the past and the present with myth and history, he unearths a new form in dramatic presentation. The play revolves around the horrendous past of warfare and destruction such as: devastation of Manipur by Burmese army; killing during the World War II; Russian revolution and the mass killings; Japanese attack on Pearl Harbour; bombing of Hiroshima and Nagasaki; genocide during Khmer Rouge regime in Kampuchea. The play is presented with a mythological background of seven sisters, the celestial nymphs, busy at the loom weaving a cloth which is the traditional symbol of love, peace and honour. They are to offer it to the Almighty, with a prayer to stop all warfare and destruction, ushering in an era of peace and brotherhood. The dramatist has personified history in the form of *Puwari* an old man. There are nymphs that fly around like birds and incarnated human beings. They recount the past bloodshed, flying around the world through the pages of history. The play climaxes as the nymphs offer the cloth they have woven to the Almighty. They become the peace loving citizens of the world.

The prologue begins with a prayer song sung with the accompaniment of *pena* (traditional Manipuri bow and string instrument), invoking Divine blessings and forgiveness.

O Lord
Lord of the Lords
O Mother Goddess
in your divine courtyard
we, Your humble servants,
are offering a length of cloth
please accept it wholeheartedly,
O Father
forgive our sins.

(Thiyam 50)

Seven dancers armed with spears and shields, recount the story of bloodshed. Seven females wearing golden masks dance as well. They are the seven sisters, the celestial nymphs who can take any form. The had flown around the world as birds and have taken human form. The nymphs are *Hi-pokpi, Yui-pokpi, Hi-leima, Yui-leima, Hikubi, Yaikubi,* and *Yaishra.* A ballad is sung about the creation of the world from bamboo leaves and the adventures of the seven nymphs. The eldest nymph remains perched on a loom in the form of a bird as the other nymphs fly away.

The first scene represents the seven sisters narrating their experience of conflict and warfare throughout the world. The nymphs act as *Maibis* (priestesses) and they communicate with an unseen Force, foreboding of a bleak future. *Puwari*, an old man, personified history recounts the prophesies on Nostradamus about Hitler's atrocities and the bombing of Hiroshima, while *Hi-leima*, the nymph, flies off to Japan to collect news of the bombing. The eldest nymph gets all the information from her six sisters. The first nymph recounts the seven years of devastation in Manipur by the Burmese forces. Several children had been killed with the smoke of burning chillies. Thousands had been tied with cane-splits passed through the slits in their ears and dragged into slavery. The second nymph speaks of the suffering meted out to the women and children by the marching soldiers. The sixth nymph gives further details of people who were killed, some while lying prostrate, others standing or sitting, unable to bear the torture. The nymphs in one voice recount the stories of suffering and death:

> *First nymph:* Seven –year devastation is over. Genocide by suffocating with the smoke of burning chillies is also over...
>
> *Second nymph:* In this gruesome age of savages, we, the weaker section, women and children, would become their beast of prey.
>
> *Third nymph:* Amidst the frightening and unfathomable tortures and extermination.
>
> *Fourth nymph:* Vanished are the humans of yesterday...
>
> *Fifth nymph:* The smell of blood is in the air; dead bodies...
>
> *Sixth nymph:* Dying while standing upright, sitting, lying prostrate, face up, sideways and upside down, before one could shout, after shouting, after moaning unable to bear the excruciating pain... (53-54).

The eldest nymphs engages in conversation with the youngest nymph, asking her to recount her experience while flying around the world. She speaks with gloom: "...A petite flower was blooming,/ a small frightened one. / The lovely tiny flower/ was quite enchantingly beautiful/...I had extended my hands/ to pluck and adorn it on my ears. / ...Taking me to be a human being/ the flower lamented...don't touch me...I hate the stench of humans"(55-6). Giving such a message of hatred for human kind for perpetrating atrocities, the nymph keeps rolling on the ground in agony. The elderly nymph consoles her saying that fighting and killing among human kind has been their heritage. She opines that even communicating with the Almighty would reveal the same. The nymphs leave and are seen communicating with each other. The Unseen Force tells them to appease the Immortal Mother to ward of disasters. After communicating with the Unseen Force, the nymphs leave. *Hi-Leima*, taking the form of a bird, perches on the loom. The old man *Puwari* is seen pulling a cart full of dead bodies and other articles he has collected. He speaks of *Konok Thengra*, a scholar, who wrote about the passage of time in *Puya* where all the dead scholars worried about the condition of the earth. He also begins to paint pictures of humanity through the ages. He calls himself 'History' personified, used to picking up dead bodies of those killed in man's inordinate hunger for power. He further begins to tell *Hi-leima* about the predictions of Nostradamus – on the World Wars and the inhuman tortures and genocide; on massacres by Hitler, Mussolini and Russian soldiers; on Japanese bombing of Pearl Harbour and the subsequent US bombing of Hiroshima and Nagasaki.

The old man busies himself making something out of the articles in his cart. After completing his task, *Puwari* begins to talk again giving details of the bombing of Hiroshima for which Naval Captain William D. Parsons was responsible:

> At 0245 hours, on the 6th of August, we took off from the Italian Air Base.
>
> At 0300 hours, we checked the trigger for dropping the bomb for the last time.
>
> At 0605 hours, we flew over Iwo Jima, towards Japan.
>
> At 0741 hours, we received weather clear report of our third target.

At 0904 hours, we changed our course to the west.

At 0915 hours 30 seconds we dropped the bomb (62).

Scene II opens as *Hi-Liema* is seen trapped under a fallen tree, experiencing excruciating pain and immobility. She recollects how she had seen children go to school in the morning when explosion took place. Bright circular objects flared up as the sky darkened. The city was covered with a mushroom shaped cloud and spiral clouds hung above the city. Countless men, women and children died. No one was there to assist the injured who cried for help. Seeing everything destroyed, *Hi-liema* agonising in pain, flies away. She limps back home as she cries aloud, "I'm dying, I'm dying. Please save me. I'm dying of thirst, a drop of water, a drop of water...please. Water...water" (64). Her sisters embrace and console her.

The third scene opens as *Puwari* is seen fixing crosses at the cemetery and offering flowers at the graves. He keeps uttering words of remembrance of the departed ones. After his round, he climbs on his cart and salutes as bugle sounds. He also reads out the names of a few soldiers who lost their lives.

In the fourth scene *Puwari* visits the house of the nymphs. The eldest nymph is busy weaving cloth. As the old man calls out and walks in, dragging his cart along, the nymph is delighted to behold him. He dances around joyfully. *Hi-pokpi* invites him to rest for a while and puff tobacco and drink *Manthak* brew from gourd-bottle. He tells her how she broods over the unsettled times of suffering. She speaks out, "The Earth is suffering like anything, *Epu*. The story of killing never ends. War after war, war-mongering cowards –I'm at a loss, *Epu*, how will the future generation survive amidst the smoke of revenge, punishment and genocide" (67). He joins her thoughts and speaks of his despair pulling his cart full of dead bodies, since love has vanished in the wake of hatred and revenge. *Yai-leima*, tells about her plan to visit Angkor Wat to see the genocide in Cambodia during the Khmer

Rouge regime. *Hi-pokpi* requests the old man to stop *Yai-leima* from her trip. But he is of the opinion that she should go on her mission. He also wishes to follow her and pick up dead bodies from the battlefields. *Puwari* pulls *Yai-leima* into his cart to make the journey. *Hi-pokpi* muses on the wisdom of human society and the untold suffering caused by warfare throughout human history.

In the fifth scene *Yai-leima* appears in the form of a widow, a victim of Khmer Rouge regime, trying to nurse her dehydrated and starved child. She tries to make her child open his eyes. She is unable to feed him with her breasts gone dry due to starvation and malnutrition. But her child doesn't respond to her call: "What happened? What happened to you? Cry, cry out – at least once, cry out, my child…my child has refused to cry, do you hear me?" (72). As she wails and sobs, she turns into a bird and flies away.

In the sixth scene, four of the nymphs fly away to West Asia and Europe to observe the devastation wrought about by warfare. *Hi-pokpi* is worried about their safety. Suddenly the nymphs transform themselves into four war victims. They are kept in prison and tortured. The soldiers rape them, leading to their giving birth to bastard children they detest. One of them cries out: "War, you have made us prostitutes/ War, you have made us prisoners/ War you have made us bonded slaves…/The lump of blood growing day by day…growing in my womb" (73). She cannot accept the babe growing in her womb, the child of rape. Though she could hear it call her 'Mother…Mother', she hated it as the leftover of some inhuman one. She even pleads, "Why don't you die in the womb. / Why are you torturing me,/ over and over again?/ It's unbearable – it's unbearable. / Mother! Mother! Mother!" (74). After she gives birth to her unwanted child, she holds it in her arms and pleads how she could purify her defiled body. "With what face can I stand before my husband and relatives? I hate myself for being alive" (75). Her anguish is so deep rooted, she decides to commit suicide. As the sequence changes, four bodies of women are shown hanging with ropes from branches of trees. A baby is shown lying in a corner. Mother Teresa comes in with her sisters and picks up the child and carries it in her arms. The four women turn into birds and fly away.

In the epilogue, the playwright presents the eldest nymph, weaving cloth as her sisters stand beside her. She sings:"O boat, o boat, you seem not to be moving. / I'm taking the Almighty on board. /...we carry humans, like small children. / But, the enemy among the humans never ceases" (76). For her, what is left behind is only a river of blood as she wants to complete weaving the cloth. They all want to cut the cloth and dance together and offer it to the Almighty, the Creator of living beings. They pray to him to put an end to conflict and war and usher in an era of prosperity, peace and harmony on earth. They put down the cloth as an offering to God praying:

> O Father forgive our sins
> save us from making mistakes,
> with these words
> at your divine feet
> we are paying obeisance (77).

As the prayer is offered, the eldest nymph comes under a spell and collapses, while her sisters, the nymphs, turn to birds and fly away. The old man *Puwari* appears crawling. He wraps himself with the cloth they had offered to the Almighty. A languished *Puwari* confesses how he had been made a weakling by the selfishness of mankind. He is determined to write human history in his chest in blood. He pleads with the nymphs to fly away to various places. He asks them to collect the dust from the demolished image of Buddha and sprinkle it all over the corners of the earth with the message of peace. He wants them to offer flowers at Ground Zero where the Twin Towers once stood. He longs for peace to dawn on human kind and meet again the nymphs. "...O birds!. . . Oh, my dear flags!/ Hey flags, all of you,/ why is United Nations,/ formed by all of you coming together,/

to make the world a better place to live in,/hiding behind the shadow/of only the rich countries?/Punishment is given to/only the weaker countries,/why this partiality?" (78). He gives a peep into the various maladies of the world such as: children dying of starvation, sick and diseased who are denied medical care, fathers selling children, humans selling their body parts and the like. Seeing the misery of the world he cries out, "I, *Puwari*, have bee made a weakling/by the selfish nature of human beings./But, I will continue to write,/history on my chest/with blood as ink" (79).

From henceforth *Puwari* would be reduced to an open history book. The play ends with an open history book lying on a wheelchair as UN flags flutter on a platform with frozen birds in flight. The playwright has very imaginatively woven the theme of his hunger for world peace and harmony, travelling through a ravaged world history, germinating hope of peace in the hearts of his readers. In the play, there is a perfect blending of the traditional Manipuri theatrical technique with contemporary issues, reaching out to a universal audience. The play, thus, projects Thiyam's deep concern for social and spiritual welfare of humanity in the midst of socio-political conflicts and warfare.

Works Cited

"Ratan Thiyam." http://en. wikipedia. org/wiki/Ratan_Thiyam.

Thiyam, Ratan. "My Earth, My Love." Manipur Trilogy. Guwahati:WordSmith Publications, 2008. 45-79.

12

Myth Criticism and Fiction Inspiration

P.V.L. Sailaja

This paper attempts a brief overview of the conceptual and philosophical grounding of myth criticism. The various theories of myth which inform myth criticism and the major mythological traditions of the world including Indian mythology have been dealt with in brief. It also traces the relationship between myth and Indian English literature. Within the vast literary canvass of Indian English writing, the novels of Chitra Banerjee Divakaruni have been located as being inspired by the ancient Indian myths and folklore. Myth criticism is regarded as one of the major literary movements of the twentieth century. It traces the relationship between myth and literary thinking. It analyses the myths originating in a particular socio-cultural context and how they influence the literary trends of that geographical region. Similarly the universality of myths and their appeal to the human imagination is another chief tenet of this school of criticism.

Myth critics try to bring out the essential unity in terms of theme, symbolism and imagery between the myths of different cultures from across the globe. Myths are regarded by these critics as reflections of a profound reality which dramatically represents the instinctual understanding of human beings. Mythology has provided themes for some of the world's greatest literary classics. Hence it becomes mandatory for the literary critic to go to the origins of the literary text, the mythical background from which it draws its inspiration. Myth, legend and folk-tale are three very basic terms utilized in folklore. They are used very loosely and have sometimes been hotly disputed. William Bascom defines folk-tales as prose narratives which are regarded as fiction. According to him, myths can be regarded as prose narratives of the society in which they are told and are considered to be truthful accounts of what happened in the remote past. Bascom argues that legends are also prose narratives which like myth, are regarded as true by the narrator and his audience, but are set in a period considered less remote and when the condition of the world is similar to what it is in the present day context.

Several reasons have been cited by critics for the invention of tales and myths. Myth is considered as an imaginative tale which has no real existence in the French language. Anonymity of its authorship is one of its major characteristic. They are the tales that have been passed on from one generation to another orally. Plato, who coined this term, defined mythology as the attempted narration of stories which in actuality have some serious underlying purpose and try to interpret and create divinity and religion. The philosophical grounding of this school of criticism can be traced to diverse multi-disciplinary strands of thought like the psychology of Jung, social and structural anthropology, the study of religions, analysis of literary metaphors and depth psychology. It is based largely on the works of C.G. Jung, Joseph Campbell, Robert Graves, Francis Fergusson, Philip Wheelwright, Leslie Fiedler, Northrop Frye, Maud Bodkin, G. Wilson Knight and myth itself. All these critics view the genres and individual plot patterns of literature as the recurrences of certain archetypes and mythic formulae. Percy S. Cohen discusses about myth in the following manner:

> The chief characteristics of myth are as follows:a myth is a narrative of events; the narrative has a sacred quality; the sacred communication is made in symbolic form; at least some of the events and objects which occur in the myth neither occur nor exist in the world other than that of myth itself; and the narrative refers in dramatic form to origins or transformations. The narrative

> quality distinguishes a myth from a general idea or set of ideas, such as a cosmology. The sacred quality and the reference to origins and transformations distinguish myth from legend and other types of folk-tale. The narration of events and reference to objects unknown outside the world of myth differentiates myth from history or pseudo-history.
>
> (Cohen 1969)

Any study of myths or theory of myth is essentially comparative as mythology has been regarded as a common trait of humanity and a way of interpreting the experiences of life and philosophy through universal narratives that transcend ethnic and cultural differences. However several objections have been raised that while bringing out the similarities between the various myths, the overt differences of the mythological traditions have been ignored by the myth critics. We may argue that all these differences of opinion arise due to the fact this school accommodates a vast area of human experience and is also open to discussion and analysis from a number of angles and perspectives which are highly divergent in their approach and methodology.

Karen Armstrong's in her book *A Short History of Myth* (2005) argues that myths emerged or developed during various historical periods and relate directly to the material and cultural circumstances of the human situation at that time. She points out that the modern age is characterized by a split between *mythos* and *logos*, between story and logic or reason. Armstrong traces the split back to the Greeks, where Plato wanted to banish poets from his ideal republic, although it is worth noting that Plato himself made effective use of myth in his own writing. Modern notions of truth are firmly grounded in *logos* and are defined by history and science. According to Armstrong, the modern world lives largely without compelling myths. She discusses how writers, artists, and poets like T.S. Eliot, Picasso, Joyce, Orwell, Conrad and Thomas Mann have stepped in to fill this void.

Marcus O'Donnell in "Myth and Meaning" in the *Good Weekend* has suggested that theories of intertextuality and narrative identity can assist in the development of a more cogent theory of myth and concludes with a multidimensional definition of myth drawn from this analysis. This is the definitional matrix he gives based on his study of myth:

"1. Myths are meaning seeking narratives that grow in narrative power through repetition, evolution and adaptation.

"2. Myths bring into dialogue past, present and emerging paradigms; they deploy interactive sets of symbolic codes; although traditionally associated with religious or sacred stories and symbols, contemporary myths draw on a range of psychological, socio-political and scientific images and frameworks.

"3. Individual myths are best understood as a node at the centre of a complex network of inter-related stories; as broad, intertextual narratives, myths can act as literary organising devices, which bring different, sometimes contradictory, textual elements into dialogue with one another.

"4. Myths are social stories, which emerge out of commonly understood cultural frameworks; they narrate themes of fundamental importance to cultural groups; they can serve to confirm or challenge broadly held cultural beliefs.

"5. Myths also provide narrative frameworks that are used by individuals to help organise experience; they influence personal identity formation; they can provide both restrictive and transformative models of subjectivity.

"6. Myth is a pervasive narrative form:myths and mythic references can be identified in common speech, literary works, religious texts, journalism and other popular cultural forms.

"7. Narratives that are not themselves myths can draw on mythic themes and serve mythic functions through strategies of allusion and explicit invocation.

"8. Different myths and mythic references function with different degrees of emotional and effective power; they can be used as a simple type of narrative shorthand ('Steve Waugh is an Australian hero') or as a powerful life-changing story ('I've been saved by Jesus').

"9. Sets of interlocking mythic stories can act together to form a cohesive mythology, which can work as a powerful ideological framework that underwrites either progressive or regressive directions for personal and cultural change.

"10. Attempts to mobilise particular mythic forms can be either intentional or unintentional, however their ultimate interpretation and use is cultural, resulting from unpredictable text audience interactions; any particular interpretation therefore is never completely foreclosed and must be recognised as a possible reading." (O'Donnell 2003)

Percy S. Cohen gives an overview of a number of influential theories on myth. Speaking about the necessity for a unified theory of myth assimilating the different extent theories, Cohen says:

> A theory of myth should explain something about the phenomenon:that is, it should explain a statement which refers to some aspect or aspects of the phenomenon. There are many theories of myth, but they are not necessarily rival theories:the reason for this is that different theories often explain different statements about myth. Particular theories may, of course, explain several statements about myth and they may therefore compete, partly or wholly, with other theories. But there is inevitable confusion in the debate between different proponents of different theories if they do not make it clear whether they are true rivals and what the area of their rivalry is.
>
> (Cohen 1969)

Cohen enumerates and explains the various theories on myth:

> There are seven main types of theory of myth:that which treats myth as a form of explanation and, in particular, a form which occurs at a certain stage in the development of human society and culture; that which treats myth as a form of symbolic statement which has the function, not of explanation, but of expression as an end in itself, and which reflects a particular type of thought, the mythopoeic; that which treats it as an expression of the unconscious; that which accounts for it in terms of its function in creating and maintaining social solidarity, cohesion, etc.; that which stresses its function in legitimating social institutions and social practices; that which treats it as a form of symbolic statement about social structure, possibly linked with ritual; and, finally, there is the structuralist theory.
>
> (Cohen 1969)

Literature employs words and the reality behind words has been one of the central concerns of twentieth century philosophy. Linguistic philosophy attempts to explain the use of linguistic signs and codes, and their reception. Structuralism describes literature as the expression of deep anthropological and often binary codes which contradict each other. Poststructuralist thought is built on the premise that words are an endless web of yet more words having no final referent or meaning. Postmodernism regards words as flat, media images, without any deeper significance.

Thus we can come to the conclusion that all the literary and philosophical schools of the twentieth century envision the infinite power of words if employed in a certain way and their deep and lasting impact on the human psyche. Mythic criticism is subsequent to literature just as history is to action. Plot and character are the skeletal requirements of literature which can be regarded as an output an artist's imagination, and myth criticism delves deep into the myth or the pictorial imagery and symbols from which the artist's inspiration emerges.

Mythology of some kind has been produced by all races. Among the mythological traditions, Greek and Roman mythology deserve a special mention. Greek mythology has served as a source of inspiration for Greek poets, then those of Rome, and later all whom Roman culture reached. For the Greeks, mythology served as a basis to explain the world and how it works. The Greeks believed that natural events, from the rising of the moon to thunderstorms were caused by the will of the gods. Some Greek myths dealt with their heroes. Each city had its own hero, real or fictional, who would slay terrible monsters and save its people. One popular example of this is the Greek hero Hercules.

Greek myths were adapted by the Romans who did not have a separate mythological tradition of their own a few tales about early Rome and events that led toward its founding. However, the Romans played an important role in preserving the Greek mythological heritage and transmitting it to later European civilizations. Roman mythology comprises a combination of beliefs, rituals, and observances of supernatural occurrences from the early periods until Christianity completely replaced the native religions of the Roman Empire.

While Roman mythology may lack an extensive body of narratives dealing with the divine or supernatural as that of Greek literature, Latin literature was more popular in Europe throughout the middle ages and the Renaissance. Hence the interpretation of Greek myths by the Romans had a greater influence on narrative and pictorial representations of classical mythology than their Greek sources. In particular, Virgil's *Aeneid* and the myths represented in Ovid's *Metamorphoses* have been given a canonical status.

Both British mythology and Bible myth have inspired English writers in their works of literature to a great extent. Indian writing in English, though a separate entity in itself, has drawn several ideas from the British literary tradition. British mythology is replete with myths of warrior kings, noble outlaws and stirring deeds. This tradition emanates from a pre-Celtic race of people who were once spread across most of Britain. This mythological tradition comes down to the present day through the Welsh and most of it was recorded in the written form around the tenth century, when it had acquired overlays of other traditions such as Christianity. Successive waves of invaders and settlers like the Romans, Saxons, Jutes, Anglos, Norse up to the French in the Norman Conquest have all influenced the myth and legend of England. Over the years, the traditions of the new settlers had infused with the existing English customs to form a unique mythological tradition.

The earliest and most influential mythical story of the British is the epic poem *Beowulf* written by a poet of unknown origin. Though brought to England by the Angles who invaded England, the story is of Scandinavian origin. It is about a young hero called Beowulf who saves his country from a monster named Grendel whom he overcomes with great bravery and valour. In the later periods, we find the emergence of several distinctive mythical folk heroes and their legends, many of which are influenced by history like the myths of King Arthur, Hereward the Wake, Robin Hood, and the lost land of Lyonesse.

Christian mythology is the vast group of myths associated with Christianity. In Christian myth there are three main characters, namely Jehovah, or God the Father, the Virgin Mary, and Jesus Christ the Savior. Christian or Bible myth also comprises several beliefs like the original sin, Jesus Christ's death by crucifixion, his resurrection on the third day, a friend and close associate who back stabs like Judas, a messiah with the power to give salvation to all which keep on recurring in several English works as figures of speech or serve as a source of inspiration to the writers who remodel these ideas in the present day context with similar situations. The myths within the New Testament Bible and other religious documents serve as the foundation of the Christian myth which has grown into a widespread mythological tradition.

Indian culture possesses an inexhaustible lore of myths, parables and legends that pattern and define it. The earliest and most ancient texts of India are the *Vedas* which have been subdivided in four, the *Rig*, *Yajur*, *Sama* and *Atharva*. Based on philological and linguistic evidence, we can come to the conclusion that the *Rig Veda*, the oldest of the *Vedas*, was composed roughly between 1700–1100 B.C., also referred to as the early Vedic period. According to common estimates, the end of the period is commonly estimated to have occurred about 500 B.C. and 150 B.C.

The *Vedas* comprise hymns and chants on several gods belonging to the Hindu pantheon. The *Vedas* were passed on from generation to generation orally. They were codified by Veda Vyasa, the author of *Mahabharata* much later in history. By that time, many portions of the *Vedas* were lost. One important observation which we can make from this is that if hymns and chants on gods and goddesses were in existence, then their myths or a tradition uniting them must belong to an earlier period.

The *Upanishads* come at a later period than the *Vedas* when we discuss ancient Indian texts. Historians and Indologists have fixed the date of composition of the *Upanishads* from 800 B.C. to 400 B.C. They were composed over a very long period of time and do not represent a coherent body of information or one particular system of belief, though there is a commonality of thought and approach. They are considered as philosophical treatises. Although there are more than two hundred *Upanishads*, only thirteen have been identified out of them as presenting the core teachings. There are several *Upanishads* whose commentary or discussion revolves round a mythical story. To cite an example, the famous *Katha Upanishad* is based on the myth of Nachiketa. The *Upanishads* are structured in the form of a dialogue between a realized soul acting as the preceptor, and a sincere seeker of truth who acts as the disciple. In *Katha Upanishad*, the teacher is Yama, the Hindu God of Death and the student is Nachiketa. This *Upanishad* is one of the most popular *Upanishads* and known for its simplicity and clarity of thought in making the subject matter regarding the highest truth easily comprehensible.

The *Puranas* and *Ithihasas* come at a later period in history. The *Puranas* were written to popularize the religion of the *Vedas*. They contain the Vedic essence and impress on the minds of the masses the teachings of the *Vedas* through concrete examples, myths, stories, legends, lives of saints, kings and great men, allegories and chronicle great historical events. The *Puranas* were meant, not for the scholars, but for the ordinary people who could not understand high philosophy or study the *Vedas*.

There are eighteen *Puranas* and eighteen *Upa-Puranas* or sub-Puranas and two major *Ithihasas* from which most of the myths and legends that inspire the Indian psyche have originated. The major *Puranas* are *Vishnu Purana*, *Naradiya Purana*, *Srimad Bhagavata Purana*, *Garuda (Suparna) Purana*, *Padma Purana*, *Varaha Purana*, *Brahma Purana*, *Brahmanda Purana*, *Brahma Vaivarta Purana*, *Markandeya Purana*, *Bhavishya Purana*, *Vamana Purana*, *Matsya Purana*, *Kurma Purana*, *Linga Purana*, *Siva Purana*, *Skanda Purana* and *Agni Purana*.

The *Upa-Puranas* are *Sanatkumara*, *Narasimha*, *Brihannaradiya*, *Sivarahasya*, *Durvasa*, *Kapila*, *Vamana*, *Bhargava*, *Varuna*, *Kalika*, *Samba*, *Nandi*, *Surya*, *Parasara*, *Vasishtha*, *Devi Bhagavatam*, *Ganesa* and *Hamsa*. The *Ithihasas* or the histories, the *Ramayana* and *Mahabharata* are an inexhaustible treasure trove of Indian myths and the Indian culture. All these constitute the Hindu way of life which is called the 'Sanatana Dharma' or an old and ancient way of life that is relevant even in the present day context. All these later texts like the *Upanishads*, the *Puranas*, the *Upa-Puranas* and the Ithihasas have their roots in the *Vedas*.

This vast mythical background has served as a wonderful canvass for the literary genius of several Indian English writers like R.K. Narayan, Raja Rao, Girish Karnad, Githa Hariharan, and Chitra Banerjee Divakaruni who have exploited it in their works. R.K. Narayan (10 October 1906–13 May 2001) is regarded as one of the pioneering figures on the scene of Indian English Writing along with Mulk Raj Anand and Raja Rao. The setting for all his novels is a fictional town called Malgudi.

A very prolific writer, Narayan has fifteen novels to his credit. He has also authored three books on Indian mythology: *Gods, Demons and Others* (1964), *The Ramayana* (1973), and *The Mahabharata* (1978). Most of his novels use metaphors and figures of speech drawn from Indian mythology. For example, three of his major novels, namely, *The English Teacher* (1945), *The Man-Eater of Malgudi* (1961) and *The Painter of Signs* (1977) make use of three popular Indian myths, the Savitri-Satyavan myth, the Bhasmasura myth and the Shantanu-Ganga myth, respectively.

Raja Rao (November 8, 1908–July 8, 2006) is regarded as one among the Indian English trinity and has works of fiction like *Kanthapura* (1938), *The Serpent and the Rope* (1960), *The Cat and Shakespeare* (1965) and *Comrade Kirilov* (1976) to his credit. Speaking about Raja Rao's use of myth, S. P. Swain points out:

> Rao makes a digressional use of myth.... Rao employs three types of myths in his novels:(1) Puranic Myths (2) Localised Myths and (3) Rites and Rituals.... The Rama-Ravana myth appears to be the central thematic motif of *Kanthapura*. The novel is a fictional rendering of a localised myth (such as that of Kenchamma), it is the legendary history of a remote hamlet in the Western Coast of India. In order to create the mythic atmosphere in the novel, Raja Rao has resorted to the depiction of the rites and rituals of ploughing, of worship and sacrifice.
>
> (Swain 2001)

In *The Serpent and the Rope*, Rao utilizes the myth of Radha and Krishna and juxtaposes the mythological parallel with the contemporary world and which constitutes the thematic motif of the novel.

Girish Karnad (1938) is a pre-eminent contemporary writer, playwright, screen-writer, actor and movie director in the language of Kannada. His plays were written in Kannada, and have later been translated into English and all the major Indian languages. He takes up fragments of historical and legendary experience and fuses them into a forceful statement. He tries to link the past and the present, the archetypal and the real, by presenting current issues of the present world with their parallels in the myths and fables of the past, and reinforcing the theme. Karnad believes in the Jung's theory of archetypes and a collective racial consciousness and turns to the past for his source of inspiration. All his plays right from *Yayati* (1961) to *Tale-Danda* (1990) are based on myths and tales with which his audience is more or less familiar. Karnad has justified himself by arguing that he has gone back to the old myths, histories and oral tales not because he does not have creative and imaginative power, but because they are very much relevant even in the present context.

Yayati is based on the story of King Yayati, one of the ancestors of the Pandavas, who was cursed to suffer the pangs of premature old age by his father-in-law, Shukracharya, as a consequence of his infidelity towards his daughter, Devyani. Yayati pleads all his sons, one by one, to sacrifice their youth for him as he wanted to enjoy youth for many more years. Puru, his youngest son agrees to this ridiculous demand. *Hayavadana* (1971) is another influential play of Karnad which draws from folk forms like Yakshagana and heavily based on folk mythology. It is based on a theme drawn from *The Transposed Heads (1*940), a novella authored by Thomas Mann. It is originally found in the *Kathasaritasagara*. *Naga-Mandala* (1988) is again influenced by a famous folk tale narrated to him by A.K. Ramanujam. *The Fire and the Rain* (1995) centers round a myth found in the *Mahabharata* about two brothers, Aravasu and Paravasu and their cousin brother Yavakri.

Githa Hariharan (1958) is an Indian novelist who has written works of fiction like *The Thousand Faces of Night* (1992), *The Ghosts of Vasu Master* (1994), *When Dreams Travel* (1999), *In*

Times of Siege (2003), and *Fugitive Histories* (2009). She takes up Indian myths from the *Ramayana* and *Mahabharata* and relates them to the women characters of her first novel, *The Thousand Faces of Night.* The plot of the novel revolves around three women, Devi, the protagonist; Sita, her mother; and Mayamma, the caretaker-cum-cook. Hariharan deftly explores gender relations utilizing women characters from Indian mythology like Gandhari, Amba, Damayanthi and others, and draws the parallel between them and the characters in her novel.

In this context, we cannot ignore the contribution made by Shashi Tharoor's *The Great Indian Novel* (1989) that takes the story of the *Mahabharata* and recasts it in the context of the Indian Independence Movement and the first three decades post-independence. Figures from Indian history are transformed into characters from mythology, and the *Mahabharata* is retold as a history of Indian independence and the subsequent historical events till the 1980s.

Chitra Banerjee Divakaruni deserves a special mention when we consider the writers who have explored the mythical background of India, and have utilized concepts drawn from parapsychology, magic, and fantasy literature. After carefully analyzing her works, especially her novels, we can conclude that her works deal with diverse elements like the immigrant experience, the role of women in India and America, clash of cultures, the complexities of relationships, magic, myth, and fantasy.

Divakaruni's works have figured in over 50 literary anthologies, including *Best American Short Stories*, *The O' Henry Prize Stories* and *The Pushcart Prize Anthology*. Her book of short stories, *Arranged Marriage* won the American Book Award for the year 1996, the Bay Area Book Reviewers Award and the PEN Josephine Miles Award for fiction. *The Mistress of Spices* found its place of honour in several *Best Books* lists, including the San Francisco Chronicle's *100 Best Books of the 20th Century*. Two novels of her novels, *The Mistress of Spices (1997)* and *Sister of My Heart (*1999), have also been made into films. At present, she is teaching Creative Writing at the University of Houston.

Divakaruni's sojourn into the world of poetry begins prior to her entry into the world of fiction. She was already an acclaimed poet by the time she started writing short stories and novels. Her poems deal with a variety of themes with particular focus on the immigrant experience and the experiences of South Asian women living in America. She depicts the experiences and struggles of these women trying carve a new identity for themselves in a land and culture completely alien to their motherland.

Chitra Banerjee Divakaruni is also the editor of *Multitudes*, an anthology which she widely makes use of in her own classroom. It includes stories about communication styles across cultures, expectations from friendships, the Los Angeles riots, and prejudice against gay people. It also contains works by a variety of authors including her own students. Similarly, Divakaruni has been influenced and inspired by the Indian myths and legends which she grew up hearing from her grandfather as a child in India. Speaking about those experiences, she says:

> When I was a child in India, my grandfather would tell me stories from the *Ramayan* and *Mahabharat*, the ancient Indian epics. I loved to hear about the wondrous exploits of divine warrior heroes such as Ram and Krishna, and the magical weapons—the enormous bow, the fiery discus—with which they destroyed evil kings and demons. There were human heroes too—the prince Arjun, the greatest archer in the world and Krishna's best friend; Guha, the tribal chieftain who loved Ram with all his heart. Their friendships—unselfish, devoted, noble—were meant to inspire us to similar emotions.
>
> Even more than the men, I loved the great women of the epics. There was Ram's wife Sita, who gave up the pleasures of the palace to follow her exiled husband to the forest. There was Draupadi, who exacted a terrible vengeance for the humiliation she had to suffer at the hands of her husband's enemies. There was Queen

> Kunti, who could call down gods to father her children. There was Shabari, whose entire life was illuminated by her faith in Ram.
>
> (Divakaruni 1998)

From these lines, we can understand that the ancient Indian myths and legends have played an important part in stimulating her artistic and creative potential.

Divakaruni's first novel is *The Mistress of Spices* (1997). The protagonist of this novel is Tilo, who runs a grocery store in California and uses spices to help the customers overcome difficulties. Tilo provides spices, not only for cooking, but also to counter the homesickness and alienation that the Indian immigrants face in a foreign land where they are not fully accepted in her shop. In the process, she falls in love with a non-Indian and has to choose whether to serve her people or to follow the path leading to her own happiness. It shows Tilo's dilemma regarding which parts of her heritage she will keep and which parts she will chose to abandon.

The Mistress of Spices symbolically represents the struggles and inner turmoil faced by a population which has moved geographically, politically, socially and culturally from its homeland India, and is trying to come to terms with a new existence in an alien land. Hence it can also be read and analyzed using the concept of Diaspora. In *The Mistress of Spices*, Tilo and the customers whom she tries to help are all trying to re-establish their ties with India with the help of an ancient heritage which they share in common. The spices and their mystery is a unique link which makes them reminisce about their common past with nostalgia.

The novel ends with Tilo finding a new life and new name to give meaning to her existence. She gives herself the name Maya. The name has a number of connotations like illusion, spell and enchantment. She tells that this naming is very different from her previous naming ceremony where the Old One and other sister-

Mistresses were present to witness and bless her. This name suits her in this new world order where she has only herself to hold her up and show the right path.

This was followed up by the two novels *Sister of My Heart (1999)* and *Vine of Desire (2002)* which trace the ups and downs in the relationship Sudha and Anju and their journey in life from young budding girls into matured women who have seen the world in all its aspects, beautiful and ugly. The plot of these novels moves back and fro between India and America. Search for identity, nostalgia, the conflict of choices, women's issues, myth, and folklore are important themes which figure in both the novels. Both Anju and Sudha grow up in India hearing fairytales, myths, legends and various superstitions by their widowed aunt, Pishi who also lived with them in their ancestral house. Sudha believes in the mystery of these stories and is fascinated by them.

If we compare their childhood expectations and dreams in life, we find that almost all of them conflict with the reality. Anju's husband, Sunil leaves her at that point of time when she needs him the most. She loses her baby in a miscarriage. Neither does she travel the world nor is her life full of happiness. She experiences the loneliness and insecurity of leading a life in America, far away from the place of her birth, Kolkata. She has a very troubled married life with an authoritative mother-in-law who sees her only as a child-bearing machine who will continue the family name and an unpaid servant who will take care of the house. After five long years of marriage when she conceives, she wants her to abort it as it is a girl child. She leaves behind the safety and security of her married life in order to protect her unborn child. Neither beauty nor her goodness saves her from the fate of being a divorcee.

Sister of My Heart has been divided into two books. The first book has been titled 'The Princess in the Palace of Snakes' utilizing an ancient legend in which a little girl was brought up by the snakes in an underground lake with no knowledge of the outside world. One day she saw the outside world and fell in love with a handsome prince. But she was forced to go to the kingdom of a strange king due to various circumstances. In the myth, the princess reunites with her prince towards the end after crossing many hurdles and difficulties. The same myth recurs throughout this book with subtle changes of tone, mood and situation to suit the life of the two sisters. The original myth is transformed into an entirely new creation which has its own relevance in the life of the two sisters.

The second book of *Sister of My Heart* titled 'The Queen of Swords' utilizes the story of the historical figure of Rani Lakshmi Bai who was the queen of Jhansi. Lakshmi Bai was born on 19th November 1835 and was known as 'Jhansi Ki Rani', or the queen of Jhansi. She was one of the leading figures of the First War of Indian Independence which broke out in 1857. She is widely admired in India as one of the pioneers of the Indian struggle for independence against the British colonial rule. She is regarded as the epitome of female bravery in India. Divakaruni compares the queen's struggle to save her offspring from the evil clutches of the conspirators with Sudha's struggle to save her yet unborn daughter, Dayita. There is an intermingling of fact and fiction in this book as both Sudha and Anju recreate and reinvent the historical figure of Lakshmi Bai in their minds to suit their present day needs. As the novel progresses, the original incidents in Lakshmi Bai's life undergo a clear and perceptible change because they are more in tune with Sudha's and Anju's life. The Lakshmi Bai's life which they invent is different from that of the historical and legendary queen Lakshmi Bai. Sudha often tells the story of the brave and courageous queen of Jhansi to her daughter Dayita in order to draw strength and inspiration to face the various problems in her life.

The Vine of Desire continues the story of the two sisters, Sudha and Anju and narrates the conflict and inteplay of wishes, desires, emotions and actions of the major characters Sudha, Anju and Sunil and their impact on their respective lives. Hence the two novels have to be read in conjunction with each other for a proper understanding of their plot and content. Though there are several similarities between both the novels, there is a great deal of stylistic variation between the two novels.

The next novel *Neela: Victory Song (2002)* is set in 1939 and tells the inspiring tale of twelve-year-old Neela to free her father who has been jailed following a march against British rule. It brings to life a particular era in Indian history and the conditions at that point of time. It also talks about the potential and indomitable bravery present in every individual to overcome the odds for a good cause. Though there is considerable time gap in between and other novels from Divakaruni also appeared in the intervening period, *The Conch Bearer* (2003), *The Mirror of Fire and Dreaming* (2005), and *Shadowland* (2009) have to be considered together as all of them are parts of a trilogy dealing with a world of magic, fantasy, adventure, and myth. The trilogy revolves round a conch, a magical object with immense powers to shape, redefine, control, or even destroy the whole world. The conch is the most powerful magical object possessed by a brotherhood of healers. It is placed in a crystal shrine at the centre of this brotherhood.

Divakaruni even bestows a mythical significance to the magical conch. Originally the conch belonged to Nakul and Sahadev, the youngest of the Pandava brothers in Vyasa's *Mahabharata*. The conch is a gift from their divine fathers, the Ashwini twins who are responsible for healing and curing diseases. The conch was taken away from them when they overstepped their bounds by trying to resuscitate the dead during the battle of Kurukshetra.

After several hundreds of years, the conch resurfaced and fell into the hands of a hill tribe, who recognizing its power passed it on to a holy man. Over the years a group of like-minded people with magical powers and the noble intention of serving humanity congregated round the conch and formed the brotherhood of healers in the Silver Valley. The conch thus becomes the guiding force for this secret brotherhood established in the secret mountain folds of the Himalayas, in the pristine Silver Valley.

In the first novel of the trilogy, *The Conch Bearer*, tragedy strikes this peaceful brotherhood when Surabhanu, a black-sheep within the brotherhood, steals the conch. Abhaydatta, one of the healers, seeks the help of Anand, a twelve-year-old boy, and also the protagonist of this trilogy, to restore the conch to its rightful place in mountain reaches of the Himalayas. They are accompanied on their journey by Nisha, a spirited sweeper girl. Together they overpower the wicked intentions of Surabhanu. They come to be known the Company of the Conch and Anand is made the Keeper of the Conch by the healers of the Silver Valley when the conch is restored to its rightful place. In *The Mirror of Fire and Dreaming* and *Shadowland*, Anand and his companions travel through time to the past and the future, respectively, and mend the sorry state of affairs in those worlds, and relieve some of the sorrows and problems faced by the people of those eras. Both these novels subvert the concept of space and time and show the presence of worlds within worlds. Divakaruni portrays the victory of good over evil in this trilogy. She also tries to visualize an alternate reality through the magical world of the Silver Valley.

Queen of Dreams (2004) is a fresh, enchanting story of transformation with a lyrical as well as a dramatic quality. Divakaruni's novel, *Queen of Dreams* is based on dreams and the occult power of dream telling. Analysis and interpretation of dreams was a well-established science in ancient Indian philosophy. We find references to dreams in a wide range of texts like *Mandukya Upanishad* (*Upanishads* are the condensed essence of the *Vedas*, holiest of Hindu scriptures), *Brihadaranyaka Upanishad*, *Katha Upanishad*, *Brahma Sutras* (Doctrines on the Almighty), and the *Ramayana*. The protagonist of the novel is Rakhi, a young artist and a divorced mother living in Berkeley,

California, struggling to retain her footing with her family and with a world in alarming transition. Her mother is a dream teller, born with the ability to share and interpret the dreams of others, to foresee and guide them through their fates. Caught beneath the burden of her own painful past, Rakhi's solace comes in the discovery, after her mother's death, of her Dream Journals, which open the door to her past and also her roots which lie in India.

The Palace of Illusions (2008) takes us back in time to a period that is half-history, half-myth, and magical. The Indian writers have often turned to the great epics of *Ramayana* and *Mahabharata* for inspiration. In her novel, *The Palace of Illusions*, Divakaruni narrates the entire story of Mahabharata from the point of view of Draupadi. Draupadi or Paanchali as she is often addressed is worshipped as a cult- goddess in many temples in south India. She is the wife of the legendary five brothers, the Pandavas.

The novel traces Panchaali's life, beginning with her magical birth in fire as the daughter of a king, her spirited balancing act as a woman with five husbands who have been cheated out of their father's kingdom, their quest to reclaim their birthright, remaining at the brothers' sides through years of exile and a terrible civil war. Panchaali is a powerful and fiery female voice in a world of warriors, gods, and ever-manipulating hands of fate.

Chitra Banerjee Divakaruni chooses to retell this epic as seen through the eyes of Draupadi. The Palace of Illusions is a magical palace built by Maya, the architect of the Rakshasas or demons on receiving instructions from her and her five husbands soon after their marriage. It plays a very important part in shaping Draupadi's identity as an individual and provides her the space to grow. That is the reason why Divakaruni titles her novel, *The Palace of Illusions.* Her most recent novel, *One Amazing Thing* (2010) begins with an earthquake which rips through the afternoon lull in an unnamed American city trapping nine highly individualistic characters together. The primary focus of all these people is to survive with very little food in an office that has started flooding. At this moment when the psychological and emotional stress seems too much for them to bear, a young graduate student suggests that each one of them tell a personal tale on "one amazing thing" from their own experiences in life. The novel proves the transcendent power of stories and the meaningfulness of human expression itself.

Most of Divakaruni's novels explore the mythical background of India. In *The Palace of Illusions*, she takes up the story of Mahabharata and narrates it from a feminist perspective. In some of her other novels, she compares her protagonists and other major characters with mythological characters. She makes use of mythological themes and figures of speech related to mythology in her narrative. Elements drawn from Indian folklore also figure prominently in her novels. Her novels also incorporate the theme of magic and the occult sciences within the framework of the literary narrative. Her literary genius to a great extent has sought its inspiration from Indian myth, folklore, legend and history.

Works Cited

Armstrong, Karen. *A Short History of Myth*. New York:Reed Business Information, 2005.

Bascom,William."The Forms of Folklore: Prose Narratives". *Journal of American Folklore*. Vol. 78 (Iss. 307). 1965. pp. 3-20.

Cohen, S. Percy. "Theories of Myth". *Man, New Series*. Vol. 4 (Iss. 3). 1969. pp. 337-353.

Divakaruni, Chitra Banerjee. *One Amazing Thing*. New York:Hyperion Books, 2010.

______. *Queen of Dreams*. London: Abacus, 2005.

______. *Shadowland*. New York: Roaring Brook Press, 2009.

______. *Sister of My Heart*. United States of America: Anchor Books, 2000.

______. *The Conch Bearer*. New York: Aladdin Paperbacks, 2005.

______. *The Mirror of Fire and Dreaming*. New Delhi: IndiaInk, 2007.

______. *The Mistress of Spices*. London: Black Swan, 1997.

______. *The Palace of Illusions*. London: Pan Macmillan Ltd, 2009.

______. *The Vine of Desire*. United States of America: Anchor Books, 2003.

______. *Victory Song*. New Delhi: Penguin Books India, 2006.

Donnell, O. Marcus. "Myth and Meaning". *Good Weekend. 2003. pp. 12-29*

Freud, Sigmund. *The Interpretation of Dreams*. London: Macmillan, 1900.

Ganguli, Kisari Mohan. *The Mahabharata of Vyasa*. New Delhi: Munshiram Manoharlal Publishers Pvt. Ltd., 1990.

Ganshyam, G.A. "Myths and Legends in the Plays of Girish Karnad". *Language in India*. Vo. 9 (Iss. 4). 2009.

Handy, J. William & Max Westbrook. *Twentieth Century Criticism*. New Delhi:Light & Life Publishers: 1976.

Hiltebeitela, L. F. *The Cult of Draupadi, I. Mythologies: From Gingee to Kuruksetra*. Chicago: The University of Chicago Press, 1988.

Rajagopalachari, C. *Mahabharata*. New Delhi: Bharatiya Vidya Bhavan, 1979.

______. *Ramayana*. New Delhi: Bharatiya Vidya Bhavan, 1957.

Vega-González, Susana. "Negotiating Boundaries in Divakaruni's *The Mistress of Spices* and Naylor's *Mama Day*". *Comparative Literature and Culture*. Vol. 5 (Iss. 2). 2003.

Vireswarananda & Adidevananda. *Brahma-sutras: Sri-Bhasya*. Calcutta:Advaita Ashrama, 1986.

Wells, H. G. *The Time Machine*. St. Petersburg: Worthington Press, 1995

Wilson, Colin. *The Occult*. London: Watkins Publishing, 2006.

Websites Consulted

www. chitradivakaruni. com

http://www. time. com/time/daily/special/india/chitra. html

http://www. english. emory. edu/Bahri/CBD. html

http://www. bookbrowse. com/author_interviews/full/index. cfm/author_number/338/chitra-banerjee-divakaruni

http://en. wikipedia. org/wiki/Indian_English_literature

http://www. githahariharan. com

13

Gita Mehta's *A River Sutra*—An Exploration

T. Sasikanth Reddy

Gita Mehta's *A River Sutra* offers authentic interpretations of Indian cultural values, music, art forms and heritage. In this novel, we find her major involvement with human subsistence in modern times.

The setting of the novel is on the banks of India's holiest river the Narmada. It is not only the setting but also the principle of the novel. It includes both a meditation and an exploration of the novel and also finds the simple pattern of the pilgrims' voyage in search of Moksha. The versatility of *A River Sutra* is that most of the characters only appear once. The progress of the six stories can be seen as variations on the theme of love and the secret of the human heart.

A river in India is generally considered as sacred and has the spiritual bliss. It is also believed that gods stay on the banks of rivers and thus there are many shrines on the banks of rivers. There is an assumption that if someone takes bath in any of the sacred rivers, their sins are purified. Since it is a spiritual belief even now also people are continuing washing away their sins.

The novel, *A River Sutra,* contains many interlinked stories within it are narrated to the narrator by other characters of the novel. Mehta presents unconnected stories in the novel - stories about Hindu and Jain ascetics, courtesans and minstrels, diamond merchants and tea executives, Muslim clerics and music teachers, tribal folks. The narrator is unnamed and unidentified in the novel, and is gaining knowledge which brings on the shores of Narmada where he meets many people and learns from them various ideas of life. Unlike most first-person narrative, the narrator in this novel, reveals very little about himself. He seems to have no life story, no main event that made him choose to live a retired life on the banks of the Narmada River. In contrast to this, the people whom the narrator meets and the stories he hears, reveal the disorderly nature of human life. Without exception, the narrator meets or hears tales of extraordinary people; people who have made enormous sacrifices for love or who have been treated cruelly by life.

The novel, *A River Sutra,* set on the bank of the river Narmade, shows how the narrator is getting experiences from the people those come/reside on the banks of the river. In the novel the narrator often meets someone who comes to rescue on the banks of the river which gives shelter to everyone who comes after some disturbance in their normal life. The narrator listens to their stories and gains experience/knowledge from their experiences. Thus the shore becomes a guide to develop the narrator's knowledge by providing him the opportunity of meeting those strangers. There are six stories; The Monk's, The Musician's, The Teacher's, The Executive's, The Courtesan's and The Minstrel's. Almost all characters in different stories converge for one or the other reason on the banks of the river for renunciation and tranquillity and breathe repeated motifs of love and rebirth. Mehta presents love as the dominant motive force in the stories.

The Indian river is considered as a religious one. Dr. Mitra in this novel also narrates how the people consider the river as a religious one. He discusses about the historical memory of the Narmada saying the great Alexandrine geographer Ptolemy wrote about Narmada. He also remembers that the Greeks and the Alexandrines had heard about the river Narmada's holiness and the religious suicides at Amarkantak. He adds that people fasting to death or immolating themselves on the river's banks, or drowning in waters to gain release from the cycle of birth and rebirth. Dr. Mitra says thus:

> In the silence I can hear waves lapping at the riverbanks and I think of the ascetics meditating by the holy pool at Amarkantak, seeking through their meditations to liberate themselves from the cycle of rebirth and death.
>
> (Gita Mehta 42.)

Thus the spiritual bliss the river has was an age old belief and is being followed by many who come to the banks of the Narmada to worship her. Both the narrator and Dr. Mitra, narrator's friend, also believe that the river has some spiritual power within it. They somehow believe the stories told by the strangers. Dr. Mitra feels happy being in the banks of the river and shares his observations with the narrator as:

> A mere glimpse of Narmada's waters is supposed to cleanse a human being of generations of sinful births. Just think how pure you and I must be, gazing on this river every day.
>
> (Gita Mehta 151)

In the novel, freedom becomes the question of spiritual one. The Jain monk's story which is narrated as the first story to the narrator shows the spiritual freedom he wanted to get. On his way, he meets sturdy tribal women from the nearby village, Vano. On one occasion, he meets a Jain monk who has recently renounced the world. The bureaucrat pretends ignorance to know why Jain monks must shave their heads and cover their mouths. The monk says that non-violence is very tiring and most difficult for a man to practise and keep. A close look at the stories of the bureaucrat and the monk becomes evident that the bureaucrat retires from his active life hoping to find the meaning of life, as he has lost his wife and has no children. So, he chooses going into the forest by preferring a less important job on the banks of the Narmada. But indifference to it, the monk suddenly decides to give up wealth, wife, children, friends and all the comforts of luxurious living. Commenting on his decision, Parasuram Ramamoorthi writes, "His decision is based on intuition and faith whereas the narrator's life is one pursuit guided by reason." (Parasuram Ramamoorthi 146)

Though the monk is young, he renounces everything. The description he gives the narrator about the grand function by his father when he renounced the world shows that he is immature to renounce the world. The narrator understands his mission as:

> Then I remind myself that the purpose of the pilgrimage is endurance. Through their endurance the pilgrims hope to generate the heat, the tapas, that links men to the energy of the universe, as the Narmada River is thought to link mankind to the energy of Shiva.
>
> (Gita Mehta 8)

Haunted by the Jain monk's encounter, the bureaucrat seems disturbed. Although Tariq Mia often teases the bureaucrat, he is the man who tells stories and clarifies his doubts. Tariq Mia explains that the Jain monk loves the human heart and its secrets because it has only one secret, the capacity to love. To understand the ways of the human heart, he tells 'The Teacher's Story'. It is about Master Mohan, who has a greedy family dominated by a nagging and scolding wife. Master Mohan is a music teacher and remains as an unsuccessful ambitious singer. Though he leads an unhappy life, his gentle nature always ushers him to small acts of kindness. He stands spellbound to the voice of a young blind Muslim boy, who enters the song leading two musical lines above the others:

> I prostrate my head to the blade of Your Sword. O, the wonder of my submission. O, the wonder of Your protection.
>
> (Gita Mehta 61)

Being kind, Master Mohan becomes the guardian of the boy, Imrat, and decides to train him. He grooms him in music and discovers the boy to be a prodigy. He instructs Imrat to sing songs of Kabir, Mirabai, Khusrau, Tulasidas, Chisti and Chandidas. His singing becomes very popular and attracts the attention of a music records company. Unable to bear the rude behaviour of his wife, Master Mohan leaves the house for Imrat to continue his practice. The boy's popularity invites him to sing at a great Sahib's palace, but Master Mohan refuses. It is Master Mohan's wife who wants to make some money out of the boy, accepts the offer and receives five thousand rupees. Later, the boy is forced to sing and his singing fills the hall with ecstacy and mystic raptures. When the great Sahib rises, Master Mohan thinks the Sahib is going to dance to the music of the boy. But when he slits the throat of the boy, his cold cruel logic is revealed:

> Such a voice is not human. What will happen to music if this is the standard by which God judges us?
>
> (Gita Mehta 81)

The gruesome end drives the Master to the verge of madness. He comes to the banks of the Narmada in search of peace, but he does not get it as the story leaves him with many questions unanswered. Tariq Mia's explanation is that he does not know the answer and it is a story about the human heart. The bureaucrat questions himself whether the police catch him or not and why the Sahib kills the boy. Unable to come to a conclusion, Master Mohan commits suicide on his way back. In this context, Pradeep Trikha comments, "The story indicates distrust in the goodness of human beings. It has a sensitive emotional unfolding, which consequently mark the ways of the world and generates tolerance towards inhuman acts of man". (Pradeep Trikha 176)

The novel *A River Sutra* shows the class difference in the society. The Executive Story is a case study of Nitin Bose, who is said to be possessed. He is an executive in Calcutta's oldest tea company. He is a well-educated, orthodox person committed to duty. Unable to bear humdrum life in Calcutta, he opts for the tea estates despite the dreadful predictions of his companions. As he is a voracious reader, he has a sound knowledge of legends, myths and anthropology of tribals. To overcome his loneliness, he reads the *Rig Veda* and gradually follows the example of his predecessors with a bottle of whisky on his table. Then comes a break through in the form of a tribal woman. One day, when he is enjoying a glass of whisky, he breaks the cocoon around him and enters a new world of sensual pleasures:

> I felt a softness press against my shoulder. Stretching out my hand, I grasped the swelling firmness of a woman's breast.
>
> (Gita Mehta 124)

He usually keeps women away from him, but now he does not like to lose the new experience that awakens the sensuous man in him. The urgency of his desire stays him awake after spending a few satisfied nights with Rima, and he realises he is enchanted. As the tribal priest said, Nitin Bose, a tormented soul, takes refuge on the banks of the river to immerse the figure of a goddess to weaken his possession. When the bureaucrat finishes the diary, Tariq Mia struggles to understand the power of the tribal woman and it makes no sense to him. But his assistant Chagla understands it intuitively and explains:

> It is Mr. Bose who is making no sense, pretending desire is some kind of magic performed with black arts. . .
>
> (Gita Mehta 143)

Chagla explains that there is no life without desire, everything will stand still and it becomes empty. Analysing the story, Pradeep Trikha sagely comments, "The story suggests that man suffers from emotional and spiritual limitations but despite these there is a realization of achievement". (Pradeep Trikha 176)

Another story narrated in the novel shows the freedom of the soul in the next birth. The story is narrated by a woman, whose daughter is kidnapped by Rahul Singh, a bandit. The narrator can meet the daughter and she states that Rahul Singh and she were married in their previous births too, so he wants her to marry in this birth also. She too believs that they were married together in the previous births and since he is a bandit she cannot stay with him for a long time and therefore, she returns to her mother. When her mother gets back her daughter, she thanks the river and when she loses her daughter dead in the river she fels that her daughter is lucky to die in the holy river,

> Only that she was happy her daughter had died in the Narmada because she would be purified of all her sins.
>
> (Gita Mehta 190)

The narrator thus understands that the river plays a major role in their religious and mythological beliefs, and the death in the river is freeing her soul. In the novel, the river remains as a hope-giver by giving them a peaceful mind to worship. The Narmada is portrayed from different points of view by many characters in all those stories. The main characters in those six stories come to the river banks of the river Narmada to find solution to their problems. Therefore the river is taken for granted as the life-giver, mind-consoler and remains as the symbol of hope for those who suffer in their life. When the narrator is discussing about the river and the relationship to those with Dr. Mitra, another character who shares his ideas with the narrator talks about the river:

> Her holiness is believed to dispel the malevolent effects of Saturn so all manner of epileptics, depressives, and other unfortunates rush to her bands. And yet, the Narmada is also a magnet to scholars. Towns on the banks of the river are renowned for the learning of their Brahmins.
>
> (Gita Mehta 152-153)

The same experience is seen by one of the characters in the novel where the girl is expecting a major change in her living and finally starts worshipping the river. The Musician's Story is about an ugly female musician, who learns to perfect her singing all her life. The bureaucrat meets her on the river bank when she is collecting glass fragments. The bureaucrat cannot find any trace of beauty in it, but she admits that her father can understand it because he is a genius. The purpose of teaching music to his daughter is to free her from her own image. In this connection, Pradeep Trikha writes, "There is a purpose in teaching music to his ugly daughter; through music, he tries to free her from her own image so that she could love beauty wherever she finds it". (Pradeep Trikha 176)

Gradually, they respond to each other until the silence between them grows electric with desire. But the man delays the marriage till he completes the Bhairav, the raga of Shiva. After completing the last music performance, the pupil leaves for his family as the woman's mother is making preparations for marriage. Shortly, he sends thanks to the music teacher for teaching him. Later, it is revealed that the young man gets married to someone else. To cure her physical attachment, the music teacher brings her to the river bank. But, Tariq Mia says that it is the bureaucrat's misfortune because he is too young to understand the world, "To hear of love without ever having melted in its embrace" (14). Commenting on the bureaucrat's immature knowledge of the world, Indira Bhatt writes, "The man who has not loved a man is a man who has learned nothing from life." (Indira Bhatt 75)

The bureaucrat is left in ambiguity of the woman's broken engagement and unrequited love, and how the river can exorcise her grief. But Tariq Mia tells that the river is born of penance, and named by laughter where the forests are heavy with wild jasmine. He says Naga Babas usually sing the song of the Narmada. He tells The Minstrel's Story to understand the bureaucrat about the Naga Babas. It is about the Naga Baba who rescued a girl eight years from the clutches of a prostitute and who later became a minstrel. The Naga Baba sits in the cremation ground without food and water for nine days. The people, who cross the road, fear the Naga's sight, as his skin is grey, matted hair and the human skull from which he eats and drinks. And they also believe the Naga possess super human powers, the ability to levitate and curse anyone who displeases them. On the night of Shiva, the Naga are supposed to beg at the houses of those who are unclean, untouchable or profane. So he sets out to beg alms from a third unclean house. He chooses a brothel house and accepts a child as alms. The woman tells she is not responsible for the trouble the child brings. The Naga Baba names her Uma, peace in the night, and they live in caves where he teaches the child how to read and write and at night trains to sing the song of the Narmada. In this connection, PradeepTrikha comments, "He takes the child with him, meditates in a cave, makes the girl sing in the praise of the Narmada a minstrel is born". (Pradeep Trikha 176)

The Naga Baba leaves the singer-saint to follow the next stage of his enlightenment. Leaving Uma is a foolish deed of the Naga Baba because, if the Narmada is born of Shiva's penance, Uma is born of the Naga Baba's penance. The song of the Narmada is the last narrative in the novel in which the Naga Baba, who meditated in the caves of the Narmada, reappears as Prof. Shankar and Uma as a minstrel. The bureaucrat is intrigued to discover Prof. Shankar, who renounced the world to understand the spirit of the river. He prefers its immortality to holiness. When the bureaucrat admits that he is on the banks of the Narmada for enlightenment, Prof. Shankar says that he has chosen the wrong place because so many lives converge on the banks of the Narmada. Prof. Shankar opines that the river is sacred because it has the individual experiences of human beings, who live on its banks. At this point of view, Indira Bhatt writes, "It is the active life, the life of Karma and not a passive renunciation that brings not only knowledge but also enlightenment". (Indira Bhatt 75)

Thus, the novel *A River Sutra* ends in a note of ambiguity; however all the stories are treatments of love and life-giving principles. The bureaucrat cannot believe that Prof. Shankar was once an ascetic and now an admirer of the river Narmada. Gita Mehta sketches that the river is a perennial source of life, so it has become immortal. Parasuram Ramamoorthi writes, "A River Sutra is an attempt to subversiveness to present the river as an eternal source of the flow of life." (Parasuram Ramamoorthi 153)

The progress of the six stories can be seen as variations on the theme of love and the secret of the human heart. Commenting about the uniqueness of the stories of the unsettled nature of man, swinging between happiness and despair, Asit Chandmal points out, "There are stories of obsession and renunciation, desperation, and destruction, desire and death. Above all there are stories of sexual, sensual and spiritual longings and love." (Asit Chandmal 30)

The Indian myths portray a river as a feminine being and the Narmada River is also not exempted from it. Dr. Mitra discusses the myth of the Narmada to the narrator, he tells that, when Shiva, Creator and Destroyer of Worlds, was in an ascetic trance the perspiration from his body flowed down the hills. The stream took the form of a woman and become dangerous to the ascetics tempting them by appearing as a dancer one moment and then as a romantic dreamer and as a seductress loose-limbed with the lassitude of desire. These attracted Shiva and he named her Narmada, the Delightful One, blessing her with the words,

> "You shall be forever holy, forever inexhaustible, then he gave her in marriage to the ocean Lord of Rivers, most lustrous of all her suitors."
>
> (Gita Mehta 8)

Thus everyone looks upon the river as a woman and the narrator too, after a long period of stay on the banks of river, starts imagining the river as a woman:

> I watched the water slowly redden, catching reflections from the rose colors of dawn, and imagined the river as a woman painting

> her palms and the sides of her feet with vermilion as she prepared to meet her lover.
>
> (Gita Mehta139)

Later the discussion between Dr. Mitra and the narrator leads to the point whether the river is a whore or not Dr. Mitra points out, "So Narmada is unlike to mean whore" (Gita Mehta 151). The narrator denies saying that the river Narmada is not a whore. These kinds of representations such as, the river as a woman/goddess/whore are possible in Indian writings.

In the novel the river Narmada is portrayed as a river full of life and hope. It gives shelter to many living things other than human beings also. The river tries to give a sort of experience to the narrator of the novel and others who dwell on banks of it and remain as a guide giving knowledge and experience to them. The Indian river Narmada is seen with the spiritual bliss, "In the living stones of the Narmada, God is to be found". (Gita Mehta 174)

In the novel the narrator is observing the experiences of different kinds of people living on the banks of the Narmada river. It gives different experiences and so the narrator gets intellectual bliss through the real stories. The spiritual nature of the Narmada River too is realized by the narrator through other characters he meets. At the end of the novel he is moving away from the banks of Narmada but the lessons given by it are pleasant memories to him. In *A River Sutra* for the narrator the river is not only symbol of experience but also as the guide to the characters in the stories and to himself. He stays at one place, but the people come and go from him and give him experiences; therefore the river stands for experience-giver/guide of knowledge in this novel.

Works Cited

Bhatt, Indira. "Shobha De's *Sultry Days* And Gita Mehta's *A River Sutra: A Study In Orientalism*" in *Indian Women Novelists: Set III*. Ed. R. K. Dhawan. Vol. 5. New Delhi: Prestige Books, 1995.

Chandmal, Asit. "A Renaissance Woman." *The Illustrated Weekly of India.* 1993.

Mehta, Gita. *A River Sutra.* New Delhi: Penguin Books, 1993.

Ramamoorthi, Parasuram. "Triumph Of Desire Over Renunciation: Gita Mehta's *A River Sutra*" in *The Indian Novel With A Social Purpose.* New Delhi: Atlantic Publishers and Distributors, 1999.

Trikha, Pradeep. "Gita Mehta's *A River Sutra*: A Pilgrim's Progress," in *Fiction of The Nineties.* Ed. Veena Noble Dass and R.K. Dhawan, New Delhi: Prestige Books, 1994.

14

Tellers, Listeners and Communities: Bharati's *Suraj Ka Satwa Ghora*

Supriya Agarwal

Story-telling creates a cultural phenomenon and expresses a range of emotions exploring the implications of rhetoric and cross-cultural communication. The novel *Suraj Ka Satwa Ghora* of Dharamvir Bharati consists of five stories which define love and through a moral give a glimpse into the life of the middle class, emphasising the explicit and the implicit elements of the human psyche. The novel falls in the category of postmodernist writing and the paper explores how the power of storytelling is a recuperation of memory, collective identity formation and an assertion of an oral tradition in literature.

Story-telling is as old as human life for it was always a means of communicating the human desire to tell and to be heard. It has been a tool to effect changes, to underline the lessons of experience and to explain the various process associated with existence. Oratory is a form of public address whether it is to a small group within a community or to a larger one where it is used to effect social change. The physical presence of the "Teller" and the "Listener" thus becomes important and affirms many aspects of life which reflect community values and discipline. Creating a cultural space it gives impetus to the power of imagination, building the expectation and anticipation of the listener, working out a whole range of emotions.

In *Suraj Ka Satwa Ghora* the protagonist tells about his past experiences and through memory relates the tales as were told to them orally by a narrator Manik Mulla. The stories told are not simply narrated in time but also located in space and within the short space of a short narrative several spaces are traversed. W. J Ong in his work *Orality and Literacy* comments that "Semiotics and folklore in every language and ethnic group explore the implications for rhetoric and composition, interpersonal communication, cross cultural communication, postcolonial studies, rural community development and popular culture" (22). In fact when we hear a story, we feel its power and uniqueness. It is, like perceiving a new object that stimulates creativity. It causes us to gape and suspend analytic thought and sets aside the inclination to slice and criticise. Instead, the mind is prompted to search earlier examples and parallels and simultaneously prompts us for new creations and one story leads to more stories.

The subject matter which Dharamvir Bharati has expanded in this novel through the speaker and the listeners has a base which is whole and enriched. To grasp the basic meaning of the story we have to keep in mind the middle class strata of society after the Second World War, their financial condition and mental state arising there from. The neo-realism in the stories and the starkness of the human character brings life to the narrative which creates a complex matrix of human relationship. Manik Mulla the person presenting the stories is a worldly man striving to know himself through the medium of love. Bharati has adopted the telling of the stories as a narrative technique used in the post modern fiction. The telling and listening, followed by discussion and after thought is consciously used as a tool to reveal contemporary reality that the writer wishes to depict.

The novel consists of five stories, the first story told in the first afternoon titled "Earning his salt" revolves around Jamuna who could not marry her lover Tanna even if she longed to, because of her financial condition. The definition of love she had gathered from the stories she had read, she saw befalling on herself. The second story is also centred about Jamuna who married Tihaju an old man who died and she began living like a model widow with Ramdhan, the tonga puller in the same house. The third story is about Tanna who was Jamuna's lover in his youth. He spent his entire life enduring difficulties and finally died slogging as a clerk. Leela is the girl who was married off to Tanna. Her misfortune is apparent from these stories. The fourth narrative is associated with Mahesar Dayal and Manik Mulla. The story of Devasena, princess of Malwa is the sub-title which gives us a glimpse into the author's mind. The thought of Devasena in Skandgupta's play rises in the writer's mind giving rise to several dimensions in the story. The romance of Manik and Leela and ultimately Leela's marriage to Tanna is depicted in an emotional fashion. The fifth tale is a tragic tale of love between Manik and Satti. The narrative of the sixth afternoon does not usher in any new character. Manik's heart-striken version gives a true to life portrayal of Chaman Thakur, Satti and her plight.

Bharati has very dexterously woven the art of storytelling and the literary qualities of a novel. Through word pictures he has converted the tale into another medium, placing the instances aesthetically and in a cohesive and harmonised whole. The teller himself is the protagonist in each of the stories but his self perception in each is different as how he sees himself. In the first story he sees himself as a prepubescent, in another as an adolescent and in the third as an adult and suddenly we discover that these events are actually taking place simultaneously. The work considers the human capacity to evaluate, modify and move between a plurality of communal and communicative contexts in the creation of meaningful narratives of selfhood. Manik Mulla's stories, intertwined with notions of love, romance and separation lead to all kinds of social, political and literary polemics and discussions among the listeners. Titled as interludes the views of the listeners and the speaker along with that of the author himself are interwoven with great dexterity and convey several messages and morals. We get not only the glimpses of the community and its critical analysis but also learn that how our own resources can be used for betterment of the community. The book is an interesting study of the relationship between narrative, narrator and the reader. Elaborating upon the complexity of the narrative Paul Cobley points out "as soon as we start to look more closely at this phenomenon, it is evident that the apparently natural impulse of storytelling or story listening (or reading)is far from simple. Even the most 'simple' of stories is embedded in a network of relations that are sometimes astounding in their complexity" (2)

Cobley defines narrative as "a particular form of representation implementing signs which includes the telling of events and the mode selected for that to take place" (6). Selection, sequence, space, time, phylogeny and ontogeny and various other specifics are part of the process. The narrative does not necessarily posit a single, cohesive and unified world but goes on to provoke different responses and creates a multiverse. The novel is both a period piece connecting the past with the present as well as a myth which projects several connotations. Narrating six parts of the story and not penning a story of the seventh horse the writer assumes it to be a horse resplendent with sending dreams. He sees a golden dream about the future. The six horses are wounded and rendered incapable of pulling the chariot but the seventh horse remains strong and robust with his chest stretched out and head held high. He struts ahead as the horse of the future. A horse belonging to the innocent children of Jamuna, Tanna and Satti whose lives will be far more peaceful and contented. The very same seventh horse sends us dreams of the future and new readings of the present enabling us to construct a path on which the horse of the future will arrive. Helping us pen new pages of history on which *Ashwamegha's* victorious horse will stride forth.

The aspect of the sun which Dr. Dharamvir Bharati presents through the symbol of the seventh horse is one which will tear through the uncertain darkness and galloping ahead would change the existing social conditions and renew all values of humanity. In the Hindu mythology Lord Surya is the Sun god. Surya is depicted as riding seven horses which are known as *Harits* who draw the chariot of the sun across the sky. The horses symbolise the cosmic rays which radiate warmth and life, and they remove darkness and usher in light. The seven horses also symbolise the seven colours of rainbow. The rays of the sun sustain all living beings and the horses are also said to represent seven days of the week. The arrival of the sun is heralded by the beauty of the dawn. As the sun moves through the heavens in each season it is accompanied by set of hermits, celestial maiden serpents and giants who sit as envoys on the chariot. The sun in mythology is given two wives from whom many children are born, the senior one is *Samjyna* and the other *Chhaya* who always remains at a safe distance behind her fiery husband.

In these stories there is also the role of the other woman and as the sun is poetically and phenomenally associated with the power of healing, these stories too have a curative power on the listeners who are exhausted and depressed. The stories thus veer between the intensely personal and the mythically grand. The events of the stories are not piled up upon each other but are spinned carefully. There is a combination of the real and the fantastic and also the virtues and vices that exist in it. The stories are not really the stories of love but the sort of life which the lower middle class of today lives. In this life, the importance of love has been over shadowed by economic struggle and moral disintegration resulting in chaos, bitterness and dark despair that envelops the middle class and yet deep down somewhere there is something which has always urged us to pierce the darkness and look forward to change the social structure - gives us not only the desire but the strength to reassert and establish the simple basic value of human life.

That something can be called faith, courage, fortitude, integrity or truth but whatever it is, it is that essential something which steers us forward just as the sun's horses draw his chariot relentlessly ever forward. The six horses are exhausted and staggering while the seventh horse is still fresh with his head held high and nostrils quivering with restlessness. The last horse is the horse of the future, the horse that stands for all - the innocent infant children of Tanna, Jamuna and Satti - children of the future whose lives will be cleaner, more wholesome and more peaceful than ours, full of light and beatitude. It is the seventh horse that touches our eyes with visions of the future and gives our mind new orientations.

The novella does not tell us stories alone; it gives a direct commentary and criticism within the novel itself though the medium of interludes. All stories not only have a moral but the writer has focused on the art of storytelling by means of conversation between the teller and the listeners, highlighting the relationship between the narrative, narrator and the reader. The writer begins by a tongue in cheek definition of story as a progression from nothingness through a beginning, middle and an end to the waste paper basket. At the time of the beginning of the second story, Onkar one of the listener wants to know the title to which the narrator Manik Mulla retorts, "Are you interested in the story or in the title? Or do you think I am one of those who having nothing to tell gives it an attractive caption to bamboozle editors and readers" (37).

The narrative also points out the nuances of telling and listening. If while listening you are not on your toes all the time, you are bound to miss the essential point of the story and be left with a great deal of chaff. While commenting on the technical aspect he says that technique is merely a sign of the immature, the experimenter, the man who has not yet mastered his medium and in the end when the listeners ask for more stories the teller Manik Mulla refuses to continue saying that so many love stories in one unbroken string were enough and indeed what he had related was infact a novel which had the elements both of a comedy and a tragedy.

So, what outwardly appear as love stories when deconstructed come out in reality as stories of what love is not. The communal importance of love has also been pointed out asserting that love which doesn't contribute to social progress and individual development is meaningless. Thus the characters are situated as subjects in a variety of communal frameworks which provide a range of interpretative possibilities and different signifying practices that may be adopted by the subject at any given moment. Social identities are not constructed for once and are neither fixed rather it shifts and alters over time as that of the three woman characters—Jamuna, Lily and Satti.

The telling and listening, followed by discussion and after thought is consciously used as a tool in the fiction to reveal contemporary reality that the writer intends to depict. The stories leave us thinking about a host of issues from the wishes and demands of women in love to the commitment and suffering of men in love and explore the explicit and implicit elements of the human psyche. The characters thus become representatives of the different strata of society and reflect the economic influences which work on love and present the picture of the conditioning of emotions by it. Men become instruments or machines of the present traditions and system and their high and noble dreams wilt and die, spreading a strange numbness over them. The individual characters become archetypal, representing the community to which they belong.

Although written in 1952, the novel falls in the post modernist category, being one of the foremost instances of meta fiction in the twentieth century. Dharamvir Bharati has very dexterously converted the oral into literary narration. John Miles Foley in his work, *The Theory of Oral Composition :History and Methodology,* has pointed out that "an oral story takes us forward and backward- we break new ground and also refer back to territory we thought we have left behind" (38). The reading of this novella is more like listening and experiencing all what the immediate listeners felt and at the same time being distanced we can understand its contexts and multiple undercurrents.

It is hard to transcribe into text exact words someone says in conversation - including the pauses, repetitions, stumbles along with the atmosphere and action of the past when the story was told. There is a world of difference between the literary and the oral. Literary stories have a different style of language used and different rhythms and pacing. They may spend considerable time describing subtle qualities of atmosphere and may switch into philosophical ponderings. The oral includes subtle pacing, pausing, facial expression and even the articles physically present as the horse shoe in the second story and the knife with a black handle in the fifth have symbolic significance.

Audience response also goes a long way in oral narration, something completely unavailable to authors in writing. Once the oral is fixed to a written format it loses its quality of aliveness and establishes a fixidity to the whole thing, a permanence and it cannot change its form as the oral does. In the oral performance the author, i.e., the speaker is available for study. He is present and interacting with the audience or the listener and the interpretation of the narration is necessarily a joint product of the tellers and listeners. Postmodernis suggest that in written documents 'authorship is dead' by which they mean to say that the author is not available for study, cannot control interpretation and the author's intention gets subservient to language and context. Unlike the ordinary workings Dharamvir Bharati has explored the power of storytelling as the recuperation of memory, collective identity formation and the presence of oral tradition in literature.

Works Cited

Bharati, Dharamvir, *Suraj Ka Satwa Ghora,* Translated: *The Sun's Seventh Horse by* Sachchidanand Hiranand Vatsyayan 'Agneya'. National Book Trust: India, 1999.

Cobley, Paul. *Narrative*, The New Critical Idiom Series. Routledge: London, 2001.

Foley, John Miles. *The Theory of Oral Composition: History and Methodology*. Indiana University Press: Bloomington and Indianapolis, 1988.

Walter, J. Ong. *Orality and Literacy: The Technologizing of the Word.* Routledge: London and New York, 1982.

15

Defining Manhood: A Study of Ramamoorthi's *Hey Parashuram*

A. Sujatha

Often, we ponder over issues like what makes a man or a woman. But we have never come up with answers that offer us a total sense of satisfaction. Ramamoorthi makes a great attempt through this play in redefining manhood. Often, most writers are obsessed with the idea of redefining womanhood and get carried away by the concept of the new liberated woman. But, Ramamoorthi's case is different. He goes a step ahead. He clearly illustrates that man is incomplete without the feminine in him through the myth of Parashuram.

Manhood refers to the state of being a man. Generally, this is associated with valour, rational thinking, and determination. Womanhood is generally defined as the state of being a woman and this in turn is associated with docility, obsequiousness, empathy, and infinite patience. This brings us to the concept of female, feminine, and feminist. While the word *female* is related to biological aspects, *feminine* concerns itself more with sociological and *feminist* with political aspects. The focus of this paper is to discuss the feminine phase that not only goes towards making a woman but also a true man. *Hey Parashuram* by Parashuram Ramamoorthi is a recreation of the Parashuram myth interspersed with episodes from *The Mahabharata*.

The play is divided into twelve scenes and Ramamoorthi employs dramatic techniques like the use of the *vidhushaka* (comedian) and musicians. The *puranic* story is narrated by the vidhushaka, while Parashuram narrates the mythopoeic version. According to the Puranas, Parashuram is extolled as an ideal son, a *suputra*, who, at his father's bidding, cuts off his mother's head. But here, although the incidents are the same, the reasons attributed to the characters' actions are different.

When Jamadagni asks Parashuram to sever Renuka's head, he is depicted more as an authoritative patriarch for whom the woman is no more than a maid who takes care of the household and the children.

Parashuram: Father, I will definitely obey you. Is this what you want me to do?

Jamadagni: Yes. Kill her.

Parashuram: I shall. But tell me why.

Jamadagni: She betrayed her god.

Parashuram: She does not even know that word betrayal, father.

Jamadagni: She betrayed me.

Parashuram: Father, please don't accuse her like that.

Jamadagni: She betrayed me. I gave her four sons. She betrayed me.

Parashuram: Father, tell me what happened.

Jamadagni: I don't want to tell you anything. Just kill her. That is all. (*Sc.* 2:17-30)

Finally, Parashuram relents to his father's wish only because his mother has instructed him to do what his father asks him to do. Ramamoorthi begins to weave his mythopoeic version with Parashuram's soliloquy. According to him, his mother was his teacher who taught him to cook and to sing. But he has no choice but to obey Jamadagni. When Parashuram finally traces his way to Renuka, he finds her surrounded by tribal women. He is all the more astonished when one of the tribal women protects her and even defends her action. She states that Renuka was sexually aroused on seeing a *Gandharva* and that it was only a passing fancy. Further, she blames Jamadagni for Renuka's action.

> I Woman: Your father does not know that Renuka has a body as well. He forgot she exists in flesh and blood. He has turned her into a servant. 'Fetch water. ' 'Get me flowers. ' 'Cook for me. ' That is all. She has no other existence. But her body is alive. Look at her. She is still fresh as a flower and in full bloom. One who does not care for her body has no right to expect her to be faithful to him.
>
> (*Sc.* 2:107-116)

For the first time, Parashuram realizes the true significance of a woman. The tribal woman becomes his 'teacher' in the true sense because she tells him how the body is very important and needs to be taken care of. At the same time, moral values such as chastity that society swears by are matters pertaining merely to the mind.

Renuka, however, unlike the tribal woman, is a person of few words. When Parashuram asks her why Jamadagni told him to kill her, she in turn asks him:

> Renuka: If I tell you what happened and if you feel that I am right, then will you disobey your father? Not kill me?
>
> (*Sc* 2:55-57)

Parashuram is tongue-tied as Renuka's question raises a vital issue: Does a person act according to his conscience or according to the instructions of his parents or guru? Finally he follows his mother's instructions and kills her along with the tribal woman who tries to protect her.

The revival of Renuka brings along with it a major transition from wife/mother to goddess. Parashuram is wonderstruck by the fact that although he is unable to restore the tribal woman to life, the other tribal women are hardly incensed. They see the goddess in Renuka and call her '*Yellamma*!' Renuka however refuses to have anything to do with her past life and tells Parashuram to stay away from her. Ramamoorthi's mythopoeic narration also brings to our awareness the fact that the patriarchal world sees Yellamma only as the goddess of *devadasis* or prostitutes. It is but apparent that generally there is no room in androcentric myths for the 'rebel' woman.

Edward C. Whitmont sums up this idea in his book *Return of the Goddess*:

> The devaluation of femininity is an intrinsic feature of the dominant culture during the epoch of patriarchal ego development. Women have been regarded as second-rate human beings at best, and often as something less than human. Owing to its religious nature, this devaluation has characterized woman's own self-image as strongly as it has men's views of her. And women have been as guilty of repressing their own feminine nature as men have been or repressing the feminine component of their psyches. To see the problem only in sociological terms would miss the core of the issue. (122)

Parashuram realizes the true significance of womanhood after his encounter with Renuka and the tribal woman. To crown it all, Renuka blesses him with womanhood so that he can feel like a woman and be both male and female. While a hermaphrodite is generally a subject of curiosity and ridicule, Ramamoorthi reinforces the concept of yin and yang through the hermaphrodite sage-warrior Parashuram whose transformation is not merely biological, but also psychological. Joseph Campbell describes this concept vividly in his *Myths to Live by:*

> Yang is of the sunny side; yin, the shady. On the sunny side there is light, there is warmth, and the heat of the sun is dry. In the shade, there is the cool ...and the earth is moist. Dark, cold, and moist; light, hot, and dry; earth and sun in counteraction. These are associated, further with the female and the male as the passive and active principles. There is no moral verdict here intended; neither principle is "better" than the other, neither "stronger" than the other. They are the two equally potent grounding principles on which all the world rests, and in their interaction they inform, constitute, and decompose all things. (119)

As mentioned above, yang is associated with men and yin, with women. But most writers and philosophers fail to see the union of the two and describe these 'qualities' as purely masculine or feminine. But Ramamoorthi clearly emphasises that it is this union of the man and woman in Parashuram that makes him a good human being who is able to perceive the problems and difficulties of both men and women. Unlike most patriarchs who enrol only male pupils in their *gurukula*, Parashuram sees no gender bias and in his ashram, Amba receives education with Devavrath (Bhisma) and Salva. The pivotal point of Parashuram's education is to fuse the *Agni* and the *Ganga* or the yang and the yin in them. Agni is associated with masculinity and symbolizes strength and energy, while Ganga symbolizes creativity and love, an important aspect of femininity. This is again reminiscent of Carl Jung's concept of the *anima* and the *animus*. But Jung's anima is more submissive and obsequious unlike its yin counterpart that claims equal significance.

> What is not-I, not masculine is most probably feminine, and because the 'not-I' is felt as not belonging to me and therefore as outside me, the anima-image is usually projected upon women...biologically speaking, it is simply the greater number of masculine genes that tips the scales in favour of masculinity. The smaller number of feminine genes seems to form a feminine character, which usually remains unconscious because of its subordinate position. (27-28)

At first one sees a perfect fusion of Agni and Ganga in Amba when he indulges in rational debates and dances rhythmically. But, when Devavrat carries her and her sisters away from the *swayamvara* to become Vichitra Veeriya's brides, matters take a turn. Spurned by Salva on account of being won by another man, and rejected by Devavrat on account of his vow, Amba unleashes the Agni in her and marches angrily to Parashuram's ashram to decide on the next course of action. According to *The Mahabharata*, Parashuram was ready to fight for Amba, but was checked due to divine intervention. Here, Parashuram makes no attempt to defend Amba who is in an utterly confused state of mind, but merely asks her to strike a balance between the Agni and the Ganga in her. He senses Agni seething and boiling in Amba and advises her to cool down. But Amba is in no mood to listen.

> Amba: But what about my humiliation? Salva says he cannot marry me, because I am the prize of Devavrath. Devavrath says that he is a Brahmachari. What should I do? Sit and pine and cry.
>
> Parashu: Peace. Peace be with you.
>
> Amba: My blood boils. You are asking me to be peaceful. I want to marry Devavrat. (*Sc.* 8:54-61)

In spite of Parashuram's attempts to reason with her, Amba marches out angrily vowing to kill Devavrat and ultimately puts an end to her precious life in the present *janma* by engulfing it in flames.

The story of Karna is another episode that provides food for our thought in the play. *The Shanti Parva*, which forms Book Twelve of *The Mahabharata*, clearly describes the attempts on Karna's part to gain mastery over weapons, particularly the various astras, in order to quell Arjuna in battle. Knowing fully well that a *shudra* will not be entertained in any gurukula, he lies to Parashuram that he is a brahmin. But Karna is caught red-handed when a worm bores its way into his thigh. Fearing that his guru who was lying on his lap would be disturbed, he bears the pain quietly. But when blood flows from his thigh and touches Parashuram who is asleep, he wakes up and understands at once that this forbearance is characteristic of only a kshatriya. When Karna confesses, Parashuram curses him. The curse is well described in *The Mahabharata*

Unto the cheerless and trembling Karna, prostrated with joined hands upon earth, that foremost one of Bhrigu's race, smiling though filled with wrath, answered, "Since thou hast, from avarice of weapons, behaved here with falsehood, therefore, O wretch, this *Brahma* weapon shalt not dwell in thy remembrance. Since thou art not a Brahmana, truly this *Brahma* weapon shall not, up to the time of thy death, dwell in thee when thou shalt be engaged with a warrior equal to thyself!" (*http:// www. sacred-texts. com/hin/m12/m12a003. htm*)

But in the play, Karna is a different person who is readily accepted in Parashuram's ashram after admitting the fact that he is a charioteer's son. At first, Parashuram teaches him the basics of warfare. Then he realises that Karna is a noble being and is not fit to wage war and destroy. So he tries to stabilise the Ganga in him by asking him to cook gruel and play the table. When Karna asks him why he is not taught the nuances of warfare, Parashuram only tells him to go back as he is not fit to destroy. But Karna appeals to Parashuram to teach him how to wield various astras and is wise enough to request him to remove all traces of that knowledge once his education is complete. In other words, Karna's quest for knowledge is complete once it is gained. He does not want to use it for *naasha* or *samhara* (destruction) unlike his *Mahabharata* counterpart whose main aim is to vanquish Arjuna in the battlefield.

> Parashu: Karna is not born to wage a war. Because no war ever ends on a victory or defeat. He is born to give everything, like the river. The Agni that was glowing was only raging at some points. Discovered the Ganga. I don't know whether he fused them. But he was great when it came to giving away everything, like the knowledge he acquired. Even possession of knowledge is an obstacle to Self-realisation. Karna was set on that road. He, I think, won at the end. Self-illumination. (*Sc* 12:14-26)

To sum up, the feminine element is not static, but is a wonderful blend of the static and the dynamic. The feminine element teaches us how to empathise and view every situation with adequate poise and stability. Every man, according to Ramamoorthi should discover the feminine self in him in order to emerge as a true human being.

Works Cited

Campbell, Joseph. *Myths to Live by.* Toronto, New York, London: Bantam Books, 1973.

Jung, Carl Gustaf. *The Archetypes and the Collective Unconscious.* Trans. by R. F. C. Hull. New York: Princeton University Press, 1969.

Ramamoorthi, Parashuram. *Hey Parashuram.* Madurai: Velvi Books, 1999.

Vyas, Ved. *The Mahabharata.* Trans. by Kisari Mohan Ganguli. http://www. Ramamoorthi, sacred-texts. com/hin/m12/m12a003. htm. 2 May 2011.

Whitmont, Edward C. *Return of the Goddess.* Great Britain: Arkana. 1983.

16

Feminist Mythopoeia: A Study of Shashi Deshpande's "Mirrors"

A. Sujatha

The purpose of this paper is to discuss the feminist approach to the myth of Nahusha. While myths extol the glory of Indra and the rishis in quelling the pride of Nahusha, Deshpande's short story views the entire episode from the women's point of view – women who have almost been pushed into oblivion in androcentric myths and legends. The two women who play a vital role in this story are Sachidevi, the wife of Indra, and Ashoka Sundari, the wife of Nahusha. What is most appealing about the story is the poise with which the women keep their secrets and succeed in bringing about a revolution.

Myths have always been a source of fascination to any individual. But what is more fascinating is the ability to rewrite myths in order to throw light on a particular aspect of society. As far as Indian writing in English is concerned, mythic feminism has become one of the most significant trends, particularly with feminists. Mythic feminism has been taking giant strides in questioning the portrayal of women and goddesses in various myths and legends from an androcentric and patriarchal perspective.

According to Jane Caputi, "One of the most significant developments to emerge out of the contemporary feminist movement is the quest to reclaim that symbolizing/naming power, to refigure the female self from a gynocentric perspective, to discover, revitalize and create a female oral and visual mythic creation and use it, ultimately, to change the world" (425).

Mythopoeia is yet another term for mythmaking. The word owes its genesis to the poem 'Mythopoeia' by J.R.R. Tolkien, where he lyrically opposes C.S. Lewis', view that myths are "lies breathed through silver." According to him, "Though all the crannies of the world we filled with elves and goblins, though we dared to build gods and their houses out of dark and light, and sow the seed of dragons, 'twas our right (used or misused). The right has not decayed. We make still by the law in which we're made." (65-70)

Mythopoeia does not necessarily mean, as Tolkien asserts, designing or creating a new myth. It also refers to the modification of existing myths in order to highlight a particular perspective. As Diane Purkiss aptly remarks:

> For feminists, the rewriting of myths denotes . . . the struggle to alter gender asymmetries agreed upon for centuries by myth's disseminators. When feminists envisage that struggle, they often think of the rewriting or the reinterpretation of individual stories:for example, by changing the focus of the narrative from a male character to a female character. (441)

Indian women writers have undoubtedly proved their prowess in this realm. Sara Joseph, Shinie Antonie, Mahasweta Devi, Shashi Deshpande, and many others have conjured powerful feminine images that have decentred their male counterparts and have driven them to the margins. Mahasweta Devi's Draupadi explores the myth of Draupadi from a postmodern perspective. In this story, Dopdi Mehjen, the tribal protagonist, prefers to remain disrobed, unlike her mythical counterpart who appeals for divine intervention to save her from being disrobed. Through this story, Mahasweta Devi presents the effect of assault and oppression on the tribal woman. Another powerful mythopoeic piece is Shinie Antonie's Gandhari. The story is significant mainly because of the key symbol – the blindfold. The conclusion is most striking for it poses a question to the reader – did Gandhari control her blindfold or did the blindfold control Gandhari? Therefore, mythmaking in the hands of women writers is no doubt a powerful tool. As Paula Gunn Allen rightly says, "The feminist use of myth stems from an understanding of myth to be a language construct that contains the power to transform something (or someone) from one state or condition to another. . ." (103).

The focus of this paper is to analyse the 'mythopoeic' approach adopted by Shashi Deshpande in the short story, *Mirrors*. This short story explores the myth of Nahusha from Sachidevi's point of view. All of us have heard of the story of Nahusha, of how he was selected the King of Heaven in Indra's absence. At the outset, Nahusha was humble and ruled wisely. But, gradually he became power crazy, and power soon gave way to lust, when he desired to ravish Sachidevi or Indrani, the wife of Indra. Sachidevi, who was a *pativrata* (chaste woman) didn't want to relent to Nahusha's desires. So, she consulted Indra, who was in hiding in a lotus stem and he asked her to inform Nahusha that she would be willing to yield to him only if he comes to meet her in a palanquin borne by the *saptarishis* (seven celestial sages). Nahusha agreed and set out to meet Sachidevi in his palanquin. The sages were not swift enough, since they weren't accustomed to such tasks, particularly Agasthya, who trudged along slowly because of his short stature. Nahusha, who was eager to meet Sachidevi, became furious and kicked Agasthya shouting 'Sarpa!' (Move quickly) Agasthya cursed that he may be turned into a *be sarpa* (snake). Finally, Bhima redeemed Nahusha from his curse.

Shashi Deshpande's story however dismisses the entire myth of Nahusha as mere sham. What is most significant about the story is that it attaches a lot of importance to Nahusha's wife, Ashoka Sundari or Viraja (a rarely known name) who has always remained incognito in most myths and legends. Only the

Bhumikhand of the *Padma Purana* mentions her name and states how she was born of the Kalpaka Vriksha (the wish fulfilling tree). Sachidevi is indeed right when she muses, "You have no place in any of the stories that are being told about what happened, none at all in the court poet's poem. And it is as if you never existed" (Mirrors 76). Sachidevi reminisces the days when she was content with her position as the queen of Heaven. She was so proud of her position that she quietly endured Indra's lasciviousness. She knew that he was a coward who killed Vritrasura using guile, though poets and 'legend makers' portrayed it differently. But the identity of a queen is always coupled with qualities like meekness, docility and absolute servility to her husband, which of course, apply to any woman. Since Sachidevi is forced to adorn the mask of docility, she is unable to give vent to her anger and disillusionment at her husband's activities. Therefore, she merely relapses into silence and serves as a mirror, reflecting the reverse image of her husband as a hero, the lord of Heaven, and a great warrior.

> I wanted to shout my rage, to scream, to tear him apart. I did none of these things. I withdrew instead behind the mask of the loving wife, into the shell of the dignified, gracious queen. But behind the mask, within the shell was a bewildered woman asking herself, "Why?Why does he need those women?"
>
> (Mirrors 79)

The predicament that Sachidevi and Ashoka Sundari encounter is something that is constantly heard of in the history of civilization, in real life incidents, in myths and legends. What is most amusing is that chaste women, according to Indian myths and legends, are those who merely tolerate the whims and fancies of their spouses and revere them as incarnations of the Cosmic Divine. Fidelity in marital life applies only to women, not to men. A.S. Altekar raises this issue in his book, *The Position ofWomen in Hindu Civilization:*

> Did husbands. . . carry out their conjugal duties as devotedly as their spouses? Did they live up to the high ideal laid down for them? Did they make a serious effort to carry out the obligations laid down in marriage vows? It is not easy to answer these questions. . . But it has to be admitted that the percentage of those who honoured the marriage vows more by breach than by the observance was much greater in the case of husbands. . . . (103)

Therefore, Sachidevi and Ashoka Sundari treat the infidelity of their husbands as a feature of the androcentric world. In fact, Sachidevi is only surprised when Indra 'rapes' mortal women, for she wonders how he could lust for such ordinary-looking women. "I could understand his enjoying the skilful beautiful women he had in his court, but these.?" (Mirrors 79). The great queen of Heaven becomes panic-stricken when Indra is forced to go into hiding after killing Vritrasura. She fears a threat to her identity when Nahusha and Ashoka Sundari are made king and queen. "I had a sense of being ignored. As if Indra had been the filter through which they had seen me. I felt myself becoming invisible without him. It's not for long, I told myself, trying to give myself courage. Indra will return and things will again be normal" (Mirrors 78).

It is this sense of insecurity in Sachidevi's mind that creates an aversion towards Ashoka Sundari. She sees Ashoka Sundari as the woman who has usurped her position. But when Ashoka Sundari comes to meet Sachidevi, her simplicity and unassuming ways lead to an anagnorisis (in Aristotelian terms, realization of one's folly). Sachidevi realizes that a queen's identity is frail and ephemeral, for isn't the queen after all a woman? "Only the façade, only the costumes, nothing more. To be beautiful, dignified and gracious, to add to the king's glory, to be available to him when he wanted me – that was all!" (Mirrors 81).

When Nahusha hankers for Sachidevi, Ashoka Sundari does not protest openly. Instead, she voices her anger in her eyes. Nahusha, the power-crazy king, however ignores it. Sachidevi, who has always been meek and docile, feels helpless and doesn't know how to tackle the situation. Again, it is Ashoka Sundari who comes to her rescue. Deshpande clearly dismisses the patriarchal depiction of the story of Nahusha by portraying Ashoka Sundari as the pivotal point who puts an end to Nahusha and thereby brings about a change in order. According to her mythopoeic version, it is she who tells Sachidevi to ask Nahusha to arrive in a palanquin borne by the saptarishis. Perhaps she thought that a virtuous man like Nahusha would never consent to such a blasphemous thought. However, Nahusha is so blinded by lust that he readily consents.

As in the original myth, it is Agasthya who puts an end to the whole thing, but here it is a different move altogether. When the palanquin passes near a vast abyss, Agasthya signals to the other rishis and they tilt the palanquin with Nahusha in it, into the abyss. Sachidevi wonders if this is also part of Ashoka Sundari's plan. This leads her to yet another revelation that being a human being is more important than being a pativrata.

Towards the end of the story, we find Ashoka Sundari quietly returning to earth and Sachidevi restored to her former position as the queen of Heaven. But while she appears unchanged outwardly, her personality and attitude undergo a transformation. The story ends with an incomplete statement, "But, perhaps some day..." (Mirrors 86). This is clue that someday, perhaps, Sachidevi might also choose to end Indra's 'misrule' as well. In short, decentering of patriarchy and the replacement of matriarchy are child's play if a woman chooses to. Deshpande's myth-making is remarkable because of the decentring of the masculine realm. She exposes Indra as a coward, who goes into hiding after treacherously slaying Vritra, who rebelled against his tyranny. She highlights Ashoka Sundari's strength during times of crisis, her understanding of the world, her silent attack against her own husband when he sets eyes on Sachidevi, and her quiet return to the mortal world after everything is over. In short, the story mirrors the feelings of those women, who have hitherto been hidden from view by male-centred myths and legends.

Works Cited

Allen, Paula Gunn. T*he Sacred Hoop: Recovering the Feminine in American Indian Tradition*. Boston, Beacon Press, 1986.

Altekar, A. S. *The Position of Women in Hindu Civilization: From Prehistoric Times to the Present*. Delhi: Motilal Banarsidass Publishers Private Limited, 1999.

Caputi, Jane. "On Psychic Activism: Feminist Mythmaking." *The Feminis Companion to Mythology*. Ed. Carolyne Larrington. London: Harpe Collins, 1992. 425-440.

Deshpande, Shashi. "Mirrors". *Stories*. Vol. 1. New Delhi: Penguin Books India, 2004. 78-86.

Purkiss, Diane. "Women's Rewriting of Myth." *The Feminist Companion to Mythology*. Ed. Carolyne Larrington. London:Harper Collins, 1992. 441-457.

Tolkien, J. R. R. "Mythopoeia." 24 Jan 2010. <http://home. ccil. org/~cowan /mythopoeia. html>

17

Patriarchal Myth and Woman's Desire in Karnad's *Naga-Mandala*

Ankur Konar

> Indian playwrights deal with this multivalent cultural legacy by adjudicating between the conflicting claims of tradition and modernity, Indianness and Westernization, but their use of two major forms of retrospective narrative – myth and history – also questions received views of the past and the ways of knowing it.
>
> (Dharwadker 2005:11)

Girish Raghunath Karnad's focal point is the literalization of incidents and accidents in the pages of history. His plays were originally written in Kannada and later translated by the dramatist himself. His plays have been successfully performed all over India in spite of his own scholastic observation that "writing in English about characters who are presumably speaking in an Indian language for audiences for whom English is a second language is not a situation conducive to great drama" (1995:365). In that sense he can easily be categorized with the Indian English dramatists' socio-political instrumentality. His plays are full of the symbolic tropes and modes of myth, history, folk culture, religion and identity politics:

1972 *Tughlaq*

1975 *Hayavadana*

1990 *Naga-Mandala*

1993 *Tale-Danda*

1998 *The Fire and the Rain*

For his obsession regarding the mythic infiltration of the texts he has set a different pattern in the process of playwriting: "From one historical standpoint, the folk-based drama of Kambar, Tanvir, Panikkar, Thiyan and Karnad is paradoxically the only new postcolonial genre, exemplifying the successful assimilation of indigenous materials and conventions to contemporary theatre" (Dharwadker 2005: 71). Against the backdrop of spatial luminality, *Tale-Danda* is about Basavanna, a twelfth-century Karnataka-based social reformer, and his reconfiguration of Indian political ideology, regarding caste system. In *The Fire and the Rain* which is supposed to be "the finest of Karnad's play" (Naik and Narayan 205), Karnad delves deep into the mythical reservoir – this time it is the relational rapture with the national epic *Mahabharata*. Through the dramatic incidents and coincidences like relationship, patricide, betrayal, caste problem, the play finally, like *The Waste Land*, dramatizes the pathetic cry for water and like *The Guide*, it ends with the possibility of much desired rain to quench the fire of anger, hatred and lust. Unlike the other dramas, *Hayavadana* leaves a message of spiritual significance. [1] The political application of *Tughlaq*, through the protagonist's Machiavellian nature, confronts the readers with issues like psychological isolation, deliberate manipulation, confrontation of power politics and many more. Dharwadker very precisely sums up the standpoint of Karnad in the field of Indian English drama:

> He is not a 'political' playwright of the same kind as Utpal Dutt, G. P. Deshpande, or even Vijay Tendulkar. But like many other Indian intellectuals, since the late 1980s Karnad has had to negotiate a new phase in the politics of the nation, and his stand against religious nationalism has led inevitably to confrontation and controversy.
>
> (Introduction 2005:xxxvii-xxxviii)

Dealing with the disturbing discomfort to the viewers, Karnad pinpoints the depth of cultural queerness related to the reservoir of Indian mythology. For that reason, critics have sometimes described him as a recreational writer. Dharwadker's rigid statement that "In many respects, *Naga-Mandala* is a companion piece and 'sequel' to *Hayavadana* rather than a work of striking originality" (Introduction 2005: viii) gives the play an absolutely new dimension of meaning that ultimately has made the text much popular at least in the academic discipline. *Naga-Mandala: Play with a Cobra*, a play originally written in Kannada and later translated in English by the dramatist himself, opens with the Prologue that projects the disturbing sense of an unsatisfied Man, a failed playwright. The Man's intense desire has been put on the conditional point that has been attributed by the personified 'Story'. The story telling method discussion of this artistic method in the Prologue of the drama gives the play a cult Indian dimension because story telling method has deeply been ingrained in the Indian psychology; R.K. Narayan in *The Guide* and Raja Rao in *Kanthapura* have exploited that oral genealogy to the maximum. *Naga-Mandala* too is a powerful product of recreational zeal regarding some local folklore:

> The two Kannada tales, the 'Tale of Tales' and also the 'Rani's Tale' in the play, emerge from the Indian folklore, which, like in Karnad's other plays, also operates in this play, as the context, in which the communication in the play in general and the speech situations, or to narrow down further, the speech acts in particular are processed. As the socio-cultural ethos in Kannada tales is part of the Indian folklore, by becoming the socio-cultural context of the communication in the play, operates as a connecting factor between the real world and, the literary and the theatrical worlds.
>
> (Jagadale 116-7)

In the very beginning of the text, the achievement of the unnamed man's whims has been resisted by his previous vow: "I have just now taken a vow not to have anything to do with themes, plots or acting. If I live, I don't want to risk any more curses from the audiences." (04) Vis-à-vis such statement, Naik and Narayan read the play totally on that direction of artistic story-making:

> The tale of the failed playwright seems to suggest that art demands everything from the artist and that he will die if he cannot fulfill his mission. The Rani-Appanna-Cobra tale is evidently an allegory of the nexus between the world of art and the world of mundane reality. That the cobra finally finds permanent refuge in the hair of Rani is perhaps indicative of the permanent *alliance between art and imagination.*
>
> (203, my emphasis)

In fact, unsatisfied desires bring the divisive ideologies of abstruse subject, working through the clandestine activities. In such a socio-religious setting where the 'idol is broken' (1), fulfilment of dream is not an easy one to achieve. The Man is not sleeping at that night only because he has a tremendous whim to live: "A mendicant told me: 'You must keep awake at least one whole night this month.'" (1) The interesting Prologue also projects the unnamed Man's compressed desire of survival: "I swear by this absent God, if I survive this night I shall have nothing more to do with themes, plots or stories. I abjure all story-telling, all play-acting." (2) Compression or suppression of powerful passions is a strategic shift to the assumed identity, not the real one.

Episodic intensification of personal drives of desire and dissatisfaction brings the sense of burgeoning inequality in the stringent standards of society. The play also focuses the marital muddle and misunderstanding in the lives of Rani and Appanna through the interplay of excision of masculinity and woman awakening. Sensitive openness ["She cannot even weep" (6)] and insensitive darkness [Appanna "*pays no attention to her, goes out, shuts the door, locks it from outside and goes away*" (6)] bring the contrastive display of different human dislocation when the sense of romantic affinity is lost. Unsatisfied whims of Rani can easily be contrasted to the satisfied desire of Rani's father when he found for Rani 'a suitable husband' who was "rich and his parents were both dead" (6). Such drastic desire, be it satisfied or unsatisfied, brings the problem of influencing in fluency, a resource reliant of shape shifter. Even the 'crying' (11) of Rani's mother during Rani's leaving with her husband is one such eternal hunger of human desire to put their child very near to them eternally. And later on the statement of Rani too marks such contrast of her present life and her life in her father's house:"I am so frightened at night, I can't sleep a wink. At home, I sleep between Father and Mother. But here, alone ... I would jump into a well – if only I could" (11). Such intensification of intention heavily connotes the reflection of the obligatory presence of dizzying desire in the dazzling display of human lives.

Like Garbo in Elkunchwar's *Garbo*, Rani too is being treated as a mere machine in the patriarchal production house that captures exploration of exploitation:"Well, then, I'll be back tomorrow at noon. Keep my lunch ready. I shall eat and go."(6)

Consequently, Kappanna's sentence is not an overstatement when she questions Appanna's disruptive behaviour:"That Appanna should have been born a wild beast or a reptile. By some mistake, he got human birth. He can't stand other people." (8)

Against the backdrop of gender politics, Rani was refused to get an entry in public by her husband because public sphere was considered only for the male members of the family, while only the private trope was strictly assigned for female. A similar observation has been reflected in Tara's momentary spurt of energy in *Tara*: "The men in the house were deciding on whether they were going to go hunting while the women looked after the cave." (Dattani 328)

Unlike the other texts of Karnad, *Naga-Mandala* is not simply a literalization of mythical history; yet it definitely contains the unseen implication of folklore materials. In the projection of a contemporary scenario, Rani has nothing but only one action to 'serve' (7) Appanna food and 'snob' (7) silently. Unadjusted tune of utter dissatisfaction marks Rani, unlike Padmini in *Hayavadana*, to be the puppet of the patriarchal power: "I'm bored to death. There is no one to talk to!" (11) The present case supports the social theorist's observation that the wife who became a subject through the ideology of marriage was increasingly subjected to a husband who was supposed to appropriate her agency. [3] Rani's father found the suitable boy – in fact, 'suitable husband' ["The young man was rich and his parents were both dead." (6)] for Rani with the intention that Rani will live in wealth and there will not be any interfering parents-in-law. But Rani is now sensing the poor nature of her perverted 'lunatic' (9) husband in her lonely deracinated life:"I am sick of being alone" (23). At this time, it would be relevant to focus on a reference:"Vives in *The Duty of a Husband* is urging husbands not to neglect their wives' educations and reminding them that women were rational creatures created by God" (Wilcox 16). Rani's present existential situation of isolationism can even be read in terms of Menon's argument:"Single women are ... invisible and disempowered" (154). Years ago, Kurudavva's intention of marriage could be fulfilled by some self-imposed superstition; but achievement of intention for all the time is not a subject to such libidinal fulfillment. Desirability of a near and dear husband does not work for Rani because there was some other taxonomy of desires:

> KURUDAVVA: Didn't want to tell you. There is a woman, a bazaar woman. She has your husband in her clutches. Squeezes him dry ... (15)

Vis-à-vis such sexual perversion, woman's existence is put in an undemocratic atmosphere. At this time I will let Leonard mention his observation to the fullest:

> Women, individually or collectively, are social actors who often actively aim to surmount the disadvantages that they face within their household, community and wider society. However, women's activism should reflect the broadening context of politics that includes action at local, national and international levels. Women's

> participation in formal politics remains marginal and falls well behind that of men. (86)

By rousing the subterranean animosity like Rakesh's *Halfway House*, Karnad's textual projection and rejection of the intentional social stratification question the readers whether women's forbidden space should be cut short right from its embryonic form to safeguard the sacrosanct meaning of marital relationship. As far as Rani's relation-status is concerned, the text shows us that Appanna has "judged her wrongly and treated her badly" (40). Keeping in mind the entire gamut of Karnad's female characters, the dramatist's "deep-rooted humanism and concern for the upliftment of the Indian women have produced two sets of characters – one the traditional representing the gendered subalternity; another progressive which mark the evolution of womenfolk. Devayani, Sharmistha and Chitralekha in *Yatri*, Padmini in *Hayavadana*, Rani and Kurudavva in *Naga-Mandala*, Vishakha and Nitilai in *The Fire and the Rain*, Chandravati in *Flowers*, Manjula Nayak and Malini in *The Broken Images*, Vidula Nadkarni, Pratibha Khan and Hema, Radhabai, Mira, Vatsala and Yamuna in *Wedding Album* define the feminine world of Karnad which embodies several aspects possessing modern relevance" (Singh 135).

The incidental slapping to Rani is a customary patriarchal desire to treat woman as a mere object to mould it according to the whimsical male desire. That's why Indrani Sen observes the strategy of patriarchy which has designed the concept of home as "an area of protection from external dangers and as a space containing female sexuality, the notion of separate spheres being obviously undergirded by anxieties about female sexual energy and, in effect, imposing a 'chastity lock' on the female body through domestic confinement" (02). Consequently, 'She' becomes the 'other' to perform the assigned order according to the dialectic demand of male desire through the cult of typical manliness:

KURUDAVVA:(*Pause.*) Does he ... 'talk' to you?

RANI:Oh, that he does. But not a syllable more than required. 'Do this', 'Do that', 'serve the food'. (10)

As narrative is "a means of bestowing meaning on one's life because it provides the possibility of looking back at life from beyond the ending" (Hessie 48), Rani's narrative captures the ill-treatment thrust at her by patriarchy which is a powerful powerhouse for the suppression of woman-identity; it is an organized system of "male power that permeates all aspects of life at all times and in all places" (Lloyd 74). Vis-à-vis patriarchy, women, from cradle to grave, are mere objects to confront that devouring and devastating nature of patriarchy: "Women who dissent do not always emerge only as 'victims', but often as 'perpetrators' in upholding repressive orders" (Ghosh 7).

Limitless fragmented identity of women, as we find in Deshpande's *That Long Silence*, is the mythical focus of patriarchy much before Philomela. At this time it would be relevant to mention Vasudha's monologue in Shanta Gokhale's *Avinash*: "There's only two ways open to us. We either despair and die, or hope and live. Who knows how this baby will be – perfect or imperfect, bringing joy or sorrow. But it's a whole new life. And that's something. A new life to live with and grow with." (30-1)

At the regular proliferation of male desire, liberating space for women is being terribly restricted into the heavily enclosed space:"... patriarchy becomes an *ahistorical category* within an originating *myth of male coercion.* The strength of this position, however, lies in the fact that it foregrounds patriarchal oppression as existing within all historically known modes of production and as a socio-cultural system cutting across class divisions." (Sangari and Vaid 23, my emphasis)

The projection of Rani's dissident imagination marks it to be a meta-critical space of liberation and deliberation because delinquency always excites desire. Rani's tremendous crave for her association with the disguised lover Naga is a clear hint of desired escaping from such crude reality or real crudity imposed by patriarchal parade. Rani's rapport with Naga definitely contains the germs to bombard patriarchy by projecting the psycho-sociological gloss of elusive freedom:

> Active female sexuality is disruptive of patriarchal control, not just because it is an emblem for, or analogous to, other sorts of rebellion, but because it directly threatens the power base of patriarchy which is dependent upon its regulation and control.
>
> (Loomba 56)

Social theorists through the classificatory topography have treated the concept of 'home' as the "female sphere per excellence" (Casanova 33). The room where Rani is enclosed becomes one such female sphere where multiple female dream and achievement are negotiated through freedom in bondage and produces the fantasy figure of reclamation (Naga) who virtually becomes a liberating figure for satisfaction; it is understandable that this 'room of Rani's own' remains far away from the confined, claustrophobic domestic dynamics. Very soon, her pregnancy puts her in front of a zone of romance; but disguised Naga probably has something other in his mind that goes against the female *jouissance*:

> RANI:... What I feared has come true. What kept me silent has happened. Youare not happy about the baby. You are not proud that I am going to be a mother. Sometimes you are so cold-blooded – you cannot be human. (31)

Dealing with the feminist spin, she scripts her story rejecting any conjectural history. In the world of superstition and 'spell' (15), it is ultimately the mirror that represents the reality by reflecting the real appearance of Naga. The disembarkation card of the deceiving elf (Naga) questions the introspective reasoning of intention. In that sense, Naga can be equated to Kanhaiya of Dattani's *Bravely Fought the Queen*. Be it a problematic drama or dramatic problem of a pregnant woman, the point is to be noted is that women become more assertive during pregnancy. Benare's final soliloquy in Tendulkar's *Silence! The Court Is In Session* will prove the point. Incommensurability of interpretive dynamics of human desires, as the play dramatizes, leads the characters towards the non-identical networks of nodal points of dissatisfactory humiliation: "I am not a parrot. Not a cat or a sparrow. Why don't you take it in trust that I have a mind and explain this charade to me? Why do you play these games? Why do you change like a chameleon from day to night?" (32). The text has basically been formed through the character's flexible accumulation of the specific obsessional effect. Rani tries to make a resistance for recognition against the patriarchal pelf through her assertive tone for her child. Identical assertion generally provides a strong self that wants to construct the autonomous self power with an apparent impression of filling the prevalent social lacks. Appanna has no desire to fulfil the feminine desires of Rani, but can cast a strong desire to humiliate his wife in front of the villagers; he can "publicly question his wife's chastity" (36). Rani too, like Hardy's Tess and Tendulkar's Benare, becomes a woman under public question because the woman in the dock is a timeless mythical sensation for patriarchy. Cohen rightly observes:

> Deviance, in one shape or another, is everywhere. All societies ... have rules, whose violation excites some disapproval, anger, or indignation. And where there are rules, there is indignation. (1)

Once again it is the woman who has to examine in the time of identity crisis: "Yes, my husband and this King Cobra. Except for these two, I have not touched anyone of the male sex. Nor have I allowed any other male to tough me. If I lie, let the Cobra bite me" (39). Vis-à-vis Rani's statement of chaste resignation, it would be relevant to mention Steele's argument:

> The formation of desired notions of spirituality and of womanhood is thus a part of the formation of the middleclass itself, wherein hierarchies and patriarchies are sought to be maintained on both material and spiritual grounds. (10)

In the interplay as well as intra-play of womanhood and desire, the specific problem is: "Desire is not purely a matter of the flesh but involves the soul:the shame of desire is that the soul cannot command either its own wishes or the body" (Belsy 62). Lacking any fulfilment of her desire(s), Rani remains alone, isolated, suppressed, cornered and fragmented because there is no one to replay, rely and relay; it is pathetic that her husband comes home only 'for lunch' (11). Anindita Ghosh is absolutely right in her observation: "The apparent harmony between oppressors and the oppressed is merely a masquerade as it conceals deeper and ever present roots of disquiet and change" (5). Allied with the voice of disagreement, they are mismatched couple through their segregationist impulse of self-righteousness and self-defeating; dissatisfaction is the sense and essence of their marital life. Through the unadjusted tune and tone, Rani becomes a victim of prejudice in the existential labyrinth, full of disgraceful and disgracing elements:

> APPANNA. Aren't you ashamed to admit it, you harlot? I locked you in, and yet you managed to find a lover! Tell me who it is. Who did you go to with your sari off?
>
> RANI. I swear to you I haven't done anything wrong!
>
> APPANNA. You haven't? And yet you have a bloated tummy. Just pumped air into it, did you? And you think I'll let you get away with that? You shame me in front of the whole village, you darken my face, you slut - ! (33)

It is not understandable that why Appanna leaves the 'tender bud' (19) and 'a pretty jasmine' (13) like Rani alone in the home. The picture of an 'ailing mother' (03) and 'insomnia' (08) of Kurudavva are not the isolated picture of society but it is a general image of 'ailing' women in the hegemonically patriarchal society. The following sentence brings the expression how the formation of patriarchy happens in our society – "a woman is supposed to be in the house" (9). In Padmanabhan's "Lights Out", Bhasker opines to Naina and Mohan: "A decent woman would never be with four men at once" (174). Even the jealous Harebrain in Thomas Middleton's *A Mad World, My Masters* (1608) believed that textual pleasure will definitely lead to sexual pleasure. Wendly Hallway rightly observes:

> It seems that any social relation between a woman and a man sparks off assumptions that sex is at the root of it. Women are inadvertently sexualized by a combination of male colleagues' sexually predatory behaviour and husbands' lack of faith in them. It does not need all men to behave in this way, either as husbands or colleagues, for this sexualization to pervade the organizational culture and disadvantage women. (256)

At certain times, antagonism and agonism of desire bring a pressurizing additive logic of interrogatory stance that can only cast what Vaid and Sangari call "slender representation of women" (4) in their social quest. Speaking symbolically, the image of locking up the key is a marker of locking up the female desire, by putting woman in the corner. Rani is in fact a 'caged bird' (10) who, like a living and sensitive human being must have the desire to 'talk' (10) to others. In spite of nourishing such desire she has been put away from speech: "In its most general sense, voice can be defined as the reward for the successfully battling oppressive systems that enforce, or it may represent the very means by which the battle was fought" (232). Like Benare in Tendulkar's *Silence*, Rani too expresses her innermost feeling to the disguised Naga that contains the dark travesty of female consciousness:

> RANI. I was a stupid, ignorant girl when you brought me here. But now I am a woman, a wife, and I am going to be a mother. I am not a parrot. Not a cat or a sparrow. Why don't you take in on trust that I have a mind and explain this charade to me? Why do you play these games? Why do you change like a chameleon from day to night? Even if I understood a little, a tiny bit – I could bear it. But now – sometimes I feel my head is going to burst! (32)

In *Sakharam Binder*, women, in a derogatory sense, have been treated as birds and are put in the "bird's cage". Rani's assertive feminocenric tone nurtures the germs to dismantle the monolithic paradigmatic unity where the male members are the sole decision maker. Pradip Basu, in his analysis of Kinship Theory, has rightly observed:

> Every society has some system for deciding who can marry whom, who inherits what from whom, and how all of these relationship are named .... Kinship systems explain what Levi-Strauss called the 'exchange of women', wherein family groups 'give' women to another family to be a wife, and receive in exchange something of value (a dowry). (44)

Undoubtedly, Rani, throughout the text, has been projected as the 'second sex', the other, the cornered, the marginalized, the victimized and it culminates with the sense how the female being 'becomes' woman through the criss-cross layers of women's subjection and subjugation:

> Karnad's *Naga-Mandala* is a sociological study of Indian women; richly textured dramatic transmutation of two folk tales of Karnataka. It not only exposes the ugliness of a society where woman is considered "second sex", other, "subject", "non-man" – women are taught in the process of being socialized, to internalize the reigning patriarchal ideology – e.g. male superiority; and so conditioned to derogate their own sex and to cooperate in their own subordination. (Singh 137)

Though 'she' is depicted as the other, 'she' has also been given a minimum space of self-realization and self-induced sensitivity at the end of the text when the text suddenly takes a u-turn through the deification of woman:

> ELDER I. Appanna, your wife is not an ordinary woman. She is a goddess incarnate. Don't grieve that you judged her wrongly and treated her badly. That is how goddesses reveal themselves to the world. You were the chosen instrument for revealing her divinity. (40)

It is a new space of abstention, bringing together epistemological error and ontological turn. Almost at the end of the critical convergence, the pathetic cry of Kurudavva ["Son! Where are you?" (43)] is the desired search of every mother for her own child. To see her child visually she can only wish for eyes verbally: "If only I had my eyes" (38). Much like this blind Kurudavva, Andhaka too in *The Fire and the Rain*, has an immense desire to look the way of the world. Her static situation can well be described in the social theorists' words:

> Deprived of access to the (dark, satanic) places of subsistence and survival, disabled people joined the growing ranks of itinerants and became a 'social problem'. Forced into idleness, they became categorized as 'unproductive' and consequently burdensome.
>
> (Peterson 37)

By mixing memory with desire, Kurudavva realizes how Appanna's mother could not fulfil her unsatisfied desire of rearing up her child as she "died bringing him into this world" (8). In fact, desire, through its intensification of the gap between self and society, has a tremendous mechanism of social disintegration:

> The political and ideological necessity to redefine the nature and status of women becomes obvious in the face of unprecedented changes that included gender relations. These changes span the economic and social status of women, their demography and spatial placement within society, and also the ideologies of their containment and scope for resistance.
>
> (Loomba 67)

In addition, the total play can also be read in terms of dissatisfaction of everyday mundane world and crave for dissident imaginative world – particularly from the perspective of women realization to construct the 'identity': "... identity categories provide modes of articulating and examining significant correlations between lived experience and social location" (Moya 4). Any society constructs gender roles and this text promotes that construction: "As we create masculinity and feminity, so we also make love. Sexuality is a construct." (Snitow and Thompson 10)

The sense of loose patriarchal authority has been implied here: "The woman's role ... is rigidly defined by male authority structure" (Hall and Londsey 250). Appanna threats Rani further with violent outcomes through the managerial strategies of spatial reordering:

> APPANNA. Open the door! Open the door, you whore! All right then, I'll show you. I'll go to the Village Elders. If they don't throw that child into boiling oil and you along with it, my name is not Appanna. (33)

In this psychodrama of sublimated self-expression, the readers sometimes get the elements that contain the crisis of masculinity. As the Village Elders are mentioned by Appanna as referrals in the oasis of radical reform, they are now ready to cast their customary vigilance on the woman which has been described by Ghosh as women's 'discursive trappings' (6) through the dispassionate mode of address:

> ELDER II. It brings no credit to the village to have a husband publicly question his wife's chastity. But Appanna here says:Since the day of our wedding, I have not once touched my wife or slept by her side. And yet she is pregnant. He has registered the complaint, so we must judge its merits. (36)

The cacophony and commands of the Village Elders' put taxation on Rani's relaxation by forcing her to take the ordeal.[4] The Village Elders' decision regarding the 'traditional test' (37) related to "inter-religious and intra-religious perspectives" (Dharwadker, Introduction 2005: x) has havoc conformity with Cohen's observation:

> Every system can tolerate a certain amount of ambiguity, and even confusion, and there are no doubt many rules that regulate conduct with such precision and detail that they thwart rather than facilitate the accomplishment of human purposes. It may be arguable whether any particular rule is necessary or even useful. There must, however, be rules that set some limits to discretion and inclination. (4)

Moreover, dogs and mongoose, in a similar pattern to the folk tales, are even used to watch and guard a woman and the deaths of these animals are the markers of falling down of the continuous mythical patriarchal vigilance upon woman. At this critical juncture it would be relevant to mention the aspects of folklore:

> The emergence of Indian folklore, as the socio-cultural context, is doubtlessly supported by the very concept of the folk theatre, which very often brings together the folklore and the theatre, the combination skillfully exercised by Karnad. The folk values in the folklore, the various literary techniques (like introducing the comic interludes and the amalgam of human and non-human worlds) in literature, and the various theatrical conventions (like the use of music, chorus, costumes, light effects etc) in the theatrical performances.
>
> (Jagadale 117)

Folk culture is sometimes taken as nation's self-expression through the emotional spillover of the characters' conflux. Even the heavily conflictual ending of unfinalizability marks the desired notion of dissatisfaction. *A la* Kermode, the ending of a literary work marks a much necessary reflection for a desired temporal propriety of ordered force. To conclusive, through the "recurrent patterns of thematic engagement with ancient myth" (Dharwadker, Introduction 2005: vii), Karnad's text, by projecting two different endings, is indeed a practical case in point. The text also proves age old belief as reflected in Charlott Lucas's statement of socio-historic metaphor:"Happiness in marriage is entirely a matter of chance." Irrespective of time and space, the classified folk rituals like woman's salvation – be it Rani of *Naga-Maṇdala* or Sita of *Mahavarata* and *satidaha* (widow immolation) bears the sense of unassimilated otherness in male dominant society. The mythical reification of the collective effervescence against a single woman is going on and on through the politics of gender that always cabins, cribs and confines women's polemicist position.

References

1. Critics like Dalmia have categorized Bharati's *Andha Yug*, Tendulkar's *Gashiram Kotwal* and Karnad's *Hayabadana* as the "classics of modern Indian theatre" (194).
2. See Wilcox 68.
3. For a detailed discussion regarding the assertive female voice, see Subramanyam's thesis.
4. See Chapter 6 of Austen's *Pride and Prejudice.*

Works Cited

Basu, Pradip. *Postmodernism, Marxism, Postcolonialism*. Kolkata: Avenel, 2010. Print.

Belsy, Catherine. *Shakespeare in Theory and Practice.* Edinburgh: Edinburgh UP, 2008. Print.

Casanova, Jose. "Private and Public Religions." *Social Research* 59. 1. 1992. Print.

Cohen, Albert K. *Deviance and Control.* New Jersey: Princeton-Hall, 1966. Print.

Dalmia, Vasudha. *Poetics, Plays and Performances: The Politics of Modern Indian Drama.* New Delhi: Oxford UP, 2006. Print.

Dattani, Mahesh. *Collected Plays.* New Delhi: Penguin, 2000. Print.

Dharwadker, A. B. *Theatres of Independence: Drama, Theory, and Urban Performance in India since 1947.* New Delhi: Oxford UP, 2005. Print.

_______ Introduction. *Girish Karnad: Collected Plays,* V II. New Delhi: Oxford UP, 2005. Print.

Ghosh, Anindita, ed. *Behind the Veil: Resistance, Women, and the Everyday in Colonial South Asia.* New Delhi: Permanent Black, 2007. Print.

Gokhale, Shanta. "Avinash." *City Plays.* Calcutta: Seagull, 2004. Print.

Hall, Calvin S. and Gardner Londsey. *Theories of Personality.* Wiley, 1985. Print.

Hallway, Wendly. "Separation, Integration and Difference:Confrontations in a Gender Regime." Eds. H. L. Radtke and H. J. Stam. *Power/ Gender: Social Relations in Theory and Practice.* London: Sage, 1994. Print.

Heise, Ursula K. *Chronoschisms: Time, Narrative, and Postmodernism.* Cambridge: Cambridge UP, 1997. Print.

Jagadale, Umesh S. "Pragmatic Analysis of a Speech Situation from Girish Karnard's *Naga-Mandala.*" *Re-exploring Indian Drama in English.* Eds. S. B. Barure and M. A. Sami Siddiqui. Jaipur: Vital, 2011. Print. 116-31

Karnad, Girish. *Naga-Mandala:Play with a Cobra.* New Delhi: Oxford UP, 1990. Print. [Page reference has been made from this edition.]

_______ "Performance, Meaning, and the other Materials of Modern Indian Theatre." Interview with Aparna Bhargava Dharwadker. *New Theater Quarterly 44*, 1995. 355-70. Print.

Kermode, Frank. *The Sense of an Ending*. London:Oxford UP, 1967. Print.

Leonard, Madeleine. "Women and Development:Examining Gender Issues in Developing Countries." Eds. Gerard McCann and Stephen McCloskey. *From the Local to the Global:Key Issues in Development Studies*. London: Pluto P, 2003. Print. 76-92.

Lloyd, Moya. *Beyond Identity Politics: Feminism, Power and Politics*. London: Sage, 2005. Print.

Menon, Nivedita "Power." *Political Theory: An Introduction*. Eds. Rajeev Bhargava and Ashoke Acharya. New Delhi:Pearson Longman, 2008. Print.

Moya, Paula M. L. Introduction. *Reclaiming Identity: Realist Theory and the Predicamentof Postmodernism*. Eds. Moya, Paula M. L. and Hames-Garcia, Michael. Hyderabad: Orient Longman, 2001. Print.

Naik, M. K. and Shyamala A. Narayan. *Indian English Literature 1980 – 2000: A Critical Study*. New Delhi: Pencraft, 2007. Print.

Padmanabhan, Manjula. "Lights Out." *City Plays*. Calcutta: Seagull, 2004. Print.

Peterson, Kavin and Bill Hughes. "Disabled Bodies." *The Body, Culture and Society: An Introduction*. Buckinghum: Open UP, 2000. Print.

Sangari, K. and Vaid, S. *Recasting Women: Essays in Colonial History*. Delhi: Zubaan, 2006. Print.

Sen, Indrani. *Women and Empire*. New Delhi: Orient Longman, 2002. Print.

Singh, Krishna. "The Plays of Grish Karnad: A Feminist Study." *Labyrinth*, Vol. 2 / No. 4. Ed. Lata Mishra, Gwalior: October 2011, 135-43. Print.

Snitow, A., C. Stamsell and S. Thompson, eds. "Introduction." *Powers of Desire*: *Monthly Review*, 1983. Print.

Subramanyam, Lakshmi, ed. *Muffled Voices: Women in Modern Indian Theatre*. New Delhi: Shakti, 2002. Print.

Whitson, Kathy J. *Encyclopedia of Feminist Literature*. London: Greenwood P, 2005. Print.

Wilcox, Helen, ed. *Women and Literature in Britain, 1500–1700*. Cambridge: Cambridge UP, 1996. Print.

18

The Zhadipatti Theatre of Vidharbha: An Unheard Melody

Durgesh Ravande

The researcher of the present paper intends to focus on a theatrical movement, initiated by certain indigenous tribal communities in the remote jungles of the districts like Gadchiroli, Chandrapur, Bhandara and Nagpur in Vidharbha region of Maharashtra. The earlier plays were limited to the indomitable faith of the tribes in gods, goddesses and local deities. The theatre has been dealing with the realistic issues like political and cultural oppression of the tribals, growing corruption in government schemes, terrific poverty, and sustaining inclination of adivasi youth towards Naxalite Movement. 'Consider us human beings and not beasts'—this is what The Zhadipatti Theatre urges. The term 'tribe' is applicable to an ethnic group of people who have distinct social, economic, and cultural traditions and practices. The tribal communities like the Gonds, the Santhals, the Mundas and the Great Andamanese have inhabited India for centuries.

The present research paper is an attempt to introduce an indigenous theatre in the dense jungles of Vidharbha of Maharashtra state. The theatre is about to complete one hundred and fifty years of its formation but yet it is an unheard melody for the outside world. Researchers like Dr. Ajay Joshi are doing their level best to let this glorious theatrical tradition be known to the budding theatre talent in our country. But it will take time to account the actual impression. The first performance on

Zhadipatti's rostrum was staged around 1870-80. But the first top to bottom Zhadipatti performance took place in the year 1960 with the staging of *Khedychi Mansa* (Village People). Since then this theatre has been captivating the minds of the tribes in this region and striving for social integration among the different social segements. The highly claimed postcolonial perspective of finding voice by reclaiming own's past is indisputably applicable to this *theatrum mundi.*

The villages where the theatrical performances under the banner of Zhadipatti take place, are located about 200 km from Nagpur, one of the metro cities in Maharashtra. The distance between these villages and Naxalite hideouts is absolutely modest. These villages are comprised in the districts like Chandrapur, Nagpur, Bhandara, Gondia and Gadchiroli. The natives in the region are either illiterate or less-educated. They are superstitious and unaware of the rapidly changing World. Amidst forests and wild animals and away from towns and cities, the Zhadipatti artists have been doing justice with one of the oldest arts of our country. The tribes in this area belong to Kosti, Gund, Wanjari, Manja, Dhiwar, Govari, Dhangar, Kunli, Mali, Teli and Chattisgarhi community. Agriculture is their major pre-occupation. But at the same time, their imdomitable passion for theatre cannot be kept aside. The performances under Zhadipatti's banner are being carried out further with the help of several groups working in the villages and small towns.

Wadsa, one of the villages in Gadchiroli district, has surprisingly more than 33 groups as such. These groups perform at different places and on different occasions. The theatre, in this way, has been exerting to preserve the heritage of these communities. The predominant influence of folk forms like Tamasha, Gondhal, Dandhar, Chattisgarhi Nautanki and Ghotul is observed clearly while watching the performances. Etymologically 'zhadi' means jungle whereas patti stands for a piece of land. If we take both the words together, loosely it can be a Jungle Theatre.

The Zhadipatti Theatre generally does not follow any conventional norms of presentation. The dictum *Art for Art's Sake* hence has a bit modification as *Art for Audiences' Sake*, in this regard. Total entertainment is the sole purpose of the performances staged under its banner. It is quite interesting to know the system these performances generally follow. The performance has to be booked well in advance, loosely six to eight months earlier with paying at least half of the amount. The remaining amount is to be paid between the break in two acts of the performance. Failing which means the show to be shut down midway! The performance is taken for wider popularity by sticking the posters at the prominent places in the nearby villages. The performances take place generally between October to the end of February. Being the postharvest period,the farmers afford to pay easily to watch the show. For the remaining months, the artists work in farms and the writers keep themselves busy in writing the new scripts for new seasons. The period of these performances coincides with the annual bulllock race the Shankar pat. The race participants gather in the night at performance place and spectacle it through out the night. The performance locations are considered as perfect match making places as most of the match-makings happen here.

The earlier Zhadipatti performances were limited to the stories of gods, goddesses and local deities. One of the indigenous Zhadipatti writer Chudaman Ballarpure's *Mahamritunjaya Markaandeshwar*, a one-act play, is the best example of this kind. In course of time, the performances underwent a noticeable change. At present, the performances are being staged on the cardinal issues like economical exploitation of adivasis, suicides of farmers, naxal activities, growing corruption in government schemes, and cross-fire between the naxalite and the police. One of the important features of this theatre is an intact liberty for women to take part in the performances. The actors and actresses are their own people, that's why they reciprocate affection for everything that is part of this theatre. The theatre geared for a change with the formation of All India Zhadipatti Academy in 2002. Its first conference was held in the same year. The growing television and cinema culture has no way affected the overwhelming response being noticed by this theatre for more than hundred years now. The performances were free of cost till the end of nineteen seventies. But the rapidly changing socio-political-economical equations have brought a sea-saw change in this regard. The ticket rates are between Rs. 20 and Rs. 100 at present. But there is no change in the response registered then onwards. The turnover at the end of a season is more than any professional theatre company's annual income in Maharashtra.

The Zhadipatti theatre is a kind of mobile theatre, similar to the Tamasha of Maharashtra or Jatra of West Bengal. The theatre directly or indirectly interwines with Augusto Bwal's The Theatre of the Oppressed and Brecht's Epic Theatre. The stage is erected in a large open space with a piece of land in front of the stage. The spectators into accommodate chairs would then do not obstruct the people sitting at the back on the ground. Light setting and mike system is required to be operating well. The back stage has a make- up and resting room. The make-up rooms are separate for males and females with essential security for women. The performances usually take place under a huge *shamiyana* (a tent). The show generally creates a siman-pure impression on the mind of audience. It happens sometime that one who has viewed the on going performance earlier; stands up and demands for a change in the script. The organizer has no option instead of making the expected or demanded change.

The use of local dialect is pre-dominant in these performances. The script is pre-censored carefully before the actual performance. Special insistence is given for removing obnoxious part from the manuscript. Now a days, scriptwriters are preferring urbanized language due to sustaining television soap and cinema influence. As mentioned overhead, the script is loosely-structured for editing convenience. Editing at the level of language is done according to the requirement. The response of the spectators to both funny and serious subjects is one and the same. They take similar interest in watching both kinds of performances. The subjects of these plays mostly tackle their problems. The performances on different issues compel general audience to learn more about the different factors leading to their day to day living.

Aristotle, in his magnum opus, *Poetics* illustrated *melos* (melody) as one of the essential requirements for any dramatic presentation. The indigenous Zhadipatti theatre has been following it strictly. Whatever may be the subject of the play, the use of songs is mandatory. It shows, in this way, an association with the *Natyasangeet*, (Musical Drama) a celebrated dramatic tradition in Maharashtra. The performance is taken to a great height with the help of songs. Each play starts with the *Nandi*, an invocation for the blessings of deities. The conventional folk songs are also used effectively to serve this purpose. More than one thousand artists of different tribal castes are working under the banner of Zhadipatti, presently. Noted Marathi artists have performed their celebrated plays on the Zhadipatti stage. This stage has produced its own playwrights,actors,and technicians.

The local actor,playwright and director Chudaram Ballarpure has produced plays like *Ha Khel Savalyancha* (Shadows'Play) *Navare Zhale Baware* (The Confused Husbands), and *Atmahatya* (Suicide) etc. His highly acclaimed play *Special Report* strikes at how the cheap politics is destructing the small villages. Sadanand Borkar, one more local theatre personage, is the producer of the plays like *Satichi Satvapariksha* (A Virtuous Wife's Trial), *Mahakavi Bhasava*r (Bhasavar: The Great Poet), and *Hostelchya Kholit Khansaheb* (Khansaheb in a Hostel Room) etc. He has been doing his level best to enhance the quality of these native performances. This mini industry has been putting its best for years, now. It has been a favourite for skillful handling of different subjects. Without any aid from government, the theatre is doing well without any concern of the outer world.

A tribal song unfolds precisely the genuine urge of this theatre.

What is the use?
You have taken my fingures
Now I can not use a bow
You have taken my tongue
What is the use?
Now I don't have a bhasha
What is the use?
You have taken my ears
Now I can't hear my heart
What is the use? (Khare)

Word Cited

Khare, Randhir (2001). *The Singing Bow:Song-Poems of the Bhil.* Harper Collins: New Delhi.

Kulkarni, Pratibha (2007). ed. *Vidharbhatil Natakkar* (Playwrights in Vidharbha). Reesha Books: Mumbai.

19

Ecology and History in Mamang Dai's *The Legends of Pensam* and Easterine Iralu's *A Naga Village Remembered*: A Comparative Analysis

Nigamananda Das

India's Northeast is one amongst the world's 25 biodiversity hotspots and 17 biodiversity heritage sites. Ecologically rich as it is, the literary genres from the region explore the flora and fauna and the mysterious ecology, and expose the eco-consciousness of its people and other ethnic realities. As such the ecological writings are canonical as they expose the postcolonial ecological erosions. So far Penguin India has published more than half a dozen fictional works of authors from various provinces of the Northeast. These works explore the ecology and history of the region. The paper aims at analyzing an Arunachalee writer, Mamang Dai's novel *The Legends of Pensam* (Penguin, 2006) and a Naga writer, Easterine Iralu's *A Naga Village Remembered* (2003), comparing their ecological and historical concerns. These first generation postcolonial first novels in English from the two different provinces of the Northeast India showcase to the world some unknown chapters of India's history and ecology.

As a contrast to the "toxic consciousness" (Deitering 202) represented by the post-1980s postnatural American novels, the novels in English from India's Northeast, especially *The Legends of Pensam* by Mamang Dai and *A Naga Village Remembered* by

Easterine Iralu explore the ecology and history of their respective regions which have remained unexplored in writing till date. Mamang Dai, an ecopoet and fictionist from Arunachal, has mixed history with ecology and ecotheology to provide the readers with a recipe of unique taste, which reflects an in-between place in the mountains of Arunachal Pradesh. A former civil servant, now turned journalist, Mamang interprets the "hidden spaces of heart where a secret garden grows" (vii). Her exploration of ecology in the tribal world of Arunachal has mostly been restricted to her own community of Adis. She says, "Like the majority of tribes inhabiting the central belt of Arunachal, the Adis practise an animistic faith that is woven around forest ecology and co-existence with the natural world" (i). *The Legends of Pensam* evokes the "toxic consciousness" in presenting a comparative exploration of the past. The situations and surroundings of the past were completely different from what we are in. The fictionist in the prologue voices the same:

> We make no comparisons now. The river cuts through our land as before in its long journey to the sea. In spring the red flowers still blaze against our sky. But the old people now, the few of them alive, turn slowly in their sleep as the fires burn down to a heap of ash. In the middle of the night a bird swoops low and calls out in a wild, staccato note. The thatch rustles. The bamboo creaks. The darkness is full of breath and sighs (italic mine). (4)

The paragraph above presents a few contours of ecology. It presents nature in a broader sense. It may be the total cosmos and beyond and it depicts the chasm between the past and present. That chasm depicting darkness is full of breath and sighs (italic mine) is nostalgic, chaotic, toxic and significantly disturbing. We feel that we had something better in the past which we have lost now. As such our mind is occupied in a constant comparison between the experiences felt and the present feeling. Divided into four sections, the novel consisting of an intricate web of 19 stories, presents the history of a tribe which comprises a "moving tribute to the human spirit" (blurb). These stories are like legends narrating incidents or accidents relating to popular figures in the Adi clan of Arunachal. The stories depict "pensam" (inbetweenness) of several kinds. The very first legend "the boy who fell from the sky" speaks of Hoxo who saw "a green wall of trees and bamboo, and a green waterfall that sprayed his cheek and washed the giant fern that seemed to be waving to him (7). "The colour green always soothed him. It was the colour of escape and solitude" (8). The legend concludes in informing that Hoxo's father, Lutor, the famous Chief of the Ida clan was killed in hunting accident leaving behind his widow wife and son. Before changes came in the shape of postcolonial encounters, life in the tribal world though seemed to be very difficult and uncertain, was happy, meaningful and magical.

In the tribal world of Arunachal, the mysterious prevails plentily. A married woman would become a widow at any time. Nature and spirit, even evil spirits played games with human life. The story titled "Pinyar, the widow" reveals how Pinyar who became a widow before she was 25 years old. Pinyar, in spite of oppositions from her parents and relatives, fell in love with a man named Orka from a village beyond Siyum hills, far to the north of the country (26) and bore a son named Kamur from him, but the marriage failed and Orka left her taking his son Kamur away. Pinyar remarried a man named Lekon and became widow in the third month of her marriage as her husband Lekon was struck down in a hunting accident. Her lonely life was again threatened when her hut one day was accidentally caught fire and turned into ashes and that removed her to forest seclusion as per their tribal tradition. Her son Kamur who was well settled with a government job, two sons and an infant daughter was accidentally in trouble one day due to a trance-like fit that invaded his soul and made him mad so that he killed his infant daughter and one son with a rusty *dao* and attacked his wife who fortunately survived due to the intervention of the neighbours.

The mysterious / magical trance which troubles most human in the tribal world is believed to be from two or three sources of intoxication. These sources may be rice beer which is prohibited for the hunter before his hunting expedition, or the spirits and some trees having evil spirits boarded on them. About the rice beer and the race of *miti-mili* it is said:

> Once upon a time, there lived a race of supernatural beings called miti-mili. These small, quiet people were the first to make mysterious si-ye that is the yeast used to ferment rice into beer. Before the miti-mili race disappeared, deranged by strange visions, they gave this sacred powder to mankind, and a strong belief grew that si-ye had special powers and that it was something to be handled with respect. Only women were allowed to handle it, and Pinyar herself made the best si-ye cakes. She mixed the white powder with ground rice and roots and berries and shaped it into small flat biscuits. ... they are strictly forbidden before a hunt or a journey. ... 'It makes men hallucinate, just like the miti-mili race. But sometimes some households forget to observe the rules, and then our men die in the forests.' (29)

About the peculiar trees which have magical powers that intoxicate human minds and make them commit sins, it is said:

> People talked about the peculiar trees of the place. They remembered the aubergine plant that had grown to the size of a tree. Nobody could recall who had planted it or when. It bore small poisonous looking flowers that grew into long, bloated fruit, menacing and shiny. It was a ghostly tree and no one dared to cut it down. Kamur had sometimes been seen under that tree at odd hours, doing nothing in particular. (31)

The guardians of history speculate on the troubles in the tribal surroundings and feel that there is something in the blood or some spirits and ghosts or marriages (right or wrong) that are responsible for these accidents (ibidem). Narration of ecology and ecocriticism "involves a deliberate act of prestidigitation, a problematic process in which an identity is projected onto nature" (Head 235). Again [Lawrence] Buell's 'aesthetic of relinquishment' actually involves the need to imagine 'non-human agents as bonafide partners', and in his discussion of 'Nature's Personhood' Buell considers how, in environmental law, our identity can be assigned to nature "to engineer a change in the legal and ethical status quo by a discursive innovation frankly announced as fictive" (ibidem).

Mamang Dai through her chain of stories called *The Legends of Pensam* has asserted an identity of Arunachal and its tribes by associating the tribal life and activities with nature. Everything happens here in the bosom of nature. The natural surroundings and human and non-human transactions assume unlimited dimensions. Ecology encompasses all human and non-human transactions in all the spaces. She mixes history, ecology and ecotheology / ecotheosopy to give an understanding of the total tribal ecological and historical tradition in Arunachal, especially her own Adi Tribe. The novel contains several paragraphs on the ecology–types of landscape and related traditions which Mamang calls "small histories" (36):

> Everyday I saw clouds dropping lower and lower like ominous waves. The hills were blue, their outline rimmed in black, and the trees were still. Soon, the first fat beads of water would tear the giant leaves of the wild yam. Then fierce, hissing rain would cover the land like the sea. At such times it seems the heavens brush very close to the earth. The wild fruit born of this union is of unknown family, bittersweet, pungent, often misshapen and hardy, or swollen to an unnatural size. Hidden by mountains and covered by a charcoal sky the forest and rivers become battlefields ferocious with the struggle for survival .... (36-37)

The ecology of Arunachal was unknown to the other world up to the nineteen century."The first white priests, surveyors and soldiers had begun arriving in the region almost two hundred years ago, in the early 1800s. Since then people from other worlds had come and gone, though the only records of their journeys are the stories that the older men and women remember" (37-38). After the white men's entry into this fantastic ecological paradise, changes have been rapid. The early decades of the twentieth-century witnessed great upheaval. In 1911, a British political officer set out from the plains of Assam on a mission to explore the course of the river Siang flowing through the territory of the Adis. He was Noel Williamson, with twenty years of experience in dealing with the tribes in the hill tracts of the country. But unfortunately an angry Adi struck him down in the village of Komsing. It developed into massacre where Williamson, his tea garden doctor friend Dr. Gregorson, forty seven sepoys and coolies were killed. The three men who survived told the world what really happened. News of the massacre sent shockwaves across colonial India and resulted in punitive expedition of 1912, which become known as the Abor Expeditionary Field Force. A memorial stone to Williamson was unveiled, where it stands now even looked after by the villagers as the British had instructed (48).

In the midst of the dense natural surrounding there exists the tribal theology / theosophy which is also ecological. Prior to the advent of Christianity into this ecology, there was the traditional tribal religion, which still exists. The Arunachalee tribals believe in the Almighty Donyipolo, the sun and the moon (57). The priest chants verses, tells tales to the folk who sit before him to listen. He explains, "We are not here without a purpose" (56). And adds:

> Our purpose is to fulfil our destiny. The life of a man is measured by his actions and his actions are good if their origin is pure. From nothingness we have come to be born under the stars and almighty Donyi-polo, the sun and the moon, whose light shines on all equally 161 is the invisible force that guides each one of us. All life is light and shadow; we live and we die, and the path of destiny is the quest for faith. (57) Again about the whole creation/ecology the priest says:

In the beginning, there was only Keyum. Nothingness. It was neither darkness nor light, nor had it any colour, shape or movement. Keyum is the remote past, way beyond the reach of our senses. It is the place of ancient things from where no answer is received. Out of this place of great stillness, the first flicker of thought began to shine like a light in the soul of man. It became a shimmering trail, took shape and expanded and became the Pathway. Out of this nebulous zone, a spark was born that was the light of imagination. The spark grew into a shining stream that was the consciousness of man and from this all the stories of the world and all its creatures came into being. (56)

Mamang Dai mixing memory, desire, history and religion with ecology provides a real picture in fiction. The work is a landmark in postcolonial writing and being the first English novel from Arunachal Pradesh it is very important work in contemporary Indian Writing in English. Easterine Irulu's *A Naga Village Remembered* is also the first novel in English by a Naga writer. The book being a historical account of the proud Khonoma village and the Battle of Khonoma (1879-1880) and the activities of the American Baptist Mission and the first converts, also depicts the ecology and history of the hilly terrain and the faith of its people. Consisting of 14 chapters, the novel presents a detailed account the Battle of Khonoma and bravery of the Angami tribes of the village and the surrounding hills. In the introduction to the book the novelist gives a description of the village as is given below:

> Khonoma nestles amid mountains that are as high as 7,000 feet, a little village on a small hillock, cradled by gaunt mountains which form a natural fortress. Hidden from human view by this natural fortress of mountains, Khonoma can be seen from only one direction in the Northern Angami region between Meriema and Chieswema. Though her size of 500 houses was rather average among Angami villages, her fame spread far and wide as a warrior village. Her warriors of the Semo, Thevo and Merhu clans hardly numbered over a thousand at any given time in her history. However, Khonoma's protectorate extended in every direction, to the Southern, Northern, Eastern and Western Angami and Naga villages. To her north, there was some Sopfuma villages of the

> Shepoumaranth region who lived under protective alliances with Khonoma. Still further to the north, Khonoma's fame spread as far as the Maram and Anal regions on the borders of the Manipur kingdoms. On her north-western borders her name was respected all over the Zeliangrong region right up to the forts of the Kachar kingdom. On her south-eastern borders, Khonoma's fame was known through villages under her protectorate. On her northern borders, she had alliances with many villages. The kingdom of Manipur too knew of Khonoma's fame and had at one time sent Manipuri soldiers to guard the Semoma clan while they built their first fort. The King of Manipur had even sent his troops to assist certain clans in the village in their wars against their enemies. As for the plains of Assam to her west, Khonoma was a constant thorn in Assam's flesh for the repeated raids of head hunting and booty hunting. (xi)

The first British expedition to the Naga Hills was led in AD 1832 by Captain Jenkins and Captain Pemberton. The second expedition took place in 1849, when the British Government learnt that Khonoma had aided men of Mezoma opposed to the Government. After attacking and suppressing Mezoma, they attacked Khonoma to quell what they called "Khonoma defiance". Houses of the Thevo clan and Merhu clan were th burnt (xii). The third attack came on the 10 December, 1850, in an expedition led by Captain J. Butler and Major Foquett, Lieutenant Reid and Lieutenant Bivar. In October 1879, Deputy Commissioner Damant was killed at Khonoma. The Kohima garrison was shortly attacked by men of Khonoma, Tsutuonuomia clan, and warriors of Viswema, Chedama, Secuma, Jakhma, Zotshuma, Piphema and Tsiepama. The garrison survived a long siege and then prepared for another assault on Khonoma. The final expedition on Khonoma was in November, 1879 (ibidem).

Surrounded on all sides Khonoma was attacked on 22nd November with troops of 3,369 soldiers. Greatly outnumbered by the British Army, the men of Khonoma retreated to their impregnable mountain fort and the battle turned into a siege of the tough little Angami village for four months. On 27 March 1880, a treaty between the representatives of the British

Government and the elders of Khonoma brought conclusion to the conflict. The cold night, hills and hillocks, festivals, animistic faiths and the Naga resistance to the colonial rule and the history of the battles form the bedrock of the novel. The festivals are integral to the hill ecology, e.g., on the last day of the festival the villagers followed the two young children appointed to perform the rhoutho ritual of seed-sowing. At the fields, the elder pronounced the blessing:

> My paddy, may you grow up well, though the weeds are abundant, my paddy do you grow around the tree stumps and boulder. It will be the food of generations, the food of wartime, grow bent over with full husked grain. (66)

Both the writers are conspicuously concerned about the history, ecology, ecological theosophy and the turmoil of time against their respective animistic faiths. The two novels are significant additions to the tradition of Indian English fiction and to the ecocritical "toxic consciousness" as they reflect the degradation of pristine virgin ecology.

Works Cited

Dai, Mamang. *The Legends of Pensam.* New Delhi: Penguin Books, 2006.

Deitering, Cynthia. "The Postnatural Novel: Toxic Consciousness in Fiction of the 1980s", *The Ecocriticism Reader.* Ed. Cheryll Glotfelty and Harold Fromm. Athens: The University of Georgia Press, 1996, (198-203).

Head, Dominic. "Ecocriticism and the Novel", *The Green Studies Reader.* Ed. Laurence Coupe. Oxon: Routledge, 2000, (235-241).

Iralu, Easterine. *A Naga Village Remembered.* Kohima: Ura Academy, 2003.

20

Conceptualizing the Myth and Folklore: A Study of the Plays of Girish Karnad and Mahesh Dattani in the Indian Context

Abhinandan Malas

The influence of Indian myths and folklores is prominent in the development of the dramatic themes and characterizations in the postcolonial Indian drama in English. It is a fact that the post-independence Indian writers in English have always shown a tendency to get back to the Indian culture and tradition to present the issues and complexities that are prevailing in modern India. These issues and problems are affecting the existence of the individual by intruding into the space that forms the existential domain of that individual in the Indian social context.

The amalgamation of the colonial Western influence and the Indian cultural past demarcates the social and psychological space of an individual in the Indian society. The confluence of the two helps in forming the thematic motifs of the modern Indian theatre in English. Indian drama in English has tried to identify the space of an individual that is constituted by the myths and folklores that are directly related to the development of the plot of the play and the psychology of the characters. Therefore, it is important to understand and conceptualize the presence and the use of myth and folklore in the Indian context so that the existence of the Indian past and its present can be understood in various dimensions.

In this paper I focus on the plays of Girish Karnad and Mahesh Dattani where the deliberate and explicit use of the Indian tradition of myth and folklore is observed and which are presented symbolically in various contexts to represent various problems and social issues in the postcolonial India. I also focus on how the use of myth and folklore change and reconstruct the meaning and character formation of the plays of these two playwrights. In this paper I also intend to analyze the other texts to which these plays get related through myth and folklore in the Indian context.

It has always been an obsession with the writers of the postcolonial period of any country to revive their pre-colonial culture and tradition. But, these writers also try to locate the present problems that the country is facing due to its long colonial past. Therefore, these writers often refer to the mythologies, folklores, traditions and beliefs of their country to highlight the situation of the present. Eminent Indian playwrights like Badal Sircar, Vijay Tendulkar, Girish Karnad and Mahesh Dattani have innovated several theatrical devises and stage props that have redefined the contours of the modern Indian theatre. Several theatrical experiments and innovative narrative techniques have rendered these plays with the spirit of Indian culture that are reflected through the use of myths, folklores, history and tradition of India in these plays. Therefore, myth, folktales, history and tradition play a very important role in the development of the narrative techniques and thematic motifs of the writings of these playwrights. Similar is the situation in case of Girish Karnad and Mahesh Dattani.

To understand the plays of Karnad and Dattani it is important to understand how the Indian myth and folklore form the basic motif of these plays through which the playwrights highlight the various social issues, problems and situations in the postcolonial Indian society and deconstruct the social ideologies and concepts thus, putting forth a picture of the real structure of the modern Indian society both at the physical level and also at the psychological level. Myths and folklores in India are rooted in the Indian psyche and they form a discourse that runs parallel to the other discourses relating to different fields of studies. The characters presented by both these playwrights in their plays are rooted in these Indian myths and folklores thus, presenting Indian society in its natural context. Myths and folklores help us to interpret these plays in the Indian context and also enable us to locate the individual as an Indian in Indian society thus, remaining separated from Western ethics and forms. They also provide us with the vision to realize an Indian individual with the problems and issues which occur in India and can also get related to the issues of other foreign societies thus, giving the whole scenario a universal outlook. The use of myths and folklores as narrative techniques also helps the playwright to present the psychology of an Indian individual in the modern Indian context. It is true that in India myth, oral tales, folklores and other regional tales play a prominent role in the formation of the psychology of an Indian. The problems that are occurring in modern Indian society are often related to the psychology of the people and their roots often lie in the Indian tradition and culture. Both Karnad and Dattani often take the Indian tradition and myths to present and interpret the various problems and issues of modern India. While Girish Karnad directly takes his dramatic themes from several ancient tales and myths of India, Dattani symbolically refers to this tradition in his plays to highlight the present picture of postcolonial Indian society. While talking about the influence of Indian myth, history and tradition on Karnad and their use by Karnad in his plays Aparna Bhargava Dharwadker writes.

> The dominant presence of the ancient and medieval past in Karnad's drama is a result of both personal and cultural compulsions. He has argued from the beginning that the deep-rooted narratives of myth, oral history, and legend constitute a vital connection between an author and his or her audience, and theatre is a particularly powerful medium for the communication of such culturally resonant fictions. Karnad belongs perhaps to the to the

> last generation of the ***urban*** Indian writers who encountered the 'great' and 'little' traditions of myth, poetry, history, legend, and folklore at first hand in their earliest childhood, and internalized them deeply enough to have their adult authorial selves shaped by them.
>
> (Karnad, *Collected Plays*, vol. I, x)

It is true that the influence of myth, history and folklore is already there in Karnad which form the basis for the development of the theme and characters of his plays. Karnad's obsession with the Indian culture and its rich traditional past predominates the texts of his plays that refer to several issues that are related to human psychology and the Indian society. These references often bring into consideration the human relationships, desires of the unconscious, Indian government, politics, foreign influences and several other discourses that turn the original text as an intertext of these other texts. In the case of Dattani the issues like gender discrimination, child abuse, incest, communal violence, problems of the eunuchs and the homosexuals and exploitations of women form the basic thematic motifs of several of his plays that are brought forth through several religious and social myths and conventions that are related to the Indian past and also the present. In the plays of both these playwrights the conflict mainly develops in the human psychology which is a storehouse of these myths and folktales. These myths and folklores are reciprocated through the character development and plot construction of these plays. While Karnad sets his dramatic themes in the Indian myths and history Dattani uses Indian myths and religious incidents as symbols in presenting the social issues. While talking about Dattani's plays R.K. Dhawan writes:

> Dattani's plays have a universal appeal...It may however be noted that these plays are essentially rooted in the Indian settings. Dattani makes an abundant use of Indian mythology, rituals and traditions and contemporary problems India is beset with, but he elevates these themes to higher level, touching the human chords that emanate love, happiness, sexual fulfillment and the problem of identity.
>
> (Dhawan 19)

It is important to understand and analyze the use of Indian myths and folklores in the plays of these two eminent playwrights and conceptualize them in the present Indian social context that relates not only to the existence of an individual but also his or her psychology. Myth and folklore form a separate discourse in the plays of Karnad and Dattani and which demarcates the domain where the spaces of the individual's physical and psychological existence are located. Myth becomes a theory, a concept and a symbol for these playwrights to present their dramatic concepts and character analysis.

Girish Karnad has emerged as a major playwright of modern India who has set his thematic motifs in context to the Indian history, myth, folktales and regional incidents to present the issues and problems that are occurring in the post independence Indian society. His plays include all those discourses that are related to India's past and present. It becomes quite natural for a reader to locate Karnad's thematic motifs and characters in the context of several other discourses that are related to different disciplines. Indian myths, folklores and history form a unifying pattern for Karnad's plays. *Hayavadana*, *Yayati*, *Bali:The Sacrifice*, *The Fire and the Rain*, *Naga-Mandala* and *Flowers* are some important examples of Karnad's plays which are set in the context of various myths and oral tales that depict the development of Indian culture and tradition through ages. Through the use of these myths Karnad puts forth some questions and issues for the reader regarding the present situation of modern individual in postcolonial Indian society. *Yayati* and *The Fire and the Rain* are based on the great Indian epic *Mahabharata*. The *Mahabharata* myth appears to relocate these mythical characters in the context of modern Indian society. Several issues like family relations, gender discriminations, adultery, the dalit discourse, moral degeneration, spiritual sterility and the ultimate regeneration are all presented through these mythical settings. Through these myths Karnad creates a domain where it becomes possible to recognize and discuss so many modern issues at a time and that also in the Indian context.

In *Yayati* the class conflict becomes a serious issue which is related to the other problems like male desire, adultery, extramarital affair, responsibilities and sacrifice. Like *Bali:The Sacrifice* once again Karnad brings the question of class difference on the family level in *Yayati*. The myth of King Yayati occurs in the *Adiparvan* of *Mahabharata* but Karnad relates it to the modern Indian context. King Yayati marries Devayani, a brahmin and the daughter of Shukracharya the Guru of the demons. Sharmishtha, the princess of the Rakshasas, is a friend of Devayani. Sarmishtha comes to the palace with Devayani as the latter's maid (slave). Jealousy intoxicates Sharmishtha's mind and she seduces King Yayati to indulge in physical relationship with her. The physical relationship of Yayati with an attendant girl infuriates Devayani and she leaves the palace and goes to her father Shukracharya. Shukracharya curses Yayati with old age. Yayati becomes old. He suffers. Shukracharya says that he can get back his youth if some one is ready to exchange his youth with Yayati's old age. Meanwhile, Yayati's son Pooru has arrived in the palace along with his newly married wife Chitralekha. Puru agrees to exchange his youth with his father's old age. Yayati gets back his youth and Puru becomes old.

The conflict between Devayani (a Brahmin) and Sharmishtha (a low caste Rakshasa princess) becomes the central motif of the play on which the other issues are based. The conflict between the two women lies rooted in the class difference between the two. But that also brings the issue of gender discrimination and adultery. Sarmishtha is a low caste Dalit and she cannot tolerate the contempt that Devayani has for her in spite of being a friend. Discarding the class difference that exists between her and Devayani, Sarmishtha replaces Devayani and challenges the superiority of Devayani's class by seducing King Yayati and compelling him to marry her. But this act on the part of King

Yayati leads to the act of adultery. This is also an act of gender discrimination committed by a man against a woman by misusing his position as a king and taking away the legitimate right of a wife on her husband by indulging in illegal physical relationship and marrying another woman. The whole drama portrays a family and the issues that are quite prevalent in the modern Indian society. It also brings into question the responsibility of a father, a husband and a lover. Pooru's acceptance of his father's old age is a reflection of his unconscious desire as a child to get identified with the father figure. While talking on this matter Aparna Bhargava Dharwadker writes, "The myth validates the father's authority and the son's obedience, reinforcing the counter-oedipal logic of filial relations in Hindu mythology" (Karnad, *Collected Plays*, vol. I, xv-xvi). The exchange of Yayati's old age with Puru's youth gives rise to the identity crisis.

Yayati takes the identity (the youth) of Puru which overlaps with his own identity. Puru on the other hand takes the identity of Yayati which overlaps with his own identity. This creates confusion for Chitralekha the young daughter-in-law of Yayati and the newly married wife of Puru. Her shock after witnessing the identity crisis, her cries, her remark that Yayati, who is actually her father-in-law, should take her husband's place and her ultimate suicide—all somehow symbolically indicate the shock received by the people of modern India after perceiving the corruption, both moral and social, prevailing in the postcolonial Indian society and family. The *Mahabharata* epic also talks about the dilemma of Sarmishtha to accept Yayati as her husband who is now having the youth of her son. While talking about the confused identities of Yayati and Puru Dr. Falguni P. Desai observes:

> Yayati exchanged his youth with Sharmishtha's son Puru; When Sharmishtha enjoys life with Yayati, she is tormented with the thought that whether she is enjoying with Puru or Yayati. She is living with Yayati but it is Puru's youth, which gives her the ritu embrace. Sexual relationship with one's own son is forbidden, as it is great sin according to ethics.
>
> (Desai 52)

Sharmishtha's desire for Puru's youth and her dilemma as a mother shows the unconscious unfulfilled sexual desires of a wife which show the tendency to get directed towards her son. The issue of confused identities describes the crisis that an individual faces in the postcolonial Indian scenario where he/she tries to establish his/her own identity by discarding the colonial (British) influence and reaffirming the Indian self.

In his important play *The Fire and the Rain* the loyalty and unquestioning submission of the son to the father is not visible. This play is also taken from *Mahabharata* where the myth of Arvasu is presented in various contexts which mainly include the Dalit discourse and the power politics. Arvasu (a brahmin) defies his father Raibhya and society to get engaged in lover affair with a low caste dalit girl Nittilai. He also undertakes the profession of an actor. Unlike his elder brother Paravasu and his cousin Yavakri he does perform spiritual meditations and sacrifices. But he suffers, loses his beloved and his father and brother and is ultimately blessed with salvation and regeneration.

The land of Arvasu as depicted in the *Mahabharata* can be easily identified with modern India where the issues of class difference, social and moral corruptions and spiritual degenerations are prevalent and Karnad here suggests that genuine suffering and sacrifice can bring moral and spiritual regeneration to society and the people existing in it.

In *The Fire and the Rain* the *Yajna* or the fire ceremony is being conducted to bring rain which can bring regeneration to the land. This episode of *Mahabharata* becomes a symbolic presentation of the situation of modern India where people are suffering due to all kinds of corruptions and degenerations. The water becomes a symbol of regeneration in Eliot's *The Wasteland* ('What the Thunder Said') and in Karnad's *The Fire and the Rain.* In the end of *The Fire and the Rain* the joy of regeneration, freedom and fulfilment is expressed by the crowd and also by Arvasu who calls Nittilai to share this moment of freedom from all kinds of barriers and discrimination,

> CROWDS: What's that?—You smell that?—Yes. Yes. The smell of wet earth. Of fresh rains. It's raining. Somewhere. Nearby. The air is blossoming with the fragrance of earth. It's raining—it's blossoming with the fragrance of earth. It's raining—it's raining—Rain! The rain! (Wind blows.... It pours. People dance with joy. They roll in the mud. Arvasu sits clutching Nittilai's body.)
>
> Arvasu:It's raining, Nittilai! It's raining!
>
> (Karnad, *The Fire and the Rain* 62)

The issue of class difference, female desire and identity crisis is dealt with in details by Karnad in his play *Hayavadana*. In this play Karnad uses the *Kathasaritasagara* ('The Heads That Got Switched') myth of the transposed heads to depict the modern Indian society and the individual living in it along with all other problems and complexities that affect his/her existence. *Hayavadana* presents human psychology, female desire and the Dalit discourse as other texts that define the text of the play which is a hybrid presentation of other discourses. *Hayavadana* deals with a triangular love relationship between Devadatta (the upper-caste), Padmini (Devadatta's wife) and Kapila (the lower-caste Dalit and a friend of Devadatta). Padmini's love for both these men indicates the prevailing incompleteness in society. This also reveals the female desire to achieve the love of a perfect male partner.

The myth of the transposed heads becomes an important medium for the expression of so many issues that are related to human psychology and existence. The myth aptly provides a ground, both symbolic and logical, for the playwright to present the conflicts of classes, desires and identities so that he can present a cross-section of postcolonial society through Indian tradition and culture. The heads of Devadatta and Kapila are exchanged. Now, these two individuals are having problems in identifying their own spaces in society and also in relation to Padmini who is originally the wife of Devadatta. This transposition of heads redefines the space occupied by an individual in society. This interchange leads to the intersection of the original spheres (before the transposition) which Karnad deals with as an experiment to study the modern Indian scenario where, in the postcolonial phase, the Indian society and culture have emerged as a transposed structure where the Indian tradition and culture are fitted with the Western look of modernization. It is clear that the space of Indian nationalism, culture and tradition is intersected by the space of Western modernization which has created a new space. This is common in most of the newly independent countries of the world. The people of India are still trying to interpret and locate themselves in this newly created space. Karnad has indirectly, but very skillfully, pointed out the hybrid nature of this space which is redefining the Indian culture and tradition. This spatial conflict has its origin in the history and myth of India. While talking about his plays Karnad says:

> My generation was the first to come of age after India became independent of British rule. It therefore had to face a situation in which tensions implicit until then had come out in the open and demanded to be resolved without apologia or self-justification: tensions between the cultural past of the country and its colonial past, between the attractions of Western modes of thought and our own traditions and finally between the various visions of the future that opened up once the common cause of political freedom was achieved. This is the historical context that gave rise to my plays and those of my contemporaries.
>
> (Karnad Vol. I, 301)

By using this myth of transposed heads Karnad creates an atmosphere of magic realism where the conventional concepts of human forms and desires are suspended. But through this make-believe world presentation of the plot and the other issues fit into the matter which make the theme real and the issues more relevant in every context. The sexual desire and the tendency to achieve perfection and the anxiety resulting from their negation depict the horror of the human existence that gives rise to conflict and the fear of extinction. After becoming alive Kapila with Devadatta's body claims Padmini because he thinks body is superior to head and the former contains the actual identity of the individual. While Devadatta with Kapila's body claims Padmini considering head to be more important than body. A sage tells them that the head is superior to body. Padimini and Devadatta are overjoyed. Kapila goes away into the forest. Gradually Devadatta, having Kapila's body, loses his muscular physique due to his reading and writing while Kapila, with Devadatta's body, becomes strong and muscular with labour and hard work. All this happens due to their individual lifestyle that governed by their respective classes. Padmini again feels the attraction for Kapila and finally goes to him. At that moment Devadatta also appears and both declare their love for Padmini. They fight with each other and die. Padmini hands over her son to Bhagavata and performs Sati. The core of the problem lies in the difference of classes that lies between Devadatta and Kapila. Even the head also cannot control the menace of this discrimination. The head is finally governed by the class. That is why even after the exchange of the heads the problem of imperfection returns. While talking on this matter in the 'Introduction' to *Collected Plays* Volume Two Aparna Bhargava Dharwadker writes,

> In the human world of Devadatta and Kapila, transposition offers a symbolic but temporary resolution to the problem of mind/body dualism:for a brief period of time, Devadatta-Kapila possesses the ideal mind as well as the ideal body, while the other hybrid being, Kapila-Devadatta, is deficient in both respects. But when each man's body reverts to its original qualities, the problem of dualism returns, and the human condition appears as essentially one of disunity and imperfection culminating in death. Karnad diffuses this human 'tragedy' by placing it alongside two other realms of experience—the divine and the animal.
>
> (Karnad, *Collected Plays*, vol. I, xxvi-xxvii)

In the above three plays we witness the myths get unified with the theme of the plays thus forming a continuum through which we experience and understand the development of the thematic motif of these plays.

Now, before proceeding with Karnad's other plays like *Naga-Mandala*, *Flowers* and others I would like to shift my focus to Mahesh Dattani's plays. A comparative study of the plays of these two playwrights will provide us with an idea of the Indian myth in relation to Indian psyche and society. Unlike Karnad, Dattani sets his plays in the modern Indian scenario in various contexts of Indian religion, family, society and politics. But constant references to the Indian mythology, tradition and past form a basic narrative technique that highlights the individual along with his or her psyche and social position. Without creating the make-believe world of magic realism Dattani makes his dramatic themes more relevant through several symbolic or direct references to various Indian myths, tradition, folklore and history. Marriage rituals, worshipping, the myths and conventions of Gods and Goddesses, and above all religion constitute the myth culture presented by Dattani in his plays. They also bring into consideration the gender roles and discriminations faced by both men and women in a typical Indian society.

The issue of women, desire, self control and lack of identity also form the basic themes of Dattani's plays that are quiet frequent in the plays of Girish Karnad discussed above. But, what is most interesting among these plays is the human psychology and behaviour that are analyzed in relation to the Indian culture and tradition through some myths and folktales. It is interesting to see that while Karnad projects the inner unconscious of the individual on the surrounding objects, in case of Dattani the present issues become a matter of the individual's psychological concern. Since the myth, tradition, and culture are deeply rooted in the individual's psyche and are communicating with the individual and the real surroundings simultaneously. Human psyche and the outer society get associated together thus, supporting each other and maintaining a new form of interpretations.

In the plays of Dattani several religious myths occur which serve several purposes in the development of the action of his plays. In his award winning play *Final Solutions* Dattani has used the religious myth and ceremony to undertake a huge role in describing the problem of communalism, the age old evil of religious fanaticism and the characters who try to highlight the cross-section of society. Dattani takes the occasion of Rath yatra ceremony to provide a background to the play. The use of such myth goes with the main theme of the play. Lord Krishna (the Avatar/incarnation of the Hindu God Vishnu) is a symbol of preserver and tolerance. But, the riot occurs when Javed, unidentified by the mob, pelts stones at the deity of the Rath. It is ironical to say that the Hindu myth of morality and tolerance form the basis on which the playwright's ideas and concepts regarding the theme of the play develop.

It is quite interesting to see that through the Indian religious myth of tolerance and equality the playwright gets the chance to express his ideas. The story of the play deals with two Muslim boys Javed and Babban. After being chased by the angry mob, Javed and Babban take shelter in the house of Ramnik Gandhi. When Javed and Babban seek shelter at the night of the riot Ramnik Gandhi decides to provide them with security in spite of his wife Aruna's protest. The sense of guilt is there in Ramnik Gandhi. He knows that his forefathers ruined the family of Javed by burning their ancestral shop. On the other hand Javed and Babban know that what they are doing (encouraging communal violence) is wrong. But their sense of guilt is countered (justified) by the fire of revenge that is there in their heart because of the sufferings and discriminations they have gone through in the Hindu dominated society. Ramnik Gandhi is now ready to compensate for their losses by offering Javed a job in his shop which was originally of Javed's forefathers.

Dattani presents Ramnik Gandhi as a representative of society. The sense of guilt and tolerance in Ramnik Gandhi reflects the Hindu spirit which also influences Javed and Babban. The myth of Lord Krishna and the Holy *Gita* comes into discussion over here and Dattani suggests a probable solution to this evil of communalism that is ailing the modern Indian society at present. The philosophies of Hinduism and the mythical instances and their references create a space where an interaction between the discriminated elements and society can be carried on to create a better atmosphere. This is expressed through the words of Babban (Bobby). When Aruna says that everything has become impure in the house by the touch of these two Muslim boys Babban replies:

> Bobby. The tragedy is that there is too much that is sacred. But if we understand and believe in one another, nothing can be destroyed. (*Puts on his footwear and looks at Hardika.*) And if you are willing to forget, I am willing to tolerate.
>
> (Dattani, vol I: 225)

By putting forth the question of forgiving and toleration Dattani rejects the evils of false pride and superstitions. To forgive and to tolerate are related to the Hindu myth of Lord Krishna. Through this myth itself Dattani solves the problem of communal discrimination and difference. Dattani does this very symbolically. Ramnik's wife Aruna is afraid of the fact that the presence of these two Muslim boys is spoiling serenity of the Hindu house. Bobby takes the image of Lord Krishna in his hands and tries to prove His magnanimity and benevolence and tries to reject the false fears and beliefs of Aruna regarding the Muslims. There is no question of spiritual contamination. The Hindu myth along with its faith and purity continue to exist irrespective of any kind of touch from an individual belonging to any community other than the Hindu. After taking the image of Lord Krishna in his hands Babban says:

> Bobby. Look how He rests in my hands! He knows I cannot harm Him. He knows His strength! I don't believe in Him but He believes in me. He smiles! He smiles at our trivial pride and our trivial shame.
>
> (Dattani, vol I:224)

Through this reference to Lord Krishna, Dattani establishes the superiority of the Almighty to any kind of superstition and false belief. Through the Hindu myth Dattani brings to the table of discussion a serious question that is related to the postcolonial Indian society where the problems of communal disharmony and violence have become serious threats to the proper development of society. Instead of indulging in mutual doubts and suspicion the different communities must listen to each other so that a status quo can be maintained for the existence of the individual. Only if society listens to them, as it needs to do in case of the other oppressed classes, some solutions may be devised. *Final Solutions* ends with a possibility of a better future as shown in Ramnik's conversation with his mother Daksha. Let us have a look at that conversation:

> Hardika. Do you think...do you think those boys will ever come back?
>
> Ramnik. If you call them they will come. But then again—if it's too late—they may not.
>
> (Dattani, vol I:226)

Like Karnad, Dattani also presents postcolonial Indian society along with its various issues through the use of Indian myth. But, the presentation of these myths is different in the writings of these two playwrights. While Karnad directly takes the episodes from Indian myths and folktales and symbolically relates them to the modern Indian society, Dattani presents a cross-section of the postcolonial society and uses Indian myth as a symbolic device to interpret the problems of society. In his other two plays, *Thirty Days in September* and *Seven Steps around the Fire* Dattani uses the Hindu myths to present the psychology of individuals who suffer in the hands of various agencies and social institutions. The play *Seven Steps around The Fire* was first broadcasted as *Seven Circles Around The Fire* by B. B. C Radio in 1998-1999. The play was performed on stage in Delhi in July 2004. The very title of the play deals with the tradition of Indian marriage and the myth of Ramayana associated with this tradition. Marriage and its rituals have become a myth in the Indian context. The marriage ceremony not only refers to the union of two individuals of opposite sexes but also associates the spiritual union, moral orientation and social and familial responsibilities that define the social space of existence for a Hindu. Thus, the age old institution of marriage has become a myth and has got associated with other myths of India as well. The play is basically a whodunit that deals with the killing of Kamla, a beautiful eunuch, who was in love with Subramanyam (Subbu), the son of the government minister Mr. Sharma. Kamla and Subbu got married secretly. Subbu's father could not accept this marriage. He was against the marriage of his son with a eunuch and got Kamla killed. Gender becomes a decisive factor in this case. The question of the eunuchs and the immense poverty are the two major issues that Dattani is dealing with in his thriller *Seven Steps around the Fire*. Like the Muslims and the homosexuals the eunuchs also form a minority community in this society. The society is afraid to recognize them as a part of it.

The domain of the eunuchs remains almost invisible to the normal world. We even do not know their real identity. They can neither become a family nor can produce children. Moreover, they can never take up a camouflage of being normal like the homosexuals. They can only dance on the occasions like marriage and childbirth. Ironically, they can never take part in any of these occasions. The ritual of seven circles around the fire is a myth that refers to several promises that husband and wife make to each other. This ritual also refers to the mythical story of Rama and Sita, the hero and heroine of the epic *Ramayana*, who are considered to be the ideal married couple. But, the irony is that society never provides the eunuchs with the right to take part in this sacred ceremony. Dattani uses the Indian myth and rituals associated with marriage and ironically points out the predicament of the eunuchs in the modern Indian society who are treated as the marginalized other in society. But, this is a major issue that is gaining focus like the homosexuals or the other marginalized sections. But, the myth of the eunuchs or the 'hijras' is as old as the Ramayana. The existence of the eunuchs can never be discarded. Dattani very beautifully associates the Indian myth of marriage and *Ramayana* with the myth of the 'hijras' through the words of Uma:

> Uma (*voice-over*). Case 7...The term hijra, of course, is of Urdu origin, a combination of Hindi, Persian and Arabic, literally meaning 'neither male nor female.'...Another legend traces thrie ancestry to the Ramayana. The legend has it that God Rama was in the forest to cross the river and go into exile. All the people of the city wanted to follow him. He said, 'Men and Women, turn back'. Some of his male followers did not know what to do. They could not disobey him. So they sacrificed their masculinity, to become neither men nor women and followed him to the forest. Rama was pleased with their devotion and blessed them. There are transsexuals all over the world, and India is no exception.
>
> (Dattani, vol II:239)

Through this *Ramayana* myth Dattani associates the eunuchs with the blessed beings who are treated with importance by those who follow the Hindu religion. But, Dattani also ironically points out the fact that due to the lack of religious and social awareness the eunuchs are treated as the untouchables among the Hindus and are discriminated against at every respect in various fields of life. They are only allowed during the marriage and birth ceremony, the occasions which the Eunuchs can never be a part of, they can neither marry nor can they give birth to children. The myths associated with marriage, ceremonies, 'mantras' and customs also pose a threat to the existence of the homosexuals who are also treated as a marginalized class in the Indian society. This issue has been treated by Dattani in his important play *On a Muggy Night in Mumbai* that deals with the problems of the homosexuals in the postcolonial Indian context.

The play *Thirty Days in September* deals with the menace of incest and the sexual abuse of a girl child. In *Thirty Days in*

September, Mala admits that she has some drawbacks in her character out of which she has tried to seduce men and has even indulged in sex. But she also says that all these things are due to the frustrations and sense of guilt that she is suffering from due to the sexual abuse that she went through as a child. Once the virginity is lost, it becomes an obsession for her to perform the sexual act again and again only to make herself suffer due to the sense of that guilt. She also makes her mother Shanta suffer. Mala is having a distorted past. She was sexually abused by her maternal uncle Vinay in the childhood. Shanta also went through the same sufferings in her past in the hands of her brother. She knew what was happening to Mala. But, since she was financially dependent on her brother therefore she could not resist that evil. At present, after she has become an adult, Mala is always in conflict with her mother. She cannot tolerate her mother's silence and indifference. She considers her mother to be responsible for her distorted life. But her mother's indifference is due her helplessness.

Now, in this play Dattani portrays the relationship between the mother and the daughter. Both of them are suffering mentally and they try to seek some solace from life. While Mala indulges in illegal physical relationships with different men, Shanta seeks her mental comfort in Lord Krishna. While Mala's comfort, which is largely due to her sense of guilt, is physical Shanta's comfort is spiritual. Both are suffering and both are aware of each other's weaknesses. Here again comes the Indian religious myth where a Hindu God seems to provide some solution to their problems.

The ordeal of suffering, penance, tolerance and ultimate relief can come through patience and faith in God. Perhaps, indirectly Dattani points towards this timeless myth of the omnipotent God in the Hindu mythology who becomes a source of inspiration for Shanta. She also gets relief by confessing her guilt and helplessness to God. The mythical image of Lord Krishna provides a space to Shanta where she can escape from the harsh reality. Mala, on the other hand, is angry with the image of the Lord considering it to be only a picture which is unable to provide her with any kind of protection and relief. Mala's reaction is out of her frustrations. The myth of Lord Krishna becomes a point of conflict, interaction and discussion among the mother and the daughter. Many things about their past are revealed through this myth. In the very beginning of the play we see Dattani distributing his stage space into different areas depending on the situation. In the play the second area is the living room of Mala and Shanta and the picture of Lord Krishna is a dominant feature in that area. This shows that the image of the God not only occupies the physical space but it is also occupying the mind of these two characters. Mala is vexed with this image because she thinks that her mother is too busy in worshipping the lord and is reluctant to hear to her sufferings. While retelling her past horror to Shanta Mala cries:

Mala *(screaming)*. Listen to me!

> *Shanta covers her ears more for the scream than not wanting to listen to her.*
>
> Mala. No. No…it is so easy for you, because you can hide behind *(Pointing to the picture.)* This! Just forget what you don't want to know and then pray. I won't let you get off so easily. There is only one way I can make you listen to me. By taking this away from you!
>
> *Mala takes down the portrait. Shanta tries to prevent her.*
>
> Shanta. Mala, what are you doing? Please don't! No, no, don't—
> Mala. I can't let you hide behind this all the time! Shanta *(hanging on to the portrait)*. I will do anything you say, but leave my Krishna alone.
>
> (Dattani, vol II:27)

These lines emphasize upon the intensity of the conflict that arise between relationships. This conflict is fuelled by the surrounding incidents. After Mala breaks the image of Lord Krishna Shanta says that it was Mala who indulged in physical relationship with her uncle in her childhood days and she (Shanta) prayed to God to provide her with wisdom and moral sense. Shanta says to Mala:

> Shanta...I prayed for you Mala. *(Pointing to the portrait.)* that is what I was praying to. To our God, so He could send his Sudarshan Chakra to defend you, to defend usfrom the demon inside you, not outside you. But you wouldn't let me. You don't let me.
>
> (Dattani, vol II:28)

Both mother and the daughter are obsessed with Lord Krishna. Both are dependent on Lord and His mythical power. Shanta prays to the Lord to protect her family. Mala is angry because Lord is not providing her with any kind of relief. But Mala finally succeeds in eliminating the traumatic childhood memories. She is liberated from the sense of guilt after going through a long counseling process and the family peace is finally restored. In the end we see Shanta praying to her Lord and Mala resting her head in Shanta's lap and both are reconciled to each other. Like *Final Solutions* Dattani once again points out the benevolence of religion and God and the space created by Hindu myths in the life of the common people which provides them with strength and support to continue with their existence.

Minor, but significant myths and folklores are there in other plays of Dattani as well. The play *Tara* is an instance. In *Tara*, Dattani deals with the issue of gender discrimination that a girl child suffers from even before her birth. Tara is denied the leg which she rightfully deserves. During their birth Tara and her twin brother Chandan were conjoined. They had a common leg. Had the leg been with Tara's body, it would have survived. But Tara's mother and her maternal grandfather decided to give the leg to the male child. The leg did not survive with the male child and, as result of this, both of them were left with one leg each and Tara got a weak health and died in her childhood after long suffering. Tara is the central character of this play and she struggles a lot in a patriarchal society. In the play Tara is often teased and tortured mentally by her friends due to her weak physique and for being physically challenged.

One day Roopa tells Tara a folk-tale about the Patels. Since Tara belongs to a Patel family therefore, this reference greatly concerns Tara. Roopa tells Tara,

> Roopa...It may not be true. But this is what I have heard. The Patels in the old days were unhappy with getting girl babies—you know dowry and things like that –so they used to drown them in milk.
>
> *Pause.*
>
> Tara *(laughs suddenly)*. In milk?
>
> Roopa. So when people asked about how the baby died, they could say that she choked while drinking her milk. .
>
> (Dattani, vol I:349)

The revelation is shocking. It becomes quite relevant in this play because Tara is also a victim of gender discrimination. This story about the Patels remains in the subconscious mind of Tara and when the discrimination done to her during her birth is revealed to her she is bound to get reminded of this tale about the Patels. Although it is not stated in the play but Tara's sense of frustration is added up with this tale which also builds up the horror of the consequences of such discriminations.

The use of myth and folklore not only relates the dramatic themes of Karnad and Dattani to the Indian scenario but also contextualizes the issues and problems presented by these playwrights in these plays. The use of folktales also adds a local colour to the dramatic themes and also the characters. Girish Karnad's two important plays *Naga-Mandala* and *Bali:The Sacrifice* are based on such tales that relate to such serious issues like gender discrimination and women empowerment and their emancipation. *Naga-Mandala* is based on two oral tales from Karnataka which Karnad first heard from A. K. Ramanujan several years ago. These tales are narrated by women to the children of the family. The play is related to the oppression of women in Indian society and a woman's desire to break away from the shackles of patriarchal exploitation and to have extramarital affairs (which becomes a necessity and not an evil) to establish her own identity in society.

In the play Rani, already married to Appanna, unknowingly establishes physical relationship which Naga (the cobra in the shape of Appanna) and begets a child by him. Rani's husband Appanna has been very cruel to her, keeping her locked the whole day in the house and having the relationship with another woman. The cobra falls in love with Rani due to the effect of the root given by Kurudavva to her and which (in the form of a paste) was eaten up by the cobra without Rani's knowledge. Confusion occurs when the cobra takes the form of Appanna (Naga) and starts making love to Rani every night during Appanna's absence. Rani fails to identify the cobra. The identity of Naga and that of Appanna have overlapped with each other thus creating a state confusion among the husband and wife. Karnad has used the oral tales from Karnataka to bring out some serious issues of modern India. The use of this folktale creates a semi-realistic atmosphere where the conventional concepts of beliefs and disbeliefs are suspended and the presentation of different feminine issues and the interplay of several social problems are made possible so that we can understand the intensity of the patriarchal oppressions faced by women in the Indian society and can realize the consequences of such oppressions. We also get a look into the female psychology. Karnad seems to support the adultery committed by Rani in the play which becomes a necessary evil to counter the patriarchal exploitations of a woman. Though the conduct of Rani may seem to be a crime in the Indian social context but the use of the folktale sets the whole story in the Indian milieu and gives the whole theme a local colour of the Indian culture.

The play *Bali: The sacrifice* deals with the problem of adultery. The source of the play is an ancient Kannada epic,

Yashodhara Charite, which itself draws on several other sources. Karnad himself says:

> For *Bali:The Sacrifice*, I have drawn upon the thirteenth-century Kannada epic, *Yashodhara Charite*, by Janna, which in turn refers back through an eleventh-century Sanskrit epic by Vadiraja to the ninth-century Sanskrit epic, *Yashastilaka*, by Somadeva Suri. Some elements of the tale have been traced back to the first century.
>
> (Karnad, *Collected Plays*, vol. I, 317)

The play presents the ideological conflict between the Hinduism and Jainism. Blood sacrifice (bali) in Hinduism is challenged by the Queen who is a Jain and a follower of nonviolence. On the other hand the Queen Mother is a devotee of Hinduism and a supporter of 'bali' (blood sacrifice). The King converts himself into Jainism after his marriage to the Queen but is unable to come to terms with the new faith. The Queen is always in psychological conflict with the Queen Mother on the question of bali (the blood sacrifice). One night the Queen, enchanted by the voice of a low caste ugly Mahout (the Elephant-Keeper), visits him and indulges in physical relationship with him. When found the Queen Mother considers it as a heinous crime and decides to perform 'bali' to appease God. The Queen refuses to support that. The King opts for a mock sacrifice of the dough cock. The sacrifice of the dough cock turns into the sacrifice of the Queen herself and she dies.

The act of adultery made by the Queen indicates the climax of the conflict between her and the Queen Mother and also between the ideologies. The act of adultery committed by the Queen is an act of aggression or revenge on the ideologies of violence in 'bali' or the blood sacrifice. It is not that the Queen is not satisfied with the King or she is adulterous. The indulgence in extramarital affair is a protest against violence, and in this case the Mahout, a dalit, plays an important role as a medium for the expression of that protest. This act of the Queen points out her desire to break away from the shackles of the religious morality practiced by the Queen Mother and followed by the King. The myth of the Dough Cock is an important devise used over here by Karnad to dissolve the ideological difference that exists between Hinduism and Jainism, between violence and nonviolence, between the Queen and the King.

Karnad's another play *Flowers* is an important example of the use of folktales by Karnad. This play stands out to be the first work of Karnad where he focuses on the male rather than the female desires. The play is based on the folktale or the legend of the priest Veeranna who belonged to the Chitradurg region. The folktale of Veeranna became framous when a Kannada writer T. R. Subbanna included it in his novel *Hamsageete* (1952). The priest is married but falls in love with a courtesan to whom he takes the offerings from the temple after every prayer. One day the Chieftain discovers a hair in the offerings and demands an explanation from Veeranna. Veeranna claims that the hair belongs to God. The Chieftain challenges Veeranna and the latter decides to prove his claim. Veeranna meditates. On the decisive day, when the Chieftain arrives to expose Veeranna's lie, the Shivalinga has indeed sprouted long silken hair, and when he pulls out a tuft to test its authenticity, blood begins to ooze from the crown of the Lingam. Veeranna is overwhelmed by the benevolence of God and also becomes aware of his own sin. He sacrifices himself. In this play we see the conflict between religious devotion and erotic love. Karnad very interestingly brings out the complex nature of the human psychology and the intense sexual desire that compels man to go against religion and commit the sin. Like *Naga-Mandala* Karnad brings forth the question of adultery. But, in *Flowers* the extramarital affair turns out to be an evil and the priest sacrifices himself thus, accepting his own misconduct.

Thus, both Karnad and Dattani have tried to use the Indian myths and folktales to highlight certain issues that are related to the modern Indian society. This also refers to the complex mazes of human psychology. The individual is rooted in these myths and folktales and he or she seeks refuge in them to escape the ordeals of life. Again, these myths and legends also refer to the modern Indian society with its complexities and problematic issues. In Dattani's *Thirty Days in September* Shanta and Mala tries to seek consolation and relief through the religious myths. The same is seen in case of Dattani's *Final Solutions* as well where the playwright tries to find some solution to the menace of communal disharmony in the Indian religious myths and philosophies. In Karnad's *Naga-Mandala* folklore provides a space for the emancipation of women from the oppressions of patriarchy. On the other hand, in *Hayavadana* and *Yayati* the expression of the female desire and the representation of the dalits are done skilfully through various mythical settings by Karnad. Both the playwrights stand as perfect exponents of postcolonial Indian writings in English. While writing in a foreign language they express the problems of modern India and use the Indian myth and folklore to develop the thematic motifs and the characterizations of their plays.

Works Cited

Chaudhuri, Asha Kuthari. *Contemporary Indian Writer in English :Mahesh Dattani, an Introduction*. New Delhi: Foundation Books Pvt. Ltd. , 2005. Print.

Dattani, Mahesh and Girish Karnad. "Two Faces of Indian Drama." *Indian Review of Books* 8. 6 (16 Mar-15 Apr 1999). Print.

______. *Collected Plays*. vol II. New Delhi: Penguin Books India, 2005. Print.

———. *Collected Plays*. vol I. New Delhi: Penguin Books India, 2000. Print.

———. *Collected Plays*. vol I. New Delhi: Penguin Books India, 2000. Print.

______. *Collected Plays Volume Two*. New Delhi: Penguin Books India, 2005. Print.

Desai, Falguni P. . "Girish Karnad's Yayati." *Contemporary Vibes* 4. 16 (Jul-Oct 2009): 50-53. Print.

———. "Girish Karnad's Yayati." *Contemporary Vibes* 4. 16 (Jul-Oct 2009): 50-53. Print.

Dharwadker, Aparna. "Historical Fictions and Postcolonial Representation: Reading Girish Karnad's Tughlaq." *PMLA* 110. 1 (Jan 1995): 43-58. Print.

Dhawan, R. K. and Tanu Pant, eds. *The Plays of Mahesh Dattani: A Critical Response.* New Delhi: Prestige Books, 2005. Print.

———. and Tanu Pant, eds. *The Plays of Mahesh Dattani:A Critical Response.* New Delhi: Prestige Books, 2005. Print.

Jha, Gauri Shankar. "Mahesh Dattani's Plays:An Outcry of the Post Colonial Dichotomy." *Cyber Literature* 11 and 12. 1 & 2(Jun-Dec 2003). Print.

Karnad, Girish. *Collected Plays.* vol I. New Delhi: O.U.P., 2010. Print.

______. 'In Search of a New Theatre.' In *Contemporary India:Essays on the Use of Tradition.* Ed. Carla Borden. Delhi: O.U.P, 1989. Print.

______. *Collected Plays.* vol II. New Delhi: O.U.P., 2010. Print.

______. *Hayavadana.* New Delhi: O.U.P., 2005. Print.

______. *The Fire and the Rain.* New Delhi: O.U.P., 2009. Print.

______. *Yayati.* New Delhi: O.U.P., 2011. Print.

Mukherjee, Tutun. *Girish Karnad's Plays: Performance and Critical Perspectives.* New Delhi: Pencraft International, 2006. Print.

Multani, Angelie. *Mahesh Dattani's Plays: Critical Perspectives.* New Delhi: Pencraft International, 2007. Print.

Naik, M. K. and Shyamala A. Narayan. *Indian English literature,1980-2000.* New Delhi: Pencraft International, 2007. Print.

Nimsarkar, P. D. . *Women in Girish Karnad's Plays: A Critical Perspective.* New Delhi: Creative Books, 2009. Print.

21

Myth, Folklore and Socio-Cultural Ethos in the Novels of Shashi Deshpande

Taniya Chakraboty & Joydeep Banerjee

Of late the Indian writings in English unanimously bring forth the holistic essence of culture of the nation. It is a postcolonial phenomenon which evolves as an effect of the postcolonial writings. Nowadays, the authors tend to exhume their respective native cultures and bring them to the limelight. It can be interpreted as a postcolonial trend in order to relocate the suppressed cultures of the colonized. The postcolonial Indian authors have relocated their cultures in their writings. In our discussion we would discuss the creative oeuvre of Shashi Deshpande as she has dealt with her native culture and society. Shashi Deshpande is among a few contemporary Indian writers whose works have been recognized in India and abroad. She holds a unique position among her contemporary writers for her excellent approach towards several social issues of contemporary India, her deep insight of human psychology and her earnest effort to bring together time and space in order to correlate with the multiple literary tradition of language, gender and culture. In an interview Shashi Deshpande says emphatically:

> I do not use Indianisms to make my writing look Indian. I never try to make India look exotic. I do not write for Western audiences at all, I write for Indians. I do not think of a western audience at all. I belong to Indian literature...
>
> (Pathak 240)

culture studies can be traced as a corollary segment of post-colonial studies. The postcolonial writers bring forth their culture, their society to the limelight in order to assert their identities in the global scenario. Shashi Deshpande's concept of culture, colours all her writing. Culture is a cumulative concept which tantalises every reader by its range of expanse. She is so devoutly dedicated to her own cultural heritage that no crisscross of cultures can be traced in her creative world. Hers is a world of typically Indian background. Even she may be easily considered as a writer of the vernacular literature with only one deviation, that her mode of writing is English. Deshpande opines:

> By writing in English I am again in another small circle, that's all. It does not make me non-Indian in any way. I do not even like the word Indo-Anglican. I am an Indian writer. My language just happens to be English, which cannot be called a foreign language at all because it is so much used in India.
>
> (Pathak 240)

Literal, topographical, psychological - all paraphernalia involved in her writings are essentially of Kannada-Marathi society. She in a way presents the real picture of the women of India. Though topographically she has restricted her concentration within a small area of Kannada–Marathi society, her readers can assume that it is an apt projection of a macrocosmic Indian society through a microcosmic order. Through presenting the life of the Indian women Deshpande presents a society that is rich in cultural ethos and simultaneously sticks to the rigid customs. She has brought a nation which is celebrating her 65th years of Independence, yet is stagnant within the quagmire of age old culture and hackneyed discourse. Even after getting the Independence in 1947, Indian society has reached the threshold of twenty-first century with the burden of child marriage, casteism, illiteracy, poverty, gender biasness, polygamy and many more. Deshpande's world portrays the saga of women's journey from 1980s to 2008 as her writing career covers up this prolong period of 28 years. In this long 28 years the condition of Indian women has changed a lot due to spread of education, globalization, industrialisation and urbanisation. Yet, the question remains, has the position of women been upgraded in Indian society? Looking back to that particular period of twenty eight years is a retrospective tribute to a journey which is equally eventful and lugubrious.

Deshpande's sensitive mind rests her concentration on educated middle-class and lower middle class women. In social history the middle-class society has been the most affected part in any social change. Deshpande presents the voice of women, especially the unheard voices of the housewives which were suppressed so far. People did not find it necessary to communicate the women of their households who might have been living at the periphery, suppressing their emotions.

Deshpande holds the idea that in this prolonged period of time men have not changed much, but there has been a sea-change in women's condition. Socio-political and economic changes have ushered in the life of the common educated women. Education makes them able to evaluate their situations. Even among the working class women, a sense of defiance has developed against their situations. In her writings we find the changes. But the most interesting fact is, though Indian women claim that they have changed a lot with the growing surge of education, urbanisation and globalisation, most of them still stick to the stereotype role-playing. Even in the popular TV serials or in various Indian movies the 'Patibrata' image of the Indian women is highlighted. The girls cherish this very image since their childhood. She gives emphasis on the popular cultures while concentrating on the middle-class and lower-middle class society and their several customary rituals. In her realistic portrayal, we have a miniature of the nation India, a 'melting pot' of several cultures.

What Deshpande has projected is the traditional Hindu culture. Her world is not narrowed down as dull, gloomy abode of some shadowy creatures. She depicts a flamboyant, vivacious, colourful life of an average Indian. It is like "a multi coloured patchwork quilt" that she weaves with the thread of words and images. She has dealt with almost every single aspect of a quotidian Indian life, the aspirations and inspirations, the 'fevers and frets', the joys and sorrows. From house-hold problems to politics; from marriage celebration to mourning of death, from bedroom to the outer world – Deshpande easily moves like an omnipresent seer. She takes three or four generations of women of a household into her account, thus providing the readers a space of articulating, how some attitudes of Indian women have changed from generation after generation. We stress on the word 'some' as a modern educated Indian woman still cherishes some beliefs which she imbibes with her birth. In this respect we may bring forth what Jasbir Jain has pointed out:

> . . the values with which one grows up are still rooted in traditional culture wherein myths and concepts are reflective mainly of ideas and aspirations not prevalent in actual practice. (Jain, 2)

The first thing about Deshpande's writing which attracts our attention is that her tremendous emphasis on family. Almost all her protagonists are born in a joint family. This joint family culture is a unique characteristic of the Indian subcontinent. But simultaneously Deshpande projects how of late joint families are broken into the nuclear ones for some unavoidable circumstances. Yet, the children in the Indian families are well accustomed with their grandparents, uncle, aunts and their siblings as well. A family is solely responsible for the culture a person is habituated with. The locales of Deshande's novels are shifted to the interior parts of the country, like villages and towns as the essential cultural ethos can be felt more palpably in these areas than the multicultural cities. Indian society has been class-conscious since the dawn of its civilization. From the Vedic principles society has been divided into four classes according to the professions of people. Later many customs have been banned or restricted by law but some still persist. Such a persisting system is caste-system.

Though historical evidence is that Mahatma Gandhi started a movement against the brutal maltreatment of the lower caste people by the upper caste brahmins, society did not respond much to his call. Deshpande writes about such an incident in her novel *Moving On.* Badri Narayan's father, a brahmin disciple of Mahatma Gandhi marries a harijan orphaned girl out of loyalty to his beliefs. Consequently he is thrown out of his family and has to live alone for the rest of his life. Much later Sarita's mother refuses to marry her daughter to Manohar, a lower-caste boy. From various characters' voices it is evident that Indian people are very much aware of the class-division of the society.

Class is a social construct which depends mostly upon economic affluence and social stratification. So-called upper class people look down upon the lower class people. When in *The Binding Vine* Kalpana becomes a victim of physical violence some people consider her to be responsible for the incident. The Police Officer says with disgust, "But, if you ask me, the man said, she must have been out with a boy friend – girls of that class always have boyfriends the families know nothing about it." (88)

From Deshpande's portrayal it is evident that though Indian women have changed their attitudes to life by the influence of western education, the huge cultural gap in which they are brought up since childhood, restricts them to follow their own wills.

To begin with Deshpande's narrative oeuvre from *The Dark Holds No Terrors* which happens to be her first novel, we find the description of a society which sends women to the margins. Even then, Sarita, the protagonist gets the enlightenment of education. She becomes a successful doctor, resists the male-dominance over her profession and wins public trust. The subtext describes how a woman is reared up in a middle-class background, how she is made aware of her puberty by restricting her from public appearance; how she is introduced with her womanhood with the first menstruation cycle; how a girl is made conscious of marriage (for Saru was barred from playing in the sun as that could damage her complexion); how society interferes an inter-caste marriage and above all how the death of a male-child could affect the lives of all the living members of a household.

Deshpande describes a society which is bigoted against girl child. In *That Long Silence*, Jaya's house maid Nayana takes several attempts to have a boy child. She whispers to Jaya, "This time, *behenji*... this time it is going to be a boy." (27). In *A Matter of Time*, Shripati stops all sort of communication with his wife Kalyani only because their mentally retarded son was lost from her custody in a crowded railway platform. In *Dark Holds No Terrors*, Sarita meets three teenage sisters in the hospital who are the victims of syphilis. Their father developed the disease and he in order to be cured had applied the ancient remedy of having intercourse with a virgin. And where could he get pure virgins than his own daughters? Such case of heinous crime makes one dumbfounded. Is this only ignorance? How cheap one could consider a girl in order to use her like this? A girl becomes the point of attack even at her childhood. Jaya remembers how a teen-age girl becomes the victim of molestation in the broad daylight. The women are treated as the dependent creatures. In her childhood, she depends on her father, in her youth on her husband and in her old age she has to depend on her son. A husband can do whatever he wishes to do with his wife as he is the 'sheltering tree'. Jaya remembers how Moan's father used to torture his mother. How he used to make her bound to make fresh chutneys even late at night, how he used to throw his food if it was a little less warm.

In *The Binding Vine* Sulu's husband humiliates her as she is suffering from some disease. Sulu does not protest as marriage provides her food and shelter and above all, security. Even in lower stratum of society, women have to struggle much for their life. Jaya in *That Long Silence* remembers the struggle of Jeeja, her maid whose husband abandons her for other woman. Jeeja has to work hard to run her family. In *The Binding Vine* Shakutai's husband, a gambler, deserts her for the other woman. Shakutai has to run the family with her meager earnings. Even men can't escape the social pressures. Sarita's husband Manohar has to face an uncomfortable question in an interview as his wife earns more than him. This weakness makes him unmanly. In a male-dominated society a man is supposed to be in more advantageous position than a woman.

Though in the mythology women have been given equal status, the reality is much different from the conceptual belief. In India, in every sphere of life women are treated brutally by their male counterparts. There is a common tendency to underestimate any professional work by the women. For instance we may cite the example of the sniffing words of the Editor to whom Jaya first submitted her writing. He ruefully suggests her, "Why don't you try for some women's magazine? ... This middle-class stuff, women's problems" (146) Madhu, in "Small Remedies", too, experiences almost the same situation as her supervisor Hamidbhai is always critical about her work. Mira, in *The Binding Vine* also becomes a butt of attack when she shows her poem to a famous poet. He suggests her to be happy with her household chores. There is a kind of discourse prevalent over people's psyche as if women can't achieve the excellence in the field of academia! Indian society has been strictly against of widow remarriage.

In earlier days a widow had to go through some strict and ascetic rituals. They had to cut their hairs if not shave the heads. The custom was in order to make their appearances ugly so that any widow, an ominous presence in society who had already lost her husband, could not attract any other man. They were used to be thrown to the periphery and their social status was reduced to a mere maid of the household. Sometimes, people used to take the undue advantage of their dreadful situations. Deshpande portrays the loathsome life of a widow through several characters.

Jaya's Ajji, the clean shaven widow who lived in almost bare room; Mukta –a young widow who bears the continuous contempt of her sharp-tongued mother-in-law in *That Long Silence* Atya, the always-working woman in *Roots and Shadows* – all are the examples of the ill fated persons whom the society has punished only for the cause that they have failed to retain their marriages. But, there is other side of the scenario. With the advancement of time the widow remarriage is in vogue among the educated middle-class society. The first instance of widow remarriage we get in *A Matter of Time* where Gopal's father married his widow brother-in-law and Gopal is the consequence of that marriage. In *In the Country of Deceit,* Sindhura, Devayani's aunt despite being a widow remarried Sudhir. In *Moving On,* Raja wants to marry Manjari, a young widow who has been his friend since childhood. But Manjari is stubborn in her decision not to marry only for the sake of her future security or her children's future. So, the perspective of women is changing day by day with the advancement of time. But, therein lies a mammoth force, i. e. society which shapes the lives of its inhabitants.

In *In the Country of Deceit* Devayani loves a married person and yet she has to end the relationship. In Indian society live-in relationship is still tabooed, particularly in small towns or villages. The children born out of the union of the live-in partners are considered illegal. That is why, in *Small Remedies* Savitribai Indorekar's daughter Munni always took the shield of a fake father in order to protect herself from the attacks of society. In such cases society does not spare the woman though the image of man remains clean. If a man is not happy in his marriage or becomes a widower, people sympathise with him and suggest him to remarry. But, if the same incidents happen in a woman's life and she remarries, everyone finds fault in that. Along with these social issues Deshpande is equally eloquent in political issues too. In her novels she gives vent to the Indo-China war, other political issues and the notorious riot in Mumbai which was responsible for a massacre. Her novel *Small Remedies* is set on the background of the riot that annihilated the lives of both Munni and Aditya.

In Deshpande's socio-cultural portrayal she rampantly uses myths in order to show their impact on the society. Shashi Deshpande is an artful story teller. In her narrative technique myths are so adroitly intertwined with the story that one can't ignore their appeal. According to her:

> I think a number of us do that in India all the time; we relate a great deal of our personal lives, our daily lives to the myths. We find parallels as matter of course. And we do this with all the myths, any myth that seems appropriate, whether they were originally about men or women. In that sense it is part of a language, a grammar that one knows and understands, rather than a conscious literary device.
>
> (Pathak 246)

Myth as a way of knowing the world implies belief in something unseen that nevertheless guides the human psyche along its way. Mythology is the fulcrum on which rests the Indian psyche and culture. In general terms a myth is a story or fable that acts as a symbolic guide or map of meaning and significance in the cosmos. In cultural studies the concept of a myth refers more to the naturalization of the connotative level of meaning, a use that somewhat is similar to the notion of ideology. Cultural studies have gained prominence in the last thirty years as an ethical and ontological resistance to myth. Indian mythology is one of the richest elements of Indian culture. It is distinguished from that of most other nations and certainly from the West, by the fact that it is still a part of the living culture of every level of Indian society. Through centuries different stories of Indian mythology have been passed from one generation to the next either orally or through carefully stored scriptures. The stories in Indian mythology vary from subtle maxim conveying tales of Panchatantra and Jataka-tales to subtle life paradigm defining stories from the *Bhagawad Gita, Ramayana* and *Mahabharata.*

In Deshpande's novels a monolithic shadow of Indian culture is immensely perceptible. Despite the fact that the Indian society Deshpande describes is still guided by some hackneyed cultural discourses, simultaneously the Indian people are affected by some recent trends. Education, industrialization, globalization, westernization etc are some inevitable events which have changed the lives of the Indian people. Particularly the attitudes of the Indian women have undergone sea-change.

In modern age, Indian women are more eloquent about their 'self' than they were before. Deshpande has projected the women who are not the unearthly, irrational, meek, submissive, contemplative creatures whom we find so far in Indian writing. Deshpande's protagonists are rational human beings whose thoughts and actions are progressive. Indian women writers are at present exploring the myths and stereotypes which are essentially entwined with the Indian psyche. This recent trend of Indian women's writing is partly influenced by the growing strength of feminist thinking.

Shashi Deshpande also like many other women novelists feels the need to explore the popular myths and stereotypes of Indian society. She deals with the issue in a very unique manner. She explores myths only from Indian mythology. With the help of myths she describes the inner turmoil of her characters. These myths or legends serve as the instruments through which she carries her message to her audience. She chooses Indian mythology deliberately because first, she belongs to India and the characters she portrays are also from this very origin; secondly, by relocating Indian myths in a changed socio-political scenario she wants to provide more humane and acceptable dimensions to these popular myths. Through these myths Deshpande not only presents the rich cultural heritage of her nation, but also the reinterpretation and relocation of myths help to enhance the credibility of Indian philosophy which is carried away through mythology.

Besides, hailing from a traditional Kannada middle-class background, she has an indebted affinity towards Indian culture.

The myths used in the novels of Deshpande are not incorporated for mere embellishments, but, they also work as the guiding force of the novels. Deshpande points out the general tendency of people in identifying themselves with the popular mythical heroes. In such situations people find solace of their predicament from the philosophy these myths impart. According to Deshpande, myths sustain the cultural heritage of the entire race and that is why they are disheveled with our lives. They help to assume the collective psyche or individual approach towards life. In her column Deshpande opines:

> How we see ourselves collectively or individually depends greatly on myths. They are part of the human psyche, part of our cultural histories. (Web)

In her novels she presents India as a nation of rich cultural heritage to the rest of the world. India is not presented as an exotic nation with some hackneyed customs and rituals; rather, it is presented as a part of global exuberance. Deshpande rationally portrays how the myths and stereotype images influence in making the archetypal figures. According to Vimala Rama Rao, Shashi Deshpande's work is one of the best instances of decolonization of Indian creative mind. In her article Vimala Rama Rao opines:

> The decolonization of the Indian creative mind is best seen in the use of myth and folklore that Deshpande makes in her fiction. Since many of her novels have women for the central consciousness, these devices are especially useful to the novelist as a means of illuminating the inner landscape of women's mind.
>
> (Pathak 208)

Deshpande consciously depicts how a common Indian's life is preoccupied by the myths and stereotyped images. In India, myths are very much effective as people tremendously believe in them. For instance, one may find names like Rama, Lakshman, Sita, Arjun, etc. bearing the legacy of the mythical figures. These are not mere names but, still very much living characters for every

Indian. People give example of Rama-Lakshman in describing a cordial relationship between two brothers; a happy married couple is often equated with Lakshmi-Narayan. Deshpande opines:

> The myths continue to be a reference point for people in their daily lives and we have so internalized them that they are part of our psyche, part of our personal, religious and Indian identity. (Web)

Myths constitute the stereotype images of various phenomena. Specially the images of women in Indian society are modeled on the mythical women. A woman is expected to be as beautiful as Lakshmi, as virtuous as Draupadi, as dutiful and devoted as Sita, as loyal and faithful as Savitri, as bountiful a provider as Annapoorna, as strong as Durga and so on. Interestingly no man is expected to be a Rama or a Krishna, or an Arjun or a Lakshman. Women writers voice their protest against this differentiation between a man and a woman in the society. They have reinterpreted the popular myths with a completely different approach.

Shashi Deshpande also worked on the myths. She has cultivated and explored the myths in several ways. She liberates the myths from the vague gender fallacy; she identifies some myths which have been included in daily rituals or cultural festivals; she provides reinterpretation or reapplication of some popular myths in a different context and finally, she deconstructs some age-old concepts which have attained the stature of myths for many centuries.

Deshpande expresses her concern over the general tendency of applying the myths only to the lives of men as they have been projected in most of the Indian myths. She feels, "myths should be liberated from the fallacy that they are relevant only to one sex because characters of that sex are portrayed" (Web). Deshpande uses the myths irrespective of sex in order to describe the human predicament. The myths are such prominent landmarks for us by which we relate ourselves with the cultural ethnicity of the race. These myths provide the philosophical precepts in order to satisfy some existential queries. In *Dark Holds No Terrors*, Sarita's mother's loneliness is equated with Duryodhana's solitude after the battle of Kurukshetra. Through the story of the legendary hero, Sarita's mother attains the revelation that every human being is basically alone.

In *The Binding Vine* Shakutai's predicament, her struggle for existence is equated with Abhimanyu's fight for escaping the chakravyuh. Urmi realizes whatever onslaughts the life offers, one has to bear until death. "You can never opt out, you can never lay it down, the burden of belonging to the human race."(202)

In *That Long Silence* almost the same philosophy is echoed. There Deshpande uses the myth of Dasharatha who killed an innocent young boy whose parents died crying out for their son. Later Dasharatha himself died calling his son's name, 'Rama, Rama'. Deshpande emphasizes on the divine justice through this myth. Man has to face his destiny. There is no escape. The protagonist Jaya feels herself in the same state as Dasharatha, the legendary king.

In *A Matter of Time* Deshpande alludes to the myth of Yaksha in which he asked Yudhisthira about the greatest wonder of this world. Man's eternal existential quest is satiated in the answer. Yudhisthira said, "We see people die and yet we go on as if we are going to live forever" (133). This is the biggest riddle in life. Man is well aware of the earthly sufferings like pain, despair, sorrow, old age, loneliness and death, but he thinks, all these sufferings are not for him. He will be saved from the maladies. In *That Long Silence* again Deshpande gives allusion to the particular episode of Mahabharata where Krishna instilled courage and knowledge to a confused Arjun saying "*Yathechchasi tatha kuru'* (Do as you desire). (192)There are many options in life, but a person has to decide himself which option he would adopt. Jaya gets rejuvenated by this philosophy when she finds her life in a cul-de-sac. So, these are some instances how we relate our lives with the mythical heroes and find solace accordingly.

Shashi Deshpande has identified some myths which have been incorporated in daily rituals of the Indian households. Indians follow some rituals based upon mythological concepts. Indian pagan culture is also based upon the ancient mythology. In *That Long Silence* Jaya's maternal aunt Vanita Mami provides her some solemn advices before her wedding regarding her impending married life. Vanita Mami's hands hold a tray full of puja things as she is returning from her everyday 'tulsi puja'. It is a very common practice in Indian household. In every Indian household the basil (tulsi) plant is worshipped as a deity. It is a cultural heritage of India. The myth of Tulsi is found in the *Srimadbhagvata Purana*. Tulsi for her dedication, perseverance and self sacrifice towards the worship of Lord Krishna becomes an inseparable part of Krishna's worship. It is believed that by worshipping the plant-deity Indian women escape widowhood. In order to achieve marital bliss and a long-lasting marital life Indian women worship Tulsi. Therefore, a tulsi-shrine is the most common site in almost all Indian households. Some more popular local festivals are mentioned in Deshpande's writing, e.g. 'Mangala-Gauri puja', 'Chaitra-gouri puja' 'sankranti haldi kumkum' ceremony etc. All these rituals are performed by women for the well-being of their family members.

In Hindu rites there is a concept of carrying a dead body with a loud chant '*Raam naam satya hai*' (literally 'God's name is the truth'). It is believed to be the most auspicious hymn that accompanies the dead on their last journey. Jaya remembers the loud voices of people who carried the dead body of her father chanting loudly '*Raam naam satya hai*'. She thinks of the 'Moksha' or salvation which is believed to attain through the death under the wheels of Lord Jagannatha ('Lord of the World', specifically the name of the God worshipped in the famous temple of Puri, on the east-coast of India) during Ratha Yatra. Thus myths have become the inseparable part of our existence.

Shashi Deshpande has captured the essence of the flamboyant Indian exuberance through some religious festivals.

It is noteworthy that most of the Hindu religious festivals are based upon the mythological concepts. Ganapati-festival is a very popular ceremony in entire Maharashtra. In *That Long Silence* Deshpande portrays a lively picture of the immersion procession of this elephant-headed deity.

According to mythology (*Shiva Purana*), Parvati, wife of Lord Shiva, once was annoyed with her husband who intruded the house even though Parvati was taking a bath. Parvati felt disturbed as she did not have any guard to keep vigilance on the door. So, she rubbed her body skin and created the shape of a boy as bright as daylight out of her own fragrant body unguents. She granted him life and named him Ganesha. Then she ordered him to keep vigil on the door. In the mean time, Lord Shiva came and was immediately obstructed by the guard Parvati appointed there. There was a heated argument between the two. In consequence Lord Shiva beheaded him. Eventually Parvati came and noticed the beheaded body of her son. She was infuriated. In order to appease her, Lord Shiva assured her to revive him provided a head is found of someone sleeping with his head to the north. In spite of a frantic search Shiva was unable to procure a child's head and he grafted an elephant's head to the dead body and gave his life back. Trying to repair his mistake Lord Shiva recognized Ganesha as his son and empowered him on all his servants; thus Ganesha became Ganapati. It is believed that annually Parvati comes to the world to bless her devotees with health and prosperity and the next day her beloved son comes to take her back. So, the images of Ganapati, after due worship are taken for the immersion to the nearby river or sea. Such images of festivity are rampant in the novels of Deshpande.

Deshpande sometimes alludes to the myths and draws some affinity between past and present which seem to be ambiguous apparently. But, a minute observation might throw some light on the apparent vagueness. For example, we can cite the Dhruva myth of the *Mahabharata* which is retold by Deshpande in *The Dark Holds No Terrors*. The unloved child of King Uttanapada was pushed off from his father's lap by his step-brother. Being hurt as well as insulted Dhruva set forth a steadfast meditation and became the constant North Star. When Sarita's younger brother Dhruva died untimely in an accident, the readers are reminded of the Dhruva myth, particularly keeping in mind that modern Dhruva was also a victim of sibling jealousy. The most interesting point is that the modern Dhruva also becomes constant in the guilt-conscious mind of her sister as she considers herself responsible for his death. In the same novel again, when Sarita returns to her parental house after a long gap, the mythological story of Krishna-Sudama readily comes in her mind. In the Mahabharata needy, ragged Sudama came to Krishna, his childhood friend, asking for help. Krishna and Sudama were friends from two different economic statuses whereas Sarita and her father share the blood relation. But, we have to consider the fact that it is not the persons or the relationships between them which are highlighted here. It is the situation, the intensity of the problem that is pointed out. Because both Sudama and Sarita went for help when there was no other way out.

Deshpande reinterprets the popular myths in a different context. She opines that whatever archetypal images of women we have are the creations of men. In the mythological books like the Mahabharata men were the main characters. So, the myths should be retold as the images of the women should be reinterpreted. How the mythical women would react in a completely changed ambience is obviously a significant query. Shashi Deshpande thinks:

> So if women are expected to behave like that today, it's very false because today's world is an altogether different world.
>
> (Thakur 19)

She is against of deifying godhood to them. Sita, Savitri, Draupadi, Arjuna – all are human beings. So their predicaments should be interpreted according to the human natures. Jaya in

That Long Silence equates herself with the mythical women like Sita, Savitri, Draupadi who followed their respective husbands in exile. Jaya also is bound to accompany her husband as she is expected to follow her husband. With a sarcastic attitude Jaya explains the predicament of the mythical heroines according to her own personal experience. She thinks, all those married women might have followed their respective husbands as they did not have any other way out. She thinks, "it is more comfortable for them to move in the same direction" (12). Later Jaya equates herself with another mythical wife Gandhari who was considered an ideal wife for her voluntary sacrifice of her vision for the sake of her blind husband. Jaya claims:

> If Gandhari, who bandaged her eyes to become blind like her husband, could be called an ideal wife, I was an ideal wife too. I bandaged my eyes tightly. I didn't want to know anything. (61)

The sarcasm is prominent in these words. We don't know whether Gandhari was really happy with her sacrifice or not, but, Jaya's bitterness against her husband's activity makes her furious. She even draws a stark contrast of attitudes between the mythical Maitreyee who renunciated her husband's property with herself who makes herself complacent with his affluence. Here also the mockery is carried out in her utterance,

> Your life, Yajnavalkya told Maitreyee, will be like the life of anyone who owns property. Well, what more does one want? Immortality? What a crazy idea! (62)

Deshpande's point is not the similarity between the ancient woman and her modern counterpart. Her point is the difference between the two attitudes. Another mythical woman Shakuntala also gets justice to Urmi in *The Binding Vine*. Urmi considers Shakuntala as a "simple village girl" who becomes the prey of Dushyanta, the "classical city roué". (37) In *A Matter of time* Deshpande retells the myth of Maitreyee and Yagnavalkya in describing the relationship between Sumitra and her husband

Gopal. When all in a sudden Gopal takes the decision to renunciate his family, Sumi does not restrict him. On the contrary, she prepares herself eligible for taking the responsibility of herself along with her three daughters. Like mythical Maitreyee, Sumitra also rejects her husband's property in order to pursue knowledge. The concept of knowledge is changed in a different ambience. Now it becomes the way of attaining selfhood. In this novel both Sumi and her mother Kalyani become Maitreyee in their quest for selfhood. Both of their husbands have renunciated the life of a commonplace householder. Both Sumi and Kalyani start their quest of their lives and in a temporal sense attain the eternal truth of life. Some critics find the myths of Parvati and Sita in the treatment of mother-daughter relationship by Deshpande. Even for some critics the Persephony-Demeter bonding is recapitulated in Kalyani's protectiveness for her daughters. Greek Persephony-Demeter myth broadly speaks about eternal bonding between a mother and her daughter. Generally, each mother is protective of her daughter. We don't find any deviation of this norm in Shashi Deshpande. The behaviours of some mothers might be a little bit different obviously, but that does not mean at all that they are not protective of their daughters. They care for their daughters in their respective individual ways.

Deshpande portrays the protagonists of the myths in the background of modern socio-political scenario. She takes liberty to explain the actions of some mythical figures like Draupadi, Sita, Savitri or Arjun as the activity of any ordinary human individual of the day-to-day life. She uses the legendary story of Draupadi's taking disguise of a 'Sairandhri' or a queen's maid from Virat Parva of the *Mahabharata* with a different interpretation. Sumitra in *A Matter of Time* explains that Draupadi's life of a Queen's maid was a relief from the monotonous life of a wife of five husbands. It was a time of emancipation for her, a time to enjoy her selfhood, "to be by herself, to sleep alone, to be free, for a while, of her five husbands." (86)

In India even a man's life is conditioned by social archetypes. In Indian society a man is often imaged as the protector, a strong and experienced personality. But, there is obviously a deviation. Men too, sometimes get tired of their perpetual duties which society imposes on them. They find a way of relaxation, may be for a brief period, but, in this transient period they seek to restore the pleasure of life. Sumitra thinks the same situation might have been occurred in the life of Arjuna, the third Pandava. This chivalrous warrior of the *Mahabharata* is famous for his valor and courage. In the *Mahabharata* he adopted the disguise of 'Brihannala', a eunuch. Sumitra thinks this activity of Arjuna must be inspired to have some relief from his tedious life of a warrior. She explains the event with a different approach:

> . . Arjuna, tired of the male world of war and violence, of relating to woman only as lord and conqueror, became Brihannala, the eunuch, so that he could enter the gentle world of women, of music and dancing and become an insider in this world. (86)

Thus, the popular myths get another facet of interpretation which is simultaneously more humane in essence and reasonable as well as broadly acceptable in modern era.

Deshpande breaks some stereotypes in her novels that have almost become myths by their use for a prolonged period of time. Such a stereotype image is of a husband as 'a sheltering tree'. In India the status of a husband was immense from time immemorial. The lives of Indian women were restricted strictly within the territory of home. Therefore, they were completely dependent on their husbands. Jaya's Vanitamami in *That Long Silence* advised her to consider her husband as 'a sheltering tree', without which a woman's life is 'unprotected and 'vulnerable'. But, with the advancement of time this concept has broken. Indian women are now stepping their feet outside of their homes and so their financial dependence on their husbands has been declined to a large extent. In various novels by Deshpande the protagonists Sarita, Urmi, Madhu – all are economically independent. Even in the lower stratum of society Jeeja, Tara, Nayana, Shakuntala – all earn their livelihoods by their own effort. So, the concept which has been prevalent so far as "a husband is a sheltering tree" is not in vogue in present day Indian society.

The second image that is shattered is the stereotype- image of a mother. In Indian books, legends, even in films this figure has become a stereotype. By various ways of idolatry, people sometimes forget that a mother is a human individual. She might have her own ways of reaction. She might not fit within the idealized concept of the archetypal mother figure. Deshpande wants to highlight this particular point in her novels. She thinks, motherhood itself is a myth that should be shattered. But, we consider 'motherhood' an experience, perhaps the most valuable and meaningful experience in any woman's life. It is not a mere concept that can be called a myth. The outcome of the experience obviously differs from person to person, but, how can an experience be conceptualized? In two novels, the experience of motherhood is described by the protagonists in two different ways. Urmi in *The Binding Vine* appears irritated with the expected roles of a mother. She reacts thus:

> Sometimes I think ... they brainwash us into this motherhood thing. They make it seem so mystical and emotional when the truth is that it's all just a myth. They've told us so often and for so long that once you're a mother you have these feelings, that we think we do. (76)

In another novel, *Samll Remedies*, Madhu, the protagonist describes motherhood as the most exiting incident of her life. She recollects the birth of her child:

> Motherhood takes over my life, it makes me over into an entirely different person. The in-control-of-herself Madhu is lost, gone forever. It's my baby's dependence that changes me; my place in the universe is marked out now. (183)

The contradiction of perspectives between two different persons proves the variety of expression from one person to another. So, this is not any 'myth' that Deshpande shatters actually; she deconstructs the general image of a mother as a soft, caring person, always ready to sacrifice herself for her family. On the contrary, Deshpande gives emphasis on the individual feelings and individual expression.

Another image which is shattered in *The Binding Vine* is the image of a happily married couple. A happily married couple is often equated with the divine couple Lakshmi-Narayan. But, Mira in one of her poems shatters the happy concept of a married life. She asks:

> But tell me, friend, did Laxmi too
> twist brocade tassels round her fingers
> and tremble, fearing the coming
> *of the dark-clouded, engulfing night?* (66)

Mira's personal bitter experience of an unwanted physical relationship spoils the ecstatic pleasures of a newly-married couple. She starts to hate the concept of love as her husband repeatedly utters "I love you" (67) in time of love-making. She is the representative of all those women who are bound to remain within the institution of marriage without their consents, as divorce is still considered to be a nuisance in Indian society.

Deshpande provides immense emphasis on individuality. That is why sometimes she describes some personal beliefs of her characters which are the expressions of the individual point of view. For example, Jaya considers love as a myth. She opines:

> Often I had told myself: love is a myth, without which sex with the same person for a lifetime would be unendurable. (97)

Love is not a concept, it is a feeling. It depends entirely on an individual human being how would he react in different phenomenon like love, hatred, and despair according to his mental condition. Jaya expresses her view in a mental condition when she is emotionally upset with her married life. Now the point is whether a momentary personal decision should be considered as an idea which is supposed to incorporate the entire ethnic group or a cult? Besides, according to the Indian philosophy love is a greater phenomenon than sex which is restricted within body. In India, love is considered to be independent of sex. Even Deshpande herself in her various novels have shown the dichotomy between love and sex. If the characters are considered to be the mouthpiece of the author, then such expressions may generate controversy which is not desirable.

Another very significant artifice which involves Deshpande's writing is folklore. Myth and folklore together create the holistic cultural ambience for the readers. The themes of domination and cunning are illustrated through folklore, the story of the Sparrow and the Crow in *That Long Silence.* This is one of the oldest fables with a moral which children hear from their predecessors. There are so many versions available in different regions. The provident little Sparrow builds her nest with wax and the foolish Crow builds his nest with dung which melts in the rain. The crow comes knocking at the door of the little Sparrow. The Sparrow takes her time to open the door; she is bathing her baby, feeding it and putting it to the bed. Finally the Crow is allowed to be in. The Sparrow instructs the drenched Crow to sit upon the roasting pan to warm himself. The foolish Crow sits on it and consequently perishes. Jaya equates herself with the little Sparrow who is virtuous and cunning and thus can manage her home efficiently.

Another folktale described in *A Matter of Time*, i. e. the tale of 'Rice and Curds' tree'. Sumi remembers the story of her childhood with myriads probable morals. There was a king who had a beautiful little princess. Every day the princess used to eat rice and curd and washed her hands at the backyard of the palace. Eventually there grew a tree. The little princess grew up to be a beautiful lady. The king arranged for her marriage. But, the princess declared she would marry only that person who would be able to identify the tree at the backyard. All the suitors failed. Only the son of the Gardener could answer it was the 'Rice and Curds' tree and consequently won the Princess's hand. Sumi thinks it to be a romantic story presented in a different way. She remembers how her Goda-mavsi used this story in order to overcome Sumi's dislike of rice and curd. Sumi thinks whatever may the purpose be, this story is very significant in the present-day life too as the story can have multiple morals, "There's the importance given to a tree, to the identification of it, there's the dismissal of the aristocracy , the triumph of the common working man" (156). Even Sumi reinterprets the story with a different angle. According to her, it is the princess who falls in love with the gardener's son. "Had she watched the gardener's son at work, noticed his muscles gleaming in the sun and decided she would have him for her husband?" (157). But, the princess knows her father would not approve of a gardener's son as his future son-in-law. So she makes a trick by setting an odd goal in front of her suitors. This is a reinterpretation of an age-old fairy tale which is represented in a changed ambience.

Deshpande's technique is unique as she concentrates her focus on the modern, educated, middle-class woman's struggle to find a balance between the traditional beliefs and individual needs. Though she equally considers the cases of both man and woman, women get a little privilege to her as she is a woman herself and she considers Indian women to be 'subordinate' in social status and a "dependent gender" (Thakur 20). Her endeavour is undoubtedly praiseworthy as she tries to catch the vein of the modern educated Indian women. She is writing back the suppressed history of the Indian women with a completely different perspective. Her endeavour is noteworthy in another sense. The rational approach in interpreting the myths would make them accessible to the common people. This can be viewed as the ushering in of a new dawn in the field of the Indian English Literature.

Works Cited

Deshpande, Shashi. "The Indian Woman – Stereotypes, Images and Realities." http://www. ch. 8m. /cgi-bin/framed/1679/shashi. htm. Web. 18 May 2011.

______. *That Long Silence.* New Delhi: Penguin Books India, 1989. Print.

______. *The Dark Holds No Terrors.* New Delhi: Penguin Books India, 1990. Print.

______. *Roots and Shadows.* New Delhi: Disha Book, 1992. Print.

______. *The Binding Vine.* New Delhi: Penguin Books India, 1993. Print.

______. *Small Remedies.* New Delhi: Penguin Books India, 2000. Print.

______. *Moving On.* New Delhi: Penguin Books India, 2004. Print.

______. *In The Country of Deceit.* New Delhi: Penguin Books India, 2008. Print.

______. *A Matter Of Time.* New Delhi: Penguin Books India, 1996. Print.

Thakur, Pallavi. "Defining Feminism: An Interview with Shashi Deshpande." *The Quest* 17. 2 (Dec 2003): 18-21. Print.

Jain, Jasbir. *Gendered Realities, Human Spaces.* New Delhi: Rawat Publications, 2003. Print.

Pathak, R. S. Ed. *The Fiction of Shashi Deshpande.* New Delhi: Disha Books, 1998. Print. Creative New Literature Series-19.

Nayar, Pramod K. *An Introduction to Cultural Studies.* New Delhi:Viva Books Private Limited, 2008. Print.

"Myths and legends about Ganesh". ganapati. perso. neuf. fr/anglais/adetmyth. html. Web. 16 March 2012.

22

Remaking Mythology as Metanarrative in Amish's *The Immortals of Meluha*

Lata Mishra

I

The present paper aims to analyze the contours of new writer, Amish's intervention into mythology. Amish's debut novel *The Immortals of Meluha* (2010) is a brilliant *tour de force* which may become a trendsetter among young writers due to its open-endedness and immense potential for varied interpretations. It has been much appreciated by various critics. The Times of India appreciates it as "Shiva's journey from cool dude. . . to Mahadev. . . is a reader's delight. . ." while the Business World lauds it as "An essentially mythological story written in a modern style." Undoubtedly, *The Immortals of Meluha* has marked the beginning of a new wave of novel-writing characterized by radical experimentation in terms of theme, form, narrative strategies and language. The cultural history of the nation is deconstructed, and the dominant myth rewritten in new permutations and combinations. The novel successfully dismantles the 'ancient myth' which sees Shiva as God and explores him as a god-in-making. He attempts to create fiction from folklore, religion and mythical facts with messages for our world that it is efforts that raise a common man to the high platform of God. Every man has a potential of being *Mahadev* (*Har Har Mahadev*).

The writer delves deep into myths and legends of India and employs them as vehicles of a new vision and interpretation. Shiva typifies the tribal society, to a large extent. In the beginning Amish presents the protagonist as a fine product of his clan. Shiva brings honour to the clan by displaying valour. He supports the entire tribe from a tender age and rises to the position of 'the protector of the village'. In Meluha the psychic rhythm of Shiva is well portrayed through beautiful anecdotes which are of immense value to the understanding of his personality. There seems to be a pattern in the way he acts and reacts; this pattern is unique and yet he is not unlike other characters.

The novel comprises 26 chapters. The opening chapter throws light on the earlier days of Shiva at Kailash, as a boisterous young man. Here attention is focused on 'Shiva, the Leader of Clan,' who defeated the Pakratis, establishing his identity and making his mark in the neighbouring area. From there, Amish leads his readers forward, giving insights and clues, depicting the psychic reflections, physical peculiarities of each character and finally leaving them to derive individual inferences. The urge for position, possessions and power is a basic human passion and often these archetypes embody themselves in varied forms. Shiva, the hero of the novel, undergoes archetypal-imaginative journey of transformation. The Hero who is usually expected to fight against villain does not do so, but the action in the plot is elevated. The task of Shiva is not to trounce evil individual but to confront the evil that attaches an individual to itself.

Since Amish is presenting Shiva as a real person and not a purely mythical character, he does make some alterations to the myth which is necessary in order to make his fiction seem realistic. He takes the characters from myth and changes them into ordinary persons who have extraordinary qualities At the same time the writer keeps true to the spirit of the ancient sources. For example, in the myth, Shiva is called Neelkanth, as he had drunk poison to save the world. Amish alters the myth by suggesting that Shiva has no such magical attributes and his neck turns blue after consuming *somras,* a drink of god (an anti-oxidant potion) scientifically prepared by Brihaspati, the senior scientist of Meluha. Fictionist's method of representing the story of Shiva and Sati shows how fact and history can become myth and folklore with the passage of time.

Myths regardless of time and culture, have been used in various forms by human societies. Involved in the discussion of the relationship between history, myth and folklore is the question of how to keep the truth of an event intact when creating a written account of the event. Mythology is inseparable from literature as through myths, writers narrate contemporary events and explain life in its varied forms. Myths explain and make sense of our environment, culture and society. To Amish, myths provide a vision of wholeness that would regenerate the fragmented civilization. He has used myth in *The Immortals of Meluha* to serve various thematic and structural purposes. The writer has presented, through myths or mythical representations, a rich and colourful world where gods and men co-exist and move freely together. His story expresses important perceptions of the society that generated myths and provides insights into the pattern of the society. He applies myths to real life situations and thus gives them meaning. Myths offer explanations of natural and other phenomena and in this way serve as extended metaphors describing situations in the reader's own life.

Even in this scientific era of drastic changes myths seem to be a relevant topic for literature as they encompass various socio-cultural and religious dimensions. The novel narrates the detailed account of journey of a Tibetan tribal chief from Mount Kailash to Kashmir and then to the plains of India. In course he comes across the various social, rational and religious beliefs of the civilization. Through his story Amish focuses on the power politics and attempts to give us a new take on the dynamics of power relations.

Levi Strauss in *Myth and Meaning* writes: "Myths give the feeling that man can understand the universe and that he does understand the universe"(17). Myths display conventional modes and mores of the society. It is argued that the past is not separate from the present, it is not something which is over but has a contemporary relevance. Tradition here offers a counterpoint to modernity, though Amish does not accept the former as such either, but questions it. Amish, throughout the novel, speaks of the social customs and observances that linked the Meluha people.

II

Structuralism sees myth as a reflection of the mind's binary organization and thus refers to highlighting the opposites in the story. Myth deals with the perception and reconciliation of these opposites. As a remarkable specimen of postmodernist thinking, this novel deals with two main postmodern issues, transgression of boundaries and travesty of logic. In the immense complexity of his narrative, however, author makes particular efforts to showcase the two above-mentioned postmodern issues amongst which the former is, of course, an iteration of Derrida's categorical extirpation of binary oppositions. Echoing a typical Derridean deconstructive spirit, Amish dismantles binary oppositions at various levels. In the chapter "Attack on Mandar," Amish brings in the Derridean play between "presence" and "absence" and concomitantly dissolves their difference. In this chapter, Pandit convinces Shiva that the existence (presence) of the world is actually constructed around its absence. In other words, it is the absence that constructs the presence and the existence of "presence" is impossible without the conception of its "absence." The Pandit engages Shiva in a dialogue and fittingly argues:

> What is the colour of that leaf? ". . . It's green.". . . . Light falls on that an object and when it reflects back from that, you see that object. . . . What normal sunlight is made of?. . . White light is nothing but the confluence of seven different colours. . . . . White sunlight falls on that leaf. The leaf's physical properties are such that it *absorbs* the colours, violet, indigo, blue, yellow, orange and red. . . . It doesn't absorb the colour green, which is then reflected back, Hence I see the leaf as green. . . . What colour it absorbs

> and what it rejects. Or is it every single colour in the world, *except* green?
>
> (Amish 295)

Martin Heidegger, does not view reason from rejects calculative, utilitarian perspective. To him reason is not the sole source of legitimate. The knowledge of *truth* cannot be confined to rationalized propositions about beings alone but ought to encompass the knowledge of the Being of beings. Rational and scientific knowledge just give the information from one particular perspective. Therefore any one kind of knowledge of beings cannot be privileged over any other. No propositional knowledge is absolute; it is all relative. The same views are echoed in the novel, *The Immortals of Meluha*:

> 'There are many realities. There are many versions of what may appear obvious,' continued the Pandit. 'Whatever appears as the unshakeable truth, the exact opposite may also be true in another context. It is the context or perspective that you're looking from that moulds which particular reality you see. (296)

The appropriated modified discourse on the Chaos Theory can be applied to the examination of the novel, *The Immortals of Meluha*. Kellert (1993) defines Chaos Theory as "the qualitative study of unstable aperiodic behaviour in deterministic nonlinear dynamical systems" (2). A determinist thinking of Suryavanshis simplifies reality. Their life and its working is as predictable as the movement of pendulum, a simple example of a dynamical system. Dynamical systems theory is the branch of mathematics devoted to the motions of systems which evolves according to simple rules. This theory was first given by Newton to model the motions of our solar system influenced by his Gravitational Law. Man is a complex being and thus cannot be studied as an isolated system. He constantly interacts with his ever-changing environment. Thought processes are generally non-deterministic in nature more like a maze, but the Meluhan rules claim that if the starting point is known, the end point is ascertained, not realizing that disorder, confusion, uncertainty, or instability prevails all the time. This is "the butterfly effect", a term used in the Chaos Theory to explain how a minor change may cause drastic and unexpected results. The Chaos Theory studies motions that do not seem cyclic or periodic. Each Meluhan who seems to be so stable in relation to his environment on deeper inspection seems to contain seeds of chaos and suppress the unstable in him. The forced orderliness of Melhuans is seen in their Maika and vikarma system. Under the Maika System:

> all children that are born in meluha are compulsorily adopted by the empire. All pregnant women have to travel there (Maika) for their delivery. . . . Once the child is born, he or she is kept in Maika for a few weeks for health reasons while the mother travels back to her own city. . . . The child is then put into the Melhuha gurukul. . . . They grow up with all the resources of the empire available to them. . . . When the children tyrn sixteen, they are allocated to the applicant parents. . . .
>
> Shiva says, 'But I guess not too many mothers would have been happy with this. . .' 'But it's for the larger good,' said Parvateshwar, 'Nothing can be worse for a mother than having a child who does not measure up to her expectations.' (*IM* 97-99)

On the other hand the Swadeepans' life appears chaotic at the surface but there is an order with their inner self as reflected to Shiva when he meets a beggar at the temple. The Swadeepans carry the motto of 'Passion. Beauty. Freedom' (*IM* 371). On the temple steps of Ayodhya, a city of Chandravanshis, Shiva meets a beggar in torn clothes who offers a share of his food on banana leaf. As Shiva is coaxed into eating with him:

> Shiva could not find the heart to look up anymore. As his heart sank deeper and his tears rose, he ate the portion the old man gave him quickly. The food was over in no time.
>
> Freedom. Freedom for the wretched to also have dignity. Something impossible in Meluha's system of governance (*IM* 386).

The novel can also be explored in the light of the colour theory. The Colour Theory is a set of principles used to create harmonious colour combinations. Melhuan cities follow either monochromatic or analogous colour schemes. Devagiri, the capital of Meluha is described as:

> The most common background colour . . , appeared to be blue. In the Melhuan mind, blue was the holiest colour ofthem all. It was the colour of the sky. It was just above green, the colour of the earth, in the colour spectrum. Melhuans who liked to see some greater design in every act of nature, thought it was marvellous that blue was above green in the colour spectrum just as the sky was above earth.

On the colour wheel, blue and green colours are adjacent to each other, hence called analogous colours. An artist chooses such colours to create harmony, an inner sense of order and a balance in the visual experience. Green, being the colour of nature, is a dominant colour while blue is used by Melhuans to enrich the scheme of nature. However the artists believe that overuse of analogous colours kills the harmony.

Shiva on entering Ayodhya reads Chandravanshi motto: *Shringar. Saundarya. Swatantrata.* The city is described as:

> Everything was painted bright- from orange buildings to parrot green ceilings to shocking pink windows! . . . A vibrant city, with exquisite beauty existing side by side with hideous ugliness, Ayodhya disgusted and yet fascinated the Meluhans. (*IM* 373)

Swadeep seems to be painted in colours opposite to each other on the colour wheel. Such colours are complementary ones and thus vibrate and draw attention. To the methodical Suryavanshis such a colour scheme of Chandravanshis seem so chaotic that they feel disgusted. They reject it as they fail to organize and understand it. Amish, while differentiating between reality and appearance or truth and perception, explains the colour of leaf in terms of its interplay with light.

> "What is the colour of that leaf?". . . "It's green." . . . . Light falls on that an object and when it reflects back from that, you see that object. . . . (295)

There are numerous such significant references to the colour spectrum in the novel.

III

In *The Literary Impact of The Golden Bough*, Vickery writes of contextual works:

> By contextual works is meant those literary creations which focus on ancient myths or rituals in order to realize their role in the ordinary, daily existence of their time, to relate them to an even more remote and primitive past, or to find in them metaphors whose continuation into the present illumines its central dilemmas. (143)

Through the application of such myths man's perception of the world becomes more clear. Carl Jung explored myths as part of the effort to understand the individual and collective human psyche. Modern psychology shows the 'self' as the psychological totality of man. Every individual, through his biological, psychological and spiritual progress aims at self-realization (Individuation). Various studies conducted by scholars emphasise the idea that myth and psychology are complementary. In myths, there are clues to the deepest hopes and fears of mankind and thus they may not be dismissed as mere stories, but ought to be studied carefully for their revelation of the depths of human nature.

To Amish myth seems to be a structural element used to express archetypal characters, situations or the collective consciousness of a community. Jung observes, "The task of analyzing the human psyche is an awesome and complex one." In his model of the psyche, at the conscious end is the *persona* which:

> ...is a complicated system of relations between individual consciousness and society, fittingly enough a kind of mask, designed on the one hand to make a definite impression upon others, and, on the other, to conceal the true nature of the individual.
>
> (*The Ego and the Unconscious* 305)

while at the unconscious end, is the shadow which is everything that an individual refuses to acknowledge about himself. Shiva is aware of shadow material in his unconscious and performs the difficult task of incorporating it into his conscious material. He in his childhood had the experience of fleeing away from the site of woman being raped by a man. The guilt of not saving the woman always lingers in his psyche.

> As he enjoyed the show, his disquiet grew. Something seemed amiss. The man was in the throes of passion while the woman lay passive - almost dead. Her hands lay lifeless by her side. Were those tears of ecstasy rolling down her cheeks? Or was she being forced? . . . . And then came the moment that would haunt him for the rest of his life. The woman's eyes suddenly fell upon him.
>
> 'HELP!' she cried out, 'Please help!'. . . . The hairy monster turned to see who the woman was calling. The boy quickly picked up his sword and fled. . . . He was terrified at the thought that the man was chasing him. (*IM* 221)

Shiva confronts his shadow in dreams. "The general function of dreams is to try to restore our psychological balance by producing dream material that re-establishes, in a subtle way, the total psychic equilibrium" (*Man and His Symbols* 50). Franz cites Jung's views, "In dreams the shadow is always the same gender as the individual" (*The Process of Individuation* 175). When Shiva fears that he had wrongly harmed Chandravanshis in the battle he dreams the same childhood event, but this time the killer of the woman is he himself.

> He was running hard, the menacing forest closing in on him. He was desperate to get beyond the trees . . . suddenly a loud cry pierced through the silence. 'Help! Please help!'

> He stopped. No. He wouldn't run away this time. He would fight that monster. He was Mahadev. It was his duty.
>
> 'Jai Shri Ram!' He yelled, as he raced back. . . . Bleeding and terrified, he ran hard.
>
> I will reach her in time.
>
> I will not fail her again.
>
> My blood will wash away my sin.
>
> . . . It was a strange laughter that finally broke his concentration.
>
> 'Oh Lord!' he shrieked in agony.
>
> The woman lay stricken on the ground, a short sword buried into her heart. The little boy stood on her side. Stunned. His hand bloodied with the struggle of his kill. The hairy monster sat on the rocky ledge, pointing at the little boy. Laughing.
>
> (Amish 361)

Shiva thus feeling guilty for leaving a woman tortured by a hairy man eventually takes up the task of doing good to humanity. Such interactions with the shadow lets Shiva know his own state of mind and assists in reaching totality. Jung observes, "Everyone carries a shadow, and the less it is embodied in the individual's conscious life, the blacker and denser it is." (*Psychology and Religion* 131)

The writer's honest endeavour to represent ancient life with contemporary issues in the mythic background with great verve needs appraisal. Even the words uttered by the characters, adorned with natural felicity, portray their psychic pattern. Amish gives a modern touch to his mythic characters at the physical and psychological level. He dramatizes the conflict of primeval psychic passions in all the characters, especially in the protagonist, Shiva. These psychic secrets of the characters, especially those of the hero, working at varied levels are brought to light, at times in their pristine primitive form or sometimes in a sophisticated style.

The psychological function of myth, Wallace W. Douglas observes, is "to fuse the perception of power with the perception of physical qualities" (*The Meaning of "Myth"* 124). At the psychological level myths throw light on the nature of man's personality with special emphasis on his psyche, thereby establishing and asserting man's lineage. Amish's characters are curious psychological specimens as they represent the totality of psychic nature with its conflicts in a universal level. The success of Amish in creating a mythic consciousness in the psychological level lies in the presentation of characters not as people of a particular nation but as man and woman in their varied roles inhabiting a timeless and wide universe. The novel seems to end at a note that life is created and sustained at the very edge of chaos.

IV

Liberty, equality and fraternity occupy a place of prominence as being instrumental in uplifting the marginalized section of the society. Through the introduction of the vikarma system the writer accommodates in its fold contemporary reality. He explores the experience of suppression and humiliation that the marginalized section of each society has to go through. Among the Melhuans giving birth to a still-born is the most shameful thing. Sati, in the novel faces personal discrimination as she had given birth to a still born and on the same day her husband had accidentally drowned. This system of labelling of vikarma is not based on caste but as Nandi explains:

> Vikarma people, my Lord are people who have been punished in this birth for the sins of their previous birth. Hence they have to live this life out with dignity and tolerate their present sufferings with grace. . . . They are not allowed to marry since they may poison others with their bad fate,. They are not allowed to touch any person who are is not related to them or is not part of their normal duties. (*IM* 93)

Sati is deeply sensitive to the pains of other oppressed vikarmas as she seems to experience their pain herself.

> Sati, who was now standing near Shiva, had heard the entire conversation. She felt sympathy for the blind, man. She knew the

> torment of having even your touch considered impure. but what he had tried to do was illegal. (*IM* 197)

Sati's tragedy is universal. This bitterness of her being an untouchable is totally understandable. This voice of vikarmas is the voice of all those who have been voiceless for centuries. India's untouchables have been forced to accept the long-silenced and long denied sufferings and the pain or poverty of a community forced to live at the bottom of India's social Pyramid. 'The Vikarma Myth' explains how men violated the divine commands in their past life and thus the present world of complexity, confusion and suffering, death, labour etc. became their lot in present one. Shiva rebels against the caste system and social prejudices, recognizing the human being as its focus. The sense of injustice created through prevailing social exclusion and victimization of untouchables or vikarmas makes Shiva to demand for a new status of the victimized group. He fights for the powerless, the oppressed, the marginalized, the exploited to win back their dignity. He says:

> I am sorry, but I think this system is completely unfair. I have heard that almost one twentieth of the people in Meluha are vikarma. Are you going to keep so many people as outcast forever? This system needs to change. (*IM* 212).

Writing in this postmodern/postcolonial era, the writer deals in his text on the issue of social/communal disharmony embedded in the post independent nation-state that India is with its claims of secularism as its democratic principle. The novel deals with the social/communal disturbances which results in the dislocation of a whole community that is marginalized within its own country. He records the testimonials of all who are the worst sufferers so as to recreate the actual situation in the perspective of the victims. In the process such attempts at reconstructing myth and history that has been told and written by those in power, challenging its ideology that is defined so finitely as the single truth, he seems to say that there are several other perspectives too. To the reader from alien land his story may not mean the same as to one born in the Indian culture.

V

In a patriarchal society, women have been occupying a marginalized position in relation to men which leads to their oppression, suppression and an innate sense of fear within themselves. That women should be meek, modest, docile and almost an angel in the house had so percolated throughout the socio-cultural set up that any deviation against it would amount to social chastisement or even ostracism in certain extreme cases. On the contrary, the ancient society of Meluha is also a patriarchal society but patriarchy seems to be just a social arrangement rather than something with other political intentions. Sati is a warrior who fights her own battles. Ayurvati is highly respected medical practitioner, while Kanakhala is a learned Prime Minister of Daksha's royal court, who takes care of all administrative, revenue and protocol matters. Sati stands as an exemplar of womanhood. She is a perfect blend of all the virtues that go into the making of an ideal woman. She is beautiful, excellent, good, moral, valorous, chaste and truly feminine. Amish does not portray her as a weak, helpless, clinging vine. The woman who is endowed with the merits is quite capable of facing all the vicissitudes of life and is a boon not merely to the family but even to the society.

The society of Suryavanshis is juxtaposed against Chandravanshis. While the former believe in Truth, Duty and Honour, the later appear to be immoral, depraved and degrading. Sexual promiscuity, gambling, cheating, lying, and small minded self-indulgence are common occurrences in their kingdom, (Swadeep). The novel deals with the theme of search for identity, alienation and loneliness. Daksha's kingdom, Melhua soars to the highest horizons only to be doomed and ruined. Harry Slochower, in *Mythopoesis: Mythic Patterns in the Literary Classics* states that "the perennial appeal and vitality of mythic thinking stems from the fact that it makes us feel that in all civilizations men face analogous situations, undergo similar experiences" (14). Daksha, an idealist, shrewd politician, impartial in his rules, practical in understanding the situation and modern in thinking, fails to establish his identity as any one of these. The different sides of his personality overlap with each other thus rendering him a confused identity. This refers to the frustrations and disillusionment of modern man resulting from clash in traditional and modern values. However understanding of human nature is Daksha'a chief strength. Love and desire can do wonders. He realizes Shiva's love for his daughter Sati. Speaking about human nature, he says:

> It is his intense desire to impress the person he loves most,' expounded Daksha. 'Look at me. I have always loved my father. My desire to impress him is what is driving me even today. Even after his death, I still want to make him proud of me. It is driving me to my destiny. . . . And when the Neelkanth develops a deep desire to make Sati proud of him, he will rise to fulfil his destiny. (*IM* 152)

Parvateshwar conceals his tender feelings since its manifestation was a sign of weakness to him. The indifferent attitude to Sati, his daughter presents him as a psychological misfit far removed from normal human happiness. He suppresses simple human virtues like affection, sympathy and gentleness. He cannot afford in his eyes to show feelings, which others interpret, as unmanly and weak. That is why even on the social and informal occasions, he played the role of a man, hiding the true spirit which results in an isolation even from his kith and kin. Though Parvateshwar repressed all feelings of gentleness, affection and tolerance as he considered them unethical qualities for the Commander, his parental affection gives vivid manifestation at times. His affection for Sati echoes in the novel.

VI

The novel also deals with the contemporary themes such as immigration for new settlements and commercial purposes as well as terrorism and its impact on public life. Immigration and settlement have been a regular phenomenon. Today diaspora is a process and outcome of globalization. The migrant communities largely have no alternative but to assimilate with the host society socially and culturally in the course of time. But in Meluha, the immigrants are divided into two categories. First are those who are invited to settle and assimilate as the tribe of Shiva and the others are the traders who come to port cities for commercial purposes only. Nandi the Meluhan chief places an offer before Shiva, the chief of the tribe, Gunas:

> Come to our land. . . . Indeed the richest and most powerful empire in whole world. Our government has an offer for immigrants. You will be given fertile land and resources for farming. . . . Meluha offers you a lifestyle beyond your wildest dreams. We ask for nothing in return. Just live in peace, pay your taxes and follow the laws of the land. (*IM* 2)

Shiva accepts the offer and leaves the native land because the weather is too hard and there are constant wars with neighbouring Pakratis. Shiva convinces his tribe:

> This will change our lives completely. I believe the change will be for the better. Anything will be better than the pointlessness of violence we face daily. I have told you what I want to what I want to do. But the choice to go or not is yours. Let the Gunas speak. (*IM* 6)

Meluha is a developed nation and thus cannot afford to keep itself insulated and isolated. So it opens its doors to foreign nations at its port cities such as Karachapa but restricts alien access only to the commercial capital so as to preserve its native culture.

VII

In the opening part, the land, Melutha is in the peak of glory. But very soon its eminence is questioned. The reader comes face to face with the contradictory traits of the Laws of the country. The central and pervasive irony of Meluha's problem is that it may be destroyed not because of its flaws but because it performs more than is expected of it. The land is a victim in the sense that it is sacrificial and upright and works for the benefit of the community. In such a society law is unquestionably revered. The blend of myth and religion is one of the most remarkable feature in Amish's fiction. Myth at the religious level embodies man's conscious and unconscious motivations, his wish fulfillments like yearning for a paradise. To experience God is an ardent longing in each and every man and for that he conforms to the varied forms or expressions of religion.

Myths have incarnated a paradise of religious beliefs and the readers find Daksha's longing for Ram Rajya (a lost paradise) in his attempts to save the kingdom from Chandravanshis and Nagas. While analysing the religious myths, we find great attention is focused on results of past Karma on present birth. Through the vikarma myth writer seems to convey the message that modern man confronted with complex problems is in need of the spiritual consolation offered by religion. The gods are the protectors of the nature, animals or inanimate things. They are responsible for fertility, wealth, possession, power etc. The river Saraswati takes care of the society and protects them from aging and death. Belief in gods and prophesies is another distinctive quality of Indian people. The Meluhan's legend speaks of the "Neelakanth" who would bring Rama Rajya back in the Land of Meluha. However, in treatment of the supernatural in this novel, it is noticeable that the writer makes supernatural events unclear, and allows for speculation. Conversely, in the myths there is no 'seems' about it; everything is clear and stark. The Pandits are revered and respected as the priests and preservers of the collective solidarity. Being the ritual and religious leaders of the kingdom they enjoy unquestioned authority from the clan when they interpret the divine will to them. In the novel, the Pandits are Vasudevs (a tribe of Vishnu).

Amish borrows the theories of physics to explain Hindu thoughts in a scientific way.The Hindus believe in the existence of the Trinity, namely, Brahma, Vishnu and Shiva, the creator, the preserver and the destroyer, respectively. These three gods are believed to balance the universe. An analogy between this thought and the Black Hole Theory of physics can be drawn out. A black hole is a region of space that has so much mass concentrated in it and such a great gravitational pull it has, that it sucks up all the nearby objects and energies into it. At the same time scientists also claim that the poles of the black hole release energy that pushes against the matter of the galaxy and thus a balance is maintained in the universe. The conversation between Shiva and Pandit in the dream probably refers to the black hole theory.

> 'Are your eyes capable of seeing another reality?' asked the Pandit.
>
> Shiva continued to stare at the leaf as it gradually altered its appearance. The colour seemed to be dissolving out of the leaf. . . till the leaf was almost transparent. . . . There appeared to be numerous curved lines of two colours, black and white, moving in and out of the leaf. It almost appeared as if the leaf was nothing but a carrier, which the black and white curved lines used as a temporary stop on their eternal journey. . . . He turned his head to soak in the panorama. Every object, from the squirrels on the trees to the pillars of the temple had all been transformed into the outlines of their selves. The same black lines and white curved lines streamed in and out of them. Turning to Pandit . . . he was stunned to see that the priest himself was also transformed into an outline of his former self. White curved lines were flooding out of him with frightening intensity.
>
> His (Shiva's) body too had been transformed. . . .Torrents of black curved lines were gushing furiously into him.
>
> 'The white waves are positive energy and the black negative,' said the Pandit's outline. 'They are both important. Their balance crucial. If they fall out of sync, cataclysm will occur.' (296-297)

Myths have originated from the oral tradition. Apart from this, myth making has been the characteristic of all ages. It can not only be confined to the primitive mind. In all ages it is created and preserved through recitation, rituals or such other practices. Joseph Campbell in *The Hero with a Thousand Faces* shows that "myth is the secret opening through which the inexhaustible energies of the cosmos pour into human cultural manifestation"(3). Durkheim comments on the myth:

> Myth basically fulfils the function of establishing, maintaining, and expressing social solidarity. Myth gives identity to a social group, binds together the members of a community and carefully sets each group apart from others. Within myth are the fundamental structures and organization of society, and within myth are the values of society. (249)

In India, dance is considered as a gift from Lord Shiva. According to Indian aesthetics, humanity gets the experience of rasa through different arts. The principles of Indian classical dance are based on a study of the relationship between an inner experience and the outer expression of that experience. For the experience of rasa, bhavas need to be successfully communicated. To experience rasa is to enter the domain of *sahrdaya. Rati* (love) *bhava* is the most celebrated one among other bhavas both in literature and performing arts. It comprises both *'sambhoga'* (love in union) and *viyoga* (love in separation). While Shiva in the novel undergoes the divine experience of self-manifestation that transports his intense emotions and transforms them into ontological passion, Sati fails to have similar experience as the persona that she carries due to the vikarma state has restrained her from the expression of the various emotional states. Shiva's dance gives *ananda* (mystic joy) to the spectators. He succeeds in sublimating his love for beloved and is transforming it into divine love. He expresses the inner experience of bliss and ecstasy, through dance.

Amish emerges as a prominent personality in the field of modern Indian literature who takes the problems prevailing in modern India and sets them against the background of Indian myth, history, culture and tradition which used to exist in ancient India. The novel obviously offers no final answers to the clash of cultures: all that is certain is that the story-telling never stops. While the events of the novel took place in the remote past, the author convinces that they still have a contemporary relevance. The figures of the myth are archetypes that can be rediscovered in the present century as well. In order to bridge the gap between the past and the present, a noteworthy trend in the postmodernist fiction is the use of mythology to present the modern predicament. Mythic thoughts, in fact, are attempts to mediate the gaps between continuity and change. By using similar mythological situations, a broader dimension is given to the present-day chaotic condition in which humanity is living today. The mythical past affirms man's relationship to the transcendent. It has a value-structure. It is a rediscovery of the past for the present, and an adaptation for the future. The characters of the novel, the protagonists in particular, serve as fitting instruments for the novelist's exploration of the mystic kingdom of the unconscious. These characters are unfolded against ancient Indian culture and they gather their strength as much from the primitive myths as from their own individual existence.

VIII

In Amish's novel, one finds a shift towards the realisation that the individual's entity is just a humble part of a larger reality. Through mythology man's alienation from a life of nourishment and grace id comprehended. An attempt is made to explore the roots, find the moorings, and probe whole areas of experience, blurred during a period of extreme modernism during the last several decades, thereby understanding India's present-day existence. Thus a departure from Euro-centric modernism has created a new socio-cultural mythical code, which is used in such kind of novels. Myth is now accepted as a meaningful sub-text of the literary text that explore the relevance of some traditional values in today's changed context. *The Immortals of Meluha* is a world classic, which portrays the spiritual struggle of man in terms of the urgency of life's demands. The novel connects modern India with its ancient past, its traditions, cultural heritage and recording of history, it also emphasizes and highlights Indian tradition in the telling of Indian history and thus brings something of Indian heritage to Western readers. Indian history is told here not only from an Indian perspective but by also utilising India's cultural heritage in its structure and form. Amish Tripathi has made an effort to retrieve, rediscover, and redefine elements of culture in a creative way, by a return to pride in one's roots, while looking ahead.

Works Cited

Campbell, Joseph. *The Hero with a Thousand Faces.* New York: Bollingen Series XVII, Princeton Univ. Press, 1949.

Day, Martin S. *The Many Meanings of Myth.* America: Univ. Press of America, 1984.

Fraser, Tom & Adam Banks, *Designer's Color Manual: The Complete Guide to Color Theory and Application,* California: Chronicle Books. 2004.

Jung, C.G. "Psychology and Religion." *Collected Works of CG Jung"* Vol. 11: Psychology and Religion: West and East. 1938:131.

_______" The Relations between the Ego and the Unconscious". *Collected Works of C.G. Jung,* Vol. 7: Two Essays on Analytical Psychology. 1928:305.

_______. "Approaching the Unconscious." *Man and his Symbols* . ed. Jung. New York: Doubleday, 1964:72-73.

Kellert, S. H. *In the wake of chaos:Unpredictable order in dynamical systems.* Chicago: University of Chicago Press. 1993

Levi- Strauss, Claude. *Myth and Meaning.* New York: Schocken Press, 1978.

Slochower, Harry. *Mythopoesis: Mythic in the Literary Classics.*

Dettoit: Wayne State University Press, 1970.

Tripathi, Amish. *The Immortals of Meluha.* 2010. (abv. as IM in the text.)

Vickery, John B. , *The Literary Impact of The Golden Bough.* Princeton: Princeton Univ. Press 1973.

von Franz, Marie-Louise. "The Process of Individuation," *Man and His Symbols,* ed. C.G. Jung. New York: Dell Publishing, 1964.

Wallace W. Douglas "The Meaning Of Myth" in *Modern Criticism Myth and Literature,* ed. Vickery, John B. Lincoln: University of Nebraska Press, 1966.

William D. Blattner, *Heidegger's Temporal Idealism,* Cambridge: Cambridge University Press, 1999.

Index